Library Services
and Incarceration

ALA Neal-Schuman purchases fund advocacy, awareness, and accreditation programs for library professionals worldwide.

Library Services
and
Incarceration

RECOGNIZING BARRIERS, STRENGTHENING ACCESS

JEANIE AUSTIN

FOREWORD BY KATHLEEN DE LA PEÑA MCCOOK

CHICAGO :: 2022

Jeanie Austin earned their PhD in library and information science from the University of Illinois at Urbana-Champaign. They are a jail and reentry services librarian at the San Francisco Public Library. They have provided library services in juvenile detention centers and jails, and researched library services in carceral facilities, for over a decade. Their work has been published in *First Monday, International Journal of Information, Diversity & Inclusion* (IJIDI), *Journal of Librarianship and Information Science, Libraries: Culture, History, and Society,* and *The Reference Librarian,* among other venues.

© 2022 by Jeanie Austin

Extensive effort has gone into ensuring the reliability of the information in this book; however, the publisher makes no warranty, express or implied, with respect to the material contained herein.

ISBNs
978-0-8389-4945-0 (paper)
978-0-8389-3740-2 (PDF)
978-0-8389-3739-6 (ePub)

Library of Congress Cataloging-in-Publication Data
Names: Austin, Jeanie, author.
Title: Library services and incarceration : recognizing barriers, strengthening access / Jeanie Austin ; foreword by Kathleen de la Peña McCook.
Description: Chicago : ALA Neal-Schuman, 2022. | Includes bibliographical references and index. | Summary: "This book provides librarians and those studying to enter the profession with tools to grapple with their own implication within systems of policing and incarceration, melding critical theory with real-world examples to demonstrate how to effectively serve people impacted by incarceration"—Provided by publisher.
Identifiers: LCCN 2021033803 (print) | LCCN 2021033804 (ebook) | ISBN 9780838949450 (paperback) | ISBN 9780838937396 (epub) | ISBN 9780838937402 (pdf)
Subjects: LCSH: Prison libraries—United States. | Libraries and prisons—United States.
Classification: LCC Z675.P8 A94 2022 (print) | LCC Z675.P8 (ebook) | DDC 027.6/65—dc23
LC record available at https://lccn.loc.gov/2021033803
LC ebook record available at https://lccn.loc.gov/2021033804

Cover design by Alejandra Diaz; imagery © Adobe Stock.
Composition in the Cardea and Acumin Pro typefaces.

♾ This paper meets the requirements of ANSI/NISO Z39.48-1992 (Permanence of Paper).

Printed in the United States of America

26 25 24 23 22   5 4 3 2 1

CONTENTS

FOREWORD

Kathleen de la Peña McCook

"Can a man who's warm understand one who is freezing?"

—Shukhov, in *One Day in the Life of Ivan Denisovich*[1]

Imprisonment is a civil death. We are all surrounded by people invisible to us who are in jails, prisons, or under some sort of post-confinement surveillance. Each of these people have families and loved ones caught in the winding sheet of incarceration. The captive maternal, so painfully explored by Dr. Joy James in the *Carceral Notebooks*, amplifies the snare of the range of our punitive society.[2]

Jeanie Austin's *Library Services and Incarceration: Recognizing Barriers, Strengthening Access* leads librarians through the stark landscape of carceral realities that affect nearly 50 percent of people living in the United States—either directly for those confined in prisons and jails or supervised by e-carceration, or their family and friends whose interaction with the imprisoned constrains all aspects of contiguity.

What do we think of when we think of prisons? The most well-known book about prison in the world is the story of the illiterate Edmond Dantès in *The Count of Monte Cristo* (1844).[3] After six years of monstrous solitary confinement and flogging, Dantès encounters Abbé Faria, who secretly teaches him to read and write during an eight-year tunneling out of the prison. Do librarians imagine that we are the Abbé Farias who will aid the prisoner to a rebirth through literacy and education?

I was fifteen when I read *One Day in the Life of Ivan Denisovich*, and that spare book seared my heart. My only connections to jails or prisons have consisted of visits to Chicago's Cook County Jail in the late 1960s to visit friends arrested in political demonstrations, a book talk to a men's prison as part of an adult literacy program, visits to other county jails for students held on minor drug charges, and the images of the hooded men at Abu Ghraib prison in 2003. I planned a national research survey about librarians and jails, but this was cut short after 9/11. No large-scale or nationwide evaluation of jail and prison librarianship has been published in nearly thirty years. Jeanie Austin has stepped up to change this.

Who are the people in prisons and jails? What do we know about them? How do we think about them? Jeanie Austin helps us to expand our framework of understanding as we explore the map of the incarcerated and the extended effect of incarceration on the family members and loved ones who support them. In *Library Services and Incarceration: Recognizing Barriers, Strengthening Access* we learn about men in prison, women in prison, juveniles in prison, and the impact of the carceral state on mothers, people of color, LGBTQIA+ and gender-nonconforming people, and people who once would have been in asylums but are now in the carceral state.[4] The impact of incarceration on LGBTQIA+ people (and especially those who are Black, Indigenous, or people of color and living in poverty) is rarely explicitly mentioned in the library literature on incarceration, but

Jeanie Austin provokes readers to see all incarcerated people as part of the human family. Austin's work led me to the story of Layleen Cubilette-Polanco, a 27-year-old transgender woman who died in a solitary jail cell on Rikers Island, and to the poetry of Benji Hart that is available on SoundCloud:

> The Rikers Island compound ~~will be replaced by a series of~~
> ~~smaller, borough-based facilities~~ *will slip into the rising*
> *Atlantic, the ribs of our dead prepared to cage it.*[5]

The experiences of people in prisons and jails have been broadly researched from many points of view. *The Prison Journal*, for example, examines the attitudes of prison and jail personnel in many nations and studies the effects of incarceration on different categories of incarcerated people.[6] But *The Prison Journal* hasn't mentioned libraries in the past twenty years of its publication. As Jeanie Austin demonstrates in these pages, more information about existing library services and the need for new collaborations is sorely needed within librarianship and must be integrated across all our services. This information does not exist in the broader scholarship about prisons and jails.

Librarians have empathy for people in prisons or jails from reading prison writing. Imprisoned five years for political protest in the Qanatir Women's Prison, Dr. Nawal El Saadawi has written: "In prison, a person's essence comes to light. One stands naked before oneself, and before others. Masks drop and slogans fall. In prison, one's true mettle is revealed, particularly in times of crisis."[7]

What can librarians do to provide support to women in prison? What can librarians do to provide support to Black men in prison? Jed Tucker, writing of Malcolm X, has observed: "The answer to the kind of extreme social displacement foisted upon poor, racialized minorities in the United States since the 1970s is not awaiting individual heroism; rather, as Malcolm's life reveals, by investing in institutions that provide some hope, in even the most desperate of those spaces, it becomes possible to create the conditions for radical personal and community transformation."[8] In this book, Austin demonstrates how libraries are an investment that can use extant models of service to develop new models within our institutions to evaluate information and incarceration. Austin provides critical theoretical approaches to library and information services for those who are incarcerated, and provides deep insight into the background of how library services reflect the scale of library systems that provide those services.

Library Services and Incarceration provides librarians with pragmatic and encouraging case studies and helps us to envisage library services to the incarcerated that should exist more widely. The models of direct service and indirect service presented here are analyzed in the context of sociopolitical environments with a grounded sense of their feasibility. It is heavy lifting to look at a local correctional landscape and then try to identify the opportunities for libraries, but Austin is clear that this must be done. The recognition that there is no invariable blueprint to develop services in jails and prisons is austere, but realistic and hopeful.

And then the reader is asked to go another mile to consider services and support for incarcerated people who leave institutions. Librarians will face the rules and structures of probation and parole with increased surveillance technologies that constrain reintegration. The unseen people who are people released from incarceration are often set adrift in a society that fails to acknowledge their humanity.

Understanding the narratives of incarceration in the United States—that they either or simultaneously justify their existence through punishment or rehabilitation—provides us with the framework to assemble and create new modes of service.

Because people working in carceral institutions vary in willingness to provide services, this text clarifies the need to recognize the fact that these institutions are organized differently from place to place. They will have different security restrictions, different administrative ideologies, and different philosophies of rehabilitation. It is essential that the librarian who wishes to implement services understands these different challenges. *Library Services and Incarceration* is pragmatic and realistic about the approaches that are required in different contexts.

The alignment of library mission and carceral mission can be quite divergent, and it is the librarian's challenge to reconcile the missions. There are other educational and social services that support prisoners and their reentry, but often these do not include libraries in their scope of work. For example, library services are not even mentioned in a 2020 report from ETS on prisoner education.[9] Community engagement, a current initiative in librarianship, provides a platform to include other prisoner-serving organizations as partners or allies.

Prison writing is a way that librarians can imagine the world that Jeanie Austin writes about. This stark verse by Jimmy Santiago Baca, a Chicano Apache poet, calls us to compassion:

> Some will make it out of here with hate in their eyes
> But so very few make it out of here as human
> As they came in, they leave wondering what good they are now.[10]

The path to helping people in prison know what good they can be is shown to us in *Library Services and Incarceration: Recognizing Barriers, Strengthening Access* with its focus on restorative justice and recognition of the humanity in each person caught in the carceral systems.

NOTES

1. Alexander Solzhenitsyn, *One Day in the Life of Ivan Denisovich* (Harmondsworth, UK: Penguin, 1963). First published in November 1962 in the Soviet literary magazine *Novy Mir*. The 1991 translation by H. T. Willetts is the translation approved by Solzhenitsyn (New York: Noonday/Farrar, Straus and Giroux, 1991). This quote is from the Willetts translation as published in 1995 (London: David Campbell), 21.

2. Joy James, "The Womb of Western Theory: Trauma, Time Theft, and the Captive Maternal," *Carceral Notebooks*, vol. 12 (2016), www.thecarceral.org/cn12/14_Womb_of_Western_Theory.pdf.

3. Alexandre Dumas's novel *The Count of Monte Cristo* (1844) has been translated into many languages and made into numerous movies, radio programs, television series, plays, and even video games. Dantes's hideous treatment and years of incarceration have been the embodiment of prisons in the minds of readers and viewers worldwide for nearly two centuries.

4. Anne E. Parsons, *From Asylum to Prison: Deinstitutionalization and the Rise of Mass Incarceration* (Chapel Hill: University of North Carolina Press, 2018).

5. Benji Hart, "Layleen's Bill (with Revisions)," Trans Day of Resilience / Forward Together 2019, https://benjihart.com/portfolio/layleens-bill-with-revisions-trans-day-of-resilience-2019/. Go to SoundCloud to hear the poem: https://soundcloud.com/user-830244714/benji-hart-layleens -bill-with-revisions. Sydney Pereira, "Layleen Polanco's Family to Receive $5.9 Million Settlement

for Her Death on Rikers Island," *The Gothamist,* August 31, 2020, https://gothamist.com/news/layleen-polancos-family-receive-59-million-settlement-her-death-rikers-island.

6. Michael B. Mitchell and Jaya B. Davis, "Formerly Incarcerated Black Mothers Matter Too: Resisting Social Constructions of Motherhood," *The Prison Journal,* vol. 99 (May 29, 2019): 420-36; Rebecca Shlafer, Grant Duwe, and Lauren Hindt, "First Parents in Prison and Their Minor Children: Comparisons between State and National Estimates," *The Prison Journal,* vol. 99 (March 2019): 310-28.

7. Nawal El Saadawi, *Memoirs from the Women's Prison* (Berkeley: University of California Press, 1994).

8. Malcolm X and Alex Haley, *The Autobiography of Malcolm X* (New York, 1965); Jed B. Tucker, "Malcolm X, the Prison Years: The Relentless Pursuit of Formal Education," *Journal of African American History,* no. 2 (2017): 184-212.

9. Stephen J. Steurer, "How to Unlock the Power of Prison Education: Policy Report: ETS Center for Research on Human Capital and Education," 2020, available from Educational Testing Service, www.ets.org/research/report/opportunity.

10. Jimmy Santiago Baca, *Immigrants in Our Own Land* (Baton Rouge: Louisiana State University Press, 1979.

ACKNOWLEDGMENTS

I am extremely fortunate to have come into LIS at a moment of deep introspection and critical engagement. I thank the faculty who have guided me in this work for their lasting impact on my perspective of LIS and for their ability to envision the real possibilities that the field holds. I extend special gratitude to Nicole A. Cooke for your enduring critical insight, advice, and support, and to Soo Ah Kwon for your willingness to direct my intellectual efforts from an interdisciplinary perspective. I am very fortunate to have been advised by Christine Jenkins, and to have benefited from the acumen and imagination of Rae-Anne Montague and Carol Tilley.

I have been mentored by great and thoughtful peers, and I continue to draw on their expertise in my own academic development. Thank you to Safiya U. Noble, Sarah Roberts, and Miriam Sweeney for opening more room to interrogate many concepts that have been normalized within library and information science. Your scholarship has already changed the world.

I extend my lasting gratitude to my critical theory cohort, K. R. Roberto, LaTesha Velez, and Melissa Villa-Nicholas, who ground me and keep me going. I am so honored to be in this work with all of you. I can't wait to continue it, together.

I thank Rachel Chance, my editor at ALA, for wholeheartedly believing in the timeliness of this book and advocating for it every step of the way.

My deepest appreciation to Rachel Kinnon, my collaborator and confidant in library services, and to Alejandro Gallegos, Michelle Jeffers, and Michael Lambert. Your support has made it possible to create and sustain meaningful library services for people in the San Francisco County Jails.

This book would not exist without the ongoing efforts of my colleagues who provide library and information services to people who are incarcerated. Thank you for the models of service that you have created and advanced, despite the many barriers, whether or not they are documented in this text. Among those I consider colleagues and forebears in the work are Joan Ariel Stout and Gilda Turitz Perolman, the editors of *Inside-Outside*. Their advocacy that librarians collaborate with people who are incarcerated to improve information access continues to inform my own practice as a librarian.

Thank you also to the many professors, colleagues, and students who have worked to increase information access for people impacted by incarceration. I know that you will be part of our profession's engagement with this topic, and I thank you in advance for all that you will do.

Finally, thank you to the many patrons who have taught me to be a better, more informed, and more thoughtful librarian. Thank you for your advocacy, your willingness to express your love of reading, and your insights into how library collections and services can be improved. I imagine this book as my partial response to your ongoing and various expressions of how much access to books, information, and the library has meant to you.

INTRODUCTION

Librarians' conceptions of criminality, policing, and incarceration shape how they provide information services and define their patron bases. Even though incarceration permeates American institutions and shapes the terrain of the public, these topics have been largely overlooked within the library and information science (LIS) field. Library services to people who are incarcerated have been positioned as a niche area of interest, are rarely given prominence in LIS education, and are often overlooked as a needed and available area of service by many types of libraries. This is true despite the swelling of incarceration rates, the scope of policing and surveillance, and the public attention repeatedly given to the ways in which policing and incarceration heavily impact Black, Indigenous, and people of color, LGBTQIA+ people, people with disabilities, and people who are living in poverty. The "mass" in mass incarceration has now come to represent the likelihood that nearly 50 percent of all adults in America have an immediate family member who has been incarcerated in a jail or prison for at least one night, and this percentage is even higher for Black and Latinx adults in the United States (Enns et al., 2019). It is beyond time that librarians attend to the realities of how incarceration shapes American society.

The vastness of carceral systems in America is almost incomprehensible, which is likely why so many publications on library services to people who are incarcerated have selectively scoped to focus on a specific setting, type of service, or on personal accounts of librarians and library staff. Instead of offering a single account of library services and incarceration, this book acknowledges Ettarh's assertion that libraries and carceral systems are institutions with shared histories that have shaped their propensities toward control and harm (2018). This project draws upon previous research on library services to incarcerated people with the aim of contextualizing the existing publications on the subject and approaching library services from multiple points of view. It does so with the recognition that few librarians have been trained to work in carceral facilities (a catchall phrase used in this book to encompass immigration detention centers, jails, juvenile detentions, and prisons), and that those that do often enter these positions with a limited understanding of policing and carceral systems and are rarely provided with the resources needed to deepen their engagement with the topic, although many librarians in carceral settings have learned about the realities of incarceration on the ground (Conrad, 2017).

This book is concerned with the overlaps and intersections between information and incarceration, the histories of library services to people who are incarcerated, carceral technologies, existing library services for people who are incarcerated or detained, ideas for information services and programming that can be implemented by a variety of libraries, and tips for creating and implementing library services. It focuses on areas of service that have often been neglected and are not considered to be rights.[1] While some librarians in prisons are positioned simultaneously as academic, reference, recreational, and law librarians, this book does not cover aspects of legal librarianship with much depth.[2] This is partly because access to the court, often in the form of a legal library, is varied in its implementation and is not always the role of prison librarians. It is also because this text seeks to identify areas where information access can be augmented by both prison librarians and librarians working outside of carceral facilities.

This book is written with the intention of providing tools for many types of librarians—including academic, public, and specialized ones, as well as librarians working in carceral institutions—and for information professionals and scholars. Incarceration is a complex system that requires a nuanced approach, and it is only by working across professional and disciplinary divides that LIS professionals can begin to successfully grapple with how the control and regulation of information is an inherent aspect of carceral functions. While this book acts primarily as an introductory text, in the absence of other similar resources, it does attempt to be as comprehensive as possible as it moves between contexts of incarceration and carceral practices and the current and possible work undertaken by LIS professionals, people who are incarcerated, and community groups. It incorporates and builds on information from people who are or have been incarcerated, and utilizes the testimony and experiences of currently and formerly incarcerated people. It incorporates person-centered language (Cox, 2020; Hickman, 2015; Keller, 2015) throughout the text. This is an intentional act to prioritize the experiences of people directly impacted by incarceration, and to highlight the ways people who are impacted by incarceration value, and evaluate, information access and their own information practices.

STRUCTURE OF THIS BOOK

In order to present a comprehensive overview of library services for people who are incarcerated, theoretical, historical, and practical considerations all arise in this text. The first half of the book, which provides an overview of information, incarceration, and historically situated library services, acts as a foundation for the descriptions of library and information services that are currently being or could be implemented. This allows readers to take a wide-ranging view of incarceration and library services, one that makes room for situated approaches to increasing information access to people impacted by incarceration.

A section on technology sits between the two halves of this book. This positioning is purposeful. It acts as a reminder of the fulcrum point between current information practices and constrictions inside, and emphasizes that access to technologies in carceral facilities falls along lines of power. The lack of information about technologies in the second half of this book suggests that librarians and information professionals have not often been able to counter the carceral facility's control of information access through technology.

The second half of the book turns to actual examples of programs and services to people who are incarcerated, often in the words of the librarians and information professionals who provide those services. It ties practical aspects of information provision back to the themes treated in the earlier chapters, illustrating that critical theoretical and historical stances can lead to generative action.

CHAPTER OVERVIEW

The first half of this book, composed of chapters 1 through 4, covers critical and historical approaches to carceral systems. It draws from critical, practical, and theoretical work from fields outside of LIS, including criminology, critical carceral studies, gender and sexuality studies, history, law, political science, psychology, studies of race and racism, and surveillance studies, in order to frame library services to people who are incarcerated within the larger context of carceral systems in the United States. This positioning provides an informed understanding of how library services to incarcerated people have been implemented over time and how the circumstances of information access and control have changed or shifted over the course of the previous century. It also creates a foundation for interrogating the neutrality of LIS. The goal of the first half of this book is to illustrate the long and often obscured history of library services to incarcerated people and to introduce the myriad contexts of incarceration and carceral systems so that LIS professionals can better engage in information provision to those impacted by incarceration. This part of the book also reveals how deeply the patron bases served (or overlooked) by libraries have been impacted by incarceration. This information enables readers to interrogate how claims to neutrality within LIS often function to support and reiterate whiteness within the field. Given the extremely racialized and gendered impact of criminalization, policing, and incarceration, and the scope of these practices in structuring much of American life, it is telling that the LIS field has not paid much attention to how carceral systems function through the control of information, nor, despite ongoing calls from within the field, has it prioritized services to people who are incarcerated.

Chapter 1, "Philosophical Approaches," positions library services within the narratives that carceral institutions have used to justify their role over time. By examining how librarians have adopted the carceral justifications of imprisonment as either rehabilitative or punitive, this chapter begins to question the idea that librarians are capable of acting outside of their own philosophical approaches to information provision. Utilizing critical theoretical work, it illustrates that what has been typified as the carceral philosophical swing between rehabilitation and punishment is often much messier and more complex, and that each of these philosophies of incarceration relies, to some extent, on its counterpart. The chapter examines how information access has functioned within these philosophical approaches, and encourages LIS professionals to rethink how they have conceptualized the role and necessity of existing carceral systems. This chapter provides needed context for the following chapters.

Chapter 2, "Carceral Histories in the United States," delves into the historical antecedents of carceral practices in the United States. It connects histories of carceral practices to histories of library services in carceral facilities, illustrating that information and the control of information have been central to incarceration in America. This chapter includes an overview of how library services to people who are incarcerated have (or have not) changed over time, and uncovers the fact that current approaches to library and information services to incarcerated people have not shifted very much in the one hundred years since some of the earliest instances of professional concerns about the information available to people who were incarcerated. A historical examination of library services for incarcerated people reveals a reliance on those very same carceral philosophies that have limited or otherwise determined information access for people who are incarcerated, and also underlines the role of racial criminalization in justifying limitations on information access. By examining the brief periods when incarcerated people's collective advocacy has led to increased access and when information access has been a prominent concern within the LIS field, this historical examination provides some opportunities for identifying points of departure from ongoing practices, and underlines the extent to which these philosophies have done a disservice to both patrons who are incarcerated and their larger social support networks.

Chapter 3, "Forms of Incarceration," moves from the discussion of mass incarceration at the conclusion of chapter 2 to outline a few of the prominent forms of carceral systems within the American landscape. By bringing attention to the interlocking but differentiated functions of types of carceral institutions and practices—including state and federal prisons, jails, juvenile detention centers, immigration detention centers, and state (community) supervision (probation, supervised release, and parole)—it foregrounds how conceptions of the public and patron bases of libraries will be transformed by the recognition that people who are incarcerated or beholden to carceral systems are included in those groups. Understanding the differences between these institutions and carceral practices is a needed element when considering possible library and information services to people who are incarcerated or under state supervision.

Chapter 4, "Information and Incarceration," surveys recent publications on library services to incarcerated people and positions these alongside the latter's actual information-seeking practices. It analyzes the library literature from 1992 through 2019, the period since the most recent ALA standards for carceral library services were developed. It then turns from LIS-centric conceptions of library and information access in carceral facilities to incorporate some of the ways in which people who have experienced incarceration discuss and conceptualize their own information access while incarcerated, and the importance they place on that access. Statements from formerly incarcerated people are contextualized as consequences of the information regulation that is inherent in American carceral practice.

The interstitial section on technology, "Technologies and Flows of Power," demonstrates that tracing access to technology within carceral practices is one way to examine how power functions in and through carceral systems. This segment of the book examines the technology and data-gathering practices of information and communications technology (ICT) companies in carceral facilities, including biometric surveillance. Surveillance technologies have been applied to people in carceral facilities since the late 1980s and have proliferated widely in the last decade, but only limited research has engaged critically with these technologies. Positioning research on the practices of ICT companies at the center of the book makes room for the possibility to extend from nascent critical research on people who are incarcerated as under the compulsion to train algorithmic intelligence (AI) and to act as digital workers as an area for further study.

Technologies do not feature heavily in the second half of the book, which concerns actual practice that can be tied to the theoretical and historical information presented earlier in the text. Yet, data gathering and other practices of surveillance are professional concerns. These practices conflict with LIS philosophies that uphold access to information and advocate for patron privacy, and they have negative repercussions on the practical library and information services offered to people who are incarcerated. The lack of attention to technologies in the second half of the book is testament to the state control and regulation of information, often counter to the efforts of library and information professionals. This part of the book raises the possibility that new library services might be developed by carefully considering how to use digital technologies to facilitate greater access to information and recreational materials.

The second half of this book focuses on the practical aspects of library services in carceral institutions. It identifies ways that LIS professionals can build upon critical approaches to carceral systems and accounts from people who have been incarcerated to create more meaningful and much-needed library and information services. Chapters 5 through 7 cover three types of library services—direct (or face-to-face) services, indirect services, and reentry services—which can be implemented to support people who are incarcerated, people who have recently been incarcerated, and their families, friends, and social support networks. Chapter 8 discusses some of the nuances of creating and sustaining library services in carceral facilities. Generally speaking, the second half of the book recognizes that the spread of carceral systems and the role of information control within carceral practice leave many points of entry for library and information services, but that these must be understood within the ongoing scale of incarceration in the United States.

Chapter 5, "Models of Direct Service," examines various examples of the face-to-face provision of library materials to those who are incarcerated. The chapter discusses notable examples of collaborations between public libraries and prison libraries or carceral facilities. It offers profiles of successful, well-established, or unique public, prison, and other library services and programs in order to illustrate the possibilities for providing direct services within carceral facilities. These programs can be contrasted with the overall dearth of library and information services for people who are incarcerated across the United States. The chapter also draws upon the literature on prison libraries and public library services in prisons to address gaps in the existing LIS literature.

Chapter 6, "Models of Indirect Service," moves from models of direct services to an analysis of the stated information needs and desires of incarcerated people and how library and information professionals might work to meet their requests. The chapter highlights two forms of indirect services—reference by mail and book donations—as ways that libraries with limited institutional support or resources can work to address the carceral control and limitation of information access. It moves outside of the LIS field proper to recognize the decades-long work of community groups that have advocated for increased information access for people who are incarcerated and have continuously pushed against the censorship decisions made on the part of carceral facilities. This chapter concludes with a survey of other indirect services and forms of support which could be explored as more services for people who are incarcerated are developed by librarians and other information professionals. It offers an ethical stance on thinking through these and other possible programs and resources—that library and information services should always be developed with the goal of increasing information access for incarcerated people.

Chapter 7, "Reentry Support and Programming," digs into the realities of release from carceral facilities, and draws on research with people in the process of reentry in order to identify existing library resources that can be tailored to better meet the needs of people who have recently been released from jails and prisons. It incorporates information from popular publications and profiles one long-standing reentry program in order to outline the various approaches to reentry support and outreach. This chapter takes as a given that raising public awareness of the realities of incarceration, and of the library resources available to those impacted by incarceration, should be part and parcel of reentry services.

Chapter 8, "Building Institutional Support and Getting Started," closes the section on practical applications of critical approaches to the carceral system by touching on hot-button issues and concerns that impact library services for people who are incarcerated. These issues include building the library staff's awareness about policing, incarceration, and reentry; advocating for new or increased library services to the incarcerated in conversations with the library administration; finding ways to begin services in carceral facilities; and institutionalizing a library's services so that they are not dependent on a few passionate staff members. This chapter also addresses concerns around patron privacy and record-keeping, challenges to library materials, navigating racism in publishing and incarceration, and identifying opportunities to share resources to better support the people most impacted by policing and incarceration.

The book concludes by encouraging LIS professionals to build on the introductory information in this text and conduct further research on LIS services for incarcerated people, critically explore the oversights in librarianship's claims to neutrality, and envision new models of LIS services which push against the normalization of incarceration in the library and information science field.

CONCLUSION

Pulling together the many threads related to carceral systems and information access provides a new framework for thinking through these disparate and intertwining themes. Doing this offers critical theoretical insight alongside practical information related to information access. This book draws on existing models to envision as yet nonexistent forms of access, collaboration, and programming.

A large portion of this text was written as people inside of carceral facilities were locked down, a move that carceral systems proposed as a security measure in response to the COVID-19 pandemic. In many instances, these conditions included only one hour a day spent outside of a cell, being placed in precarious health conditions while unable to acquire needed medical protections, having no form of in-person visitation with loved ones, and rolling and continuous outbreaks of coronavirus throughout carceral facilities in the United States. The lockdowns resulted in reduced information access, including access to recreational materials and needed medical information about personal protective equipment and general health. At the same time, medical technologies that were probably developed or refined through their compulsory use on people who were incarcerated prior to the pandemic—such as telemedicine—proliferated and facilitated resource access for people who were not incarcerated.

Although local and state carceral systems were touted for their efforts to reduce the transmission of the coronavirus within their facilities—typically by releasing incarcerated people with health conditions—these piecemeal efforts were not often supported by funding to groups that had long been resources for people in reentry. While the releases presented a possible point at which to push against carceral logics, readers should be cautious in assuming that these changes will inherently lead to a decrease in incarceration. Research has shown that coronavirus-related releases were not the reason for the decreases in prison populations that occurred during the pandemic (Sharma et al., 2020). Rather, prisons, for the most part, did not accept transfers from local jails—meaning that there was not an influx of people who were incarcerated as people who had completed their sentences were released, courts that oversaw criminal proceedings were closed, and conditions of probation and parole changed in ways that led to a lessened likelihood that individual parole or probation officers requested that people be reincarcerated (Sharma et al. 2020). These trends did not represent a change in the systemic biases present in carceral systems, nor do they portend a major change in carceral functions. Rather, carceral practices of containment and restriction have made it more pressing that LIS professionals identify ways to continue to provide information access even as carceral facilities have expanded their methods of information restriction. This book offers a few examples of continuing to advocate for people who are incarcerated, community groups that have championed information access and resisted censorship, and LIS professionals who have, alongside these groups, paved the way for an analysis of and practical engagement with the control of information as a form of state-sponsored oppression.

NOTES

1. Largely due to the organizing efforts of people who were incarcerated, people who are incarcerated have a right to meaningful access to the courts, though the definition of this has been significantly reduced over time. Access to religious texts is also a right.
2. The Assistance for Prisoners group of the American Association of Law Libraries maintains a list of relevant legal resources at www.aallnet.org/srsis/resources-publications/assistance-for-prisoners.

REFERENCES

American Association of Law Libraries. 2021. Assistance for Prisoners. www.aallnet.org/srsis/resources-publications/assistance-for-prisoners/.

Conrad, S. 2017. *Prison Librarianship: Policy and Practice*. Jefferson, NC: McFarland.

Cox, A. 2020. "The Language of Incarceration." *Incarceration: An International Journal of Imprisonment, Detention, and Coercive Confinement* 1, no. 1: 1–3.

Enns, P. K., Y. Yi, M. Comfort, A. W. Goldman, H. Lee, C. Muller, S. Wakefield, E. A. Wang, and C. Wildeman. 2019. "What Percentage of Americans Have Ever Had a Family Member Incarcerated? Evidence from the Family History of Incarceration Survey (FamHIS)." *Socius: Sociological Research for a Dynamic World*, March 4: 5.

Ettarh, F. 2018. "Vocational Awe and Librarianship: The Lies We Tell Ourselves. In the Library with the Lead Pipe. www.inthelibrarywiththeleadpipe.org/2018/vocational-awe/.

Hickman, B. 2015. "Inmate. Prisoner. Other. Discussed." The Marshall Project. www.themarshallproject.org/2015/04/03/inmate-prisoner-other-discussed.

Keller, B. 2015. "Inmate. Parolee. Felon. Discuss." The Marshall Project. www.themarshallproject.org/2015/04/01/inmate-parolee-felon-discuss.

Sharma, D., W. Li, D. Lavoie, and C. Lauer. 2020. "Prison Populations Drop by 100,000 during Pandemic, but Not Because of COVID-19 Releases." The Marshall Project. www.themarshallproject.org/2020/07/16/prison-populations-drop-by-100-000-during-pandemic.

CHAPTER 1

Philosophical Approaches

S ocial and political justifications for incarceration influence the ways that librarians envision, create, and implement library services to people who are incarcerated. Various
narratives of crime and criminality have proliferated in the American social and political
consciousness. Each carries with it a certain perspective on the legitimacy and function
of incarceration. Each narrative also provides a specific viewpoint on how people who are
incarcerated should be treated and how (or even if) people who are incarcerated should
have access to programming, contact with their families and social support networks, and,
especially important to librarians, access to information.

In popular discourse, there are two widely acknowledged poles between which the
philosophy, and resulting implementation, of carceral systems swing—punishment and
rehabilitation. In punitive models, carceral facilities exist as a form of retribution, the
person who has actually or potentially engaged in conduct deemed illegal is often framed
as always (and sometimes permanently) criminal, and the sentence from the court system
reflects the trespass and individual or social damage that has occurred. In the rehabilitative model, the person who has actually or potentially engaged in conduct deemed illegal
is viewed as able to gain skills and access to resources while incarcerated that will assist
them in returning to the outside world with a capacity and desire to no longer cause harm
or otherwise breach the law. This model relies on the belief that prisons and other carceral
facilities are equipped to facilitate personal reformation. There will be more information
about these models in a moment, but it is important to highlight here that the punitive
"tough on crime" model enabled mass incarceration, which is addressed in the second
portion of this chapter.

Despite their role in anchoring discussions of the function of incarceration, and the
belief that there is a pendulum that swings between how incarceration is conceived and
implemented at the national scale, these philosophies of punishment and rehabilitation
do not encompass the myriad ways in which carceral systems are structured. Carceral
systems proliferate throughout American society. Some of the forms of these systems are
more familiar than others. For instance, police forces and detainment (in jails, prisons,
and juvenile detention centers) are the easily available archetypes that typify how incarceration occurs in the United States. In reality, incarceration extends far beyond the
carceral institutions, and some carceral facilities, such as immigrant detention centers,
are a state response to what are legally defined as civil matters rather than criminal ones.
Throughout this book, there will be examples of how incarceration permeates American society, and how technologies are being used to increase surveillance that in turn

facilitates more incarceration. This book will also discuss the wide sweep of regulations and standards that shape life for people who are formerly incarcerated.

In order to understand the vastness of the "mass" in mass incarceration, and its direct negative impacts and aftereffects, librarians will need to turn to experts who have engaged deeply with these topics. The final portion of this chapter will introduce some of the theorists and practitioners who guide the perspectives taken in the chapters ahead. In turning to theorists who critically examine incarceration, racism, technology, and information, this chapter closes by providing a set of tools for thinking beyond the discussion of carceral systems as always either punitive or rehabilitative. The carceral structures in the United States are so extensive that they can be difficult to conceptualize, but this is a necessary step for understanding the role of information in the lives of people directly impacted by carceral systems. This chapter aims to provide a framework for thinking through the immense impact that incarceration has on the everyday experiences of people in the United States.

PUNISHMENT OR REHABILITATION: MODELS OF INCARCERATION

Information and incarceration are intertwined. Creating actionable steps that can be taken from this premise involves unpacking the defining assumptions that shape how carceral institutions are discussed and justified. In the United States, legal and popular discourse has centered on whether carceral facilities exist to punish or to reform individuals, and there is often said to be an ongoing shift between these two approaches. There are many underlying assumptions at play here, including basic ideas of morality, ethics, social cohesion, and social expulsion. Central to each model, though, is the idea that incarceration can serve a specific function through the removal of individuals and through their containment. Each model also focuses on the individual as a locus of change, with little regard for social and political factors that shape how illegal acts are defined, how policing occurs, and the circumstances to which people return when they are released from carceral facilities.

The punitive model rests on a central definition of individuals as unable or unwilling to change their behavior. In the punitive framework, the best way to preserve social order is to remove individuals from society. This logic has taken shape in mandatory minimum sentences, three strikes laws, and similar modes of judicial sentencing practices. In the current moment, the rhetoric of being "tough on crime" and a disdain for what were politically viewed as ineffective rehabilitative programs is reflected in the proliferation of prisons and other types of institutions that manage where, when, and how people involved with the carceral system must conduct themselves. This is a simplistic analysis, but the takeaway is that in the punitive model prison growth and continuation is justified because there is nothing to be done for or with people who cause harm or otherwise breach the law, that individuals are inherently good or evil, and that individuals who have been convicted of crimes are, for the most part, incapable of reflection, growth, or change.

Rehabilitative models tend to espouse opposing views to punitive approaches, while still placing much of the onus of responsibility for change on the individual. In rehabilitative frames, people must be provided with the skills to assist them in becoming functioning good (law-abiding) citizens. These might include educational programs, substance use programs, and other programming that provides therapeutic and medical intercession into their lives. Rehabilitation has often been viewed as the more progressive approach to incarceration, emphasizing intervention rather than physical control and containment. To again offer a simplistic review, rehabilitative models center on the possibilities for individuals to change, given the correct (state-implemented) intercessions.

The reality of operations in carceral facilities is, of course, much messier than the two frameworks outlined above. Within carceral facilities, the individual philosophies of correctional officers influence their everyday interactions with incarcerated people, as do the overarching approaches of wardens and captains (Lerman and Page, 2012). There is scholarly debate about whether or not clear barriers can be drawn between approaches that centralize rehabilitation or punishment in the historical traditions of incarceration in the United States (Grasso, 2017; Simon, 2007). There is debate over whether the educational and other programming in prisons, which is aligned with rehabilitative models, actually decreased in the 1980s and into the 1990s following the "punitive turn" in carceral philosophies, and research has shown that even today some state prison systems have experienced little change in the amount of programming offered, if programs are available, while others have implemented drastic cuts to programs and other resources (Garland, 2001; Phelps, 2011; Phelps, 2012). On the other side of this, there has been evidence of some potential shift toward rehabilitation in punitive carceral philosophies (Green, 2015).

Punishment and rehabilitation are outlined here because they shape the perceptions of people unfamiliar with carceral systems or who have been less directly and negatively impacted by incarceration. They offer a baseline approach that can be used to interrogate how individuals' perspectives of the role of incarceration in society shape how they conduct themselves in relation to carceral systems. Yet, the two models do not stand entirely independent of one another. Rehabilitation may have been adopted in carceral systems because they were, and still are, able to take punitive measures against individuals who are viewed as resistant to state-mandated reformation (Grasso, 2017). The next chapter, on the histories of incarceration and of library and information science, will address the overlaps between these philosophical approaches in library services and how they have shaped the field in which librarians currently operate.

To be clear, critiques of the rehabilitative model—that it is dependent on neoliberal ideas of personal responsibility for reformation, that it incorporates and relies on the possibility of intense punishment for those who do not participate in rehabilitative activities, and that individuals can and should be acted upon by outside forces that can best determine their life courses—is not offered to justify a punitive model of incarceration. Both the punitive and rehabilitative models center on some level of control of individuals detained for or convicted of activities deemed criminal under local, state, or federal statutes. The bleakness of the punitive turn, as evidenced in the next section on mass incarceration, can make rehabilitation seem a desirable narrative to embrace, especially because it offers a stark contrast to what scholars have discussed as a "warehousing" approach; the "warehouse model contributes to the political order and legitimacy of the carceral state simply with respect to its capacity to contain, with no particular focus on the substance or form of imprisonment" (Simon, 2007, 494). The "carceral state" described here is one in which mass incarceration and extensive networks of policing and surveillance are normalized to the point of becoming quotidian.[1] Turning to the realities of mass incarceration reveals many of the tendencies that are not made explicit in either of these models, including the extensively racialized modes of policing and incarceration that shape the composition of the public, both politically and socially.

MASS INCARCERATION

The "mass" in mass incarceration is evident in the numbers. Nearly 2.3 million people are incarcerated or otherwise detained in the United States at any given time, and the numbers have held at or above 2 million since at least the early 2000s.[2] According to the most recent Prison Policy Initiative analysis of incarceration, which aggregates data from many sources in order to best represent how incarceration structures much of the American experience: "The American criminal justice system holds almost 2.3 million people in 1,833 state prisons, 110 federal prisons, 1,772 juvenile correctional facilities, 3,134 local jails, 218 immigration detention facilities, and 80 Indian Country jails as well as in military prisons, civil commitment centers, state psychiatric hospitals, and prisons in the U.S. territories" (Sawyer and Wagner, 2020). It is often noted that the United States leads the world in incarceration rates per capita, that the militarization of police forces and the forms of incarceration in the United States are promoted to and adopted by other countries, and that present-day rates of incarceration have had little effect on measured rates of crime (McDowell, Harold, and Battle, 2013; Stemen, 2017).

Policing and incarceration occur along racialized and gendered lines. Michelle Alexander famously redirected the course of mainstream conversations about incarceration in the United States by noting that more Black men were incarcerated at the time of her research than were enslaved in the period leading up to the Civil War (Alexander, 2010). If policing and incarceration trends established during the turn to punitive ideologies of incarceration continue, one of every three Black men and one in six Latino men who turned 18 in 2019 are predicted to be incarcerated at some point in their lifetime (Bonczar, 2003). Prison expansion, the spread of incarceration, mundane and racialized policing, and new forms of surveillance have reshaped the terrain of states and rearranged the experiences of Black, Indigenous, and people of color and white people across the board (Kaba, 2021; Davis, 2003; Gilmore, 2007).

Moreover, the growing rates of incarceration of women mean that women of color, and specifically Black women, are increasingly likely to be detained in a local jail or sentenced to prison (Kajstura, 2019). The dilemmas of women in local jails are compounded by financial circumstances and the use of cash bail systems that result in their continuing to be detained in jail until they are tried because they cannot afford to bail out. Black, Indigenous, and women of color who, due to systemic oppression, may rely on social services for survival become increasingly exposed to policing and incarceration through their interactions with state institutions (Ritchie and Craske, 2019). Davis and Dent (2001) emphasize the effect of these underlying forces on shaping the lives of people impacted by incarceration, including women incarcerated across the globe. In an analysis of how women who are incarcerated are discussed as theoretical figures in academic research, often with an orientation that relies on stereotypes, Davis reiterates the social conditions that incarceration not only relies on, but also reproduces: "the institution of the prison and its discursive deployment produce the kind of prisoners that in turn justify the expansion of prisons. As a matter of fact, the term *prison industry* can refer precisely to the production of prisoners even as the industry produces profits for increasing numbers of corporations and, by siphoning social wealth away from such institutions as schools and hospitals, child care and housing, plays a pivotal role in producing the conditions of poverty that create a perceived need for more prisons" (2001, 1238).

Examining the policing and incarceration of women reveals a trend in carceral systems that is not always highlighted in conversations about mass incarceration—people are heavily policed along lines of sexuality and gender conformity. Roughly one-quarter of the women incarcerated in jails and one-third of the women in prison in 2011 and 2012 identified as lesbian or bisexual (Meyer et al., 2017). Men openly identified as gay or bisexual at rates similar to estimated rates of men outside of prison (Meyer et al., 2017). These figures reflect self-reports in the materials used by correctional facilities, and the number of incarcerated people who identify as gay, lesbian, or bisexual may be higher. There is no reliable information on the number of gender-nonconforming, non-binary, two-spirit, or transgender people who are incarcerated, though existing surveys of LGBTQIA+ people inside of carceral institutions and individuals' own accounts suggest that many people who might be included under an umbrella definition as being transgender or gender-nonconforming are very likely to be incarcerated at some point in their lives (Lydon et al., 2015).

These statistics do not begin to tell the whole story of incarceration in America, but they do provide a way to examine the deep and troubling impact of policing and incarceration across axes of identity. Intersectional identity categories are often subject to intense state scrutiny, distrust, surveillance, punishment, and oppression because they are viewed as deviant from the dominant social order (Collins, 2008; Crenshaw, 1991). This leads to intensifying forms of surveillance and violence. Due to white supremacist historical constructions of Black, Indigenous, and people of color as inherently a threat, and to stereotypes that continue to shape policing and incarceration, Black, Indigenous, and people of color, identifiably LGBTQIA+ people, people with disabilities, people living in poverty, and people who have been historically viewed as potentially criminal in the dominant social order are much more likely to experience incarceration than white, financially stable, heterosexual, and cisgender people.

Large swathes of the general public are deeply negatively impacted by the removal and containment of groups of people to spaces in which they are confined, and in which many of their channels for communication are either foreclosed or prohibitively expensive. This has a compounding effect on the availability of resources available to those who are most impacted by incarceration, because the lines of self- and collective advocacy are often severed or curtailed when they do exist. Incarceration and other forms of involuntary confinement can strain the peer-support networks that support people with mental illness, people who are neurodivergent, and people who are disabled because incarceration physically removes them from their support networks (Institute for the Development of Human Arts, 2020; Kaufman-Mthimkhulu and Gibson, 2020). Carceral systems operate under ableist logics that are in contrast to people's needs, desires, and ways of being in the world (Ben-Moshe, 2020; Institute for the Development of Human Arts, 2020; Kaufman-Mthimkhulu and Gibson, 2020). As Ben-Moshe makes clear, "disability is central to mass incarceration and decarceration in the United States. This is true in terms of both the disabling nature of incarceration in prisons and the pervasiveness of incarceration (whether in so-called therapeutic facilities like psych hospitals or punitive ones like jails) characterizing the lives of many disabled people" (2020, 1). The next chapter, which partially covers the eugenicist legacy that informed both incarceration and library science, further explicates this claim.

In reviewing statistics about who is incarcerated, where, and for how long, it is necessary to note that the numbers are not neutral. Rather, they are symptoms of what Ritchie and Craske identify as "criminalizing webs" (2019). Oppression operates in a way that pushes people more and more into the view of, and under the purview of, the police and makes them more vulnerable to incarceration. People who experience anti-Blackness and other forms of oppression along lines of racialization and identity categories are forced into increasing contact with policing and carceral systems. This can be viewed as two sides of a coin—as people with racialized privilege (people who benefit directly from whiteness because it has been normalized in the United States context) further protect their privilege through material access, relocation to "safer" neighborhoods, and other actions that depend on the perception of racialized criminality or non-normative criminality, they are more likely to support the further policing and containment of people who are already criminalized. That's a heady statement, and one that requires a bit of supporting evidence, which is why the next section turns to several theorists whose work helps to corroborate the analysis in which this text positions library and information services for people who are incarcerated.

TURNING OUTSIDE THE FIELD

The viewpoint that librarians and information (LIS) professionals take when thinking about information access and incarceration will shape how they create library services for people who are incarcerated, whether or not they advocate for increased information access for people inside, how they defend the materials in their collections against censorship, and how they define the public served by libraries and other information providers. The vastness of carceral systems means that LIS professionals need to rethink the ideas of criminality and the practices of policing and incarceration that reinforce existing systems that have structured mass incarceration. With so many people incarcerated and incarceration most negatively impacting communities that are already in many ways made vulnerable by state and federal policies that have reduced safety nets by curtailing resources, institutions such as libraries take on a more central role. Whether they acknowledge it or not, libraries have already become hubs of information provision and resource access for people and communities that are directly impacted by incarceration. What is at issue here is the limited discussion of this reality within the field of library and information science.

Broadly speaking, public and other outside librarians writing about services to people who are incarcerated have traditionally fallen on the rehabilitative side of the debate about the proposed purposes of incarceration, while librarians who specialize in prison librarianship have tended to write about it from a more punitive position. Many public librarians have advocated for library services to incarcerated people on grounds similar to those found in the ALA's "Statement on Prisoners' Right to Read" (2019). By contrast, librarians who work in prisons have published on how the library becomes a site of security and control within the prison while others, at times, have advocated for the alignment of library services in carceral facilities with the punitive philosophies of the prisons (Bouchard and Winnicki, 2000; Coyle, 1987). In other instances, librarians have advocated for the library's role in doing work upon people who are incarcerated as a part of rehabilitation. This is most evident in the scholarship that arose around the library's role in bibliotherapy.

Most of these approaches tend toward the disciplinary (both through rehabilitation and through punishment) nature of carceral facilities. In doing so, they reiterate the narrative of the need for state intervention and punishment, and the idea that people are projects to be worked upon through incarceration. While the areas where library services and punitive approaches to incarceration are at odds are easy to elucidate (few public libraries openly embrace or adopt a rhetoric of punishment as their goal or primary motive), narratives of rehabilitation may be much more appealing for their professed faith in individual change and a functioning society. The statistics given earlier begin to highlight some of the reasons why narratives of rehabilitation might be considered suspect. The impulse toward philosophies of rehabilitation can be interrogated by asking, "rehabilitation to what?" In a context in which people routinely are subject to more frequent, repeated, and more prolonged forms of incarceration and social and political oppression along the intersections of their identities, rehabilitation to a society that often views them as already and, at times, always potentially criminal holds its own forms of cruelty (Cacho, 2012).

Interrogating the status quo of incarceration in the United States is not the same as overlooking the harm done between people. It involves investing curiosity into why certain convictions impact certain groups of people in ways that alter their lives, damage communities, and cause generational trauma. It also involves recognizing the perseverance that people who have survived incarceration and undergone reentry enact as they show up for state-mandated appointments, search for jobs, and undertake the myriad small but accumulating tasks of maintaining or reforming relationships between themselves and others that have been damaged by the mental and emotional toll of incarceration, distance, and difficulty obtaining information and recreational materials.

Information plays a key role in this discourse because it is so central to how rehabilitation or punishment is enacted within carceral facilities. Rehabilitation may be framed as depending upon the control of information, positioning some types of information as potentially dangerous given the type of conviction a person has received. In the punitive narrative, information often becomes a prized possession, and access to books and other materials may be curtailed or denied altogether as a means by which to enact punishment within the institution.

It is naive to think that librarians who have written about library services to people who are incarcerated are always transparent when discussing their own approaches to library and information services. In an environment where every misstep may be perceived as a threat to the security of the institution and clearance to enter the institution can be easily revoked, it makes good sense for librarians to speak within the carceral logics that are popularly and publicly available. Even in these types of institutions, librarians can and do navigate their power to advocate for incarcerated people, to subvert restrictions, and to challenge or align with the carceral logics of the institutions where they provide information (Arford, 2016).

Narratives of rehabilitation or punishment are not the only ways in which librarians providing services to incarcerated people have described their work. For instance, the Public Library Association's guide on services to incarcerated people, *Get Inside: Responsible Jail and Prison Library Service*, clearly frames the need for library services within the context of mass incarceration (Higgins, 2017). There are a few recorded (and surely many more unrecorded) instances in which librarians and other information professionals have actively used their position and skills to advocate alongside incarcerated people as they work to have greater information access. The types of services highlighted in this book speak to the possibility of providing services that move away from the philosophies of incarceration described earlier in this chapter.

Gaining insight into the processes and philosophies that have resulted in current forms of incarceration, with all its various carceral facilities, forms of policing and surveillance, and possibilities to foreclose life chances or to potentially kill, requires a step outside of library and information science and into the intellectual traditions that have examined incarceration more thoroughly. Here, LIS professionals can incorporate perspectives from fields as far reaching as criminology, critical carceral studies, gender and sexuality studies, history, law, political science, psychology, studies of race and racism, surveillance studies, and other areas of research that consider the views of incarcerated people and the communities most heavily impacted by incarceration. In order to provide a clearer picture of the role of incarceration in American society today, readers will need tools to begin to destabilize, or at least assess, their own conceptions of the role of incarceration.

This text offers an analysis of library services to people who are incarcerated that is not often found in the library and information science literature. It utilizes critical theoretical approaches as a foundation for thinking through the topics described throughout the book. The expertise of the theorists in this book, many of whom have been directly connected to incarceration through their own life experience, professional services, or ongoing community engagement, shapes the ways in which library services are described and highlighted. The theorists described here have often crafted their work in ways that are intended to be actionable, or have even created new projects based on their research. Their goal is to build a better understanding of the many forces that shape how and when individuals and communities are likely to be impacted by incarceration, and to create new and imaginative ways of standing alongside the people who bear the brunt of these systems.

Turning to critical theorists also provides a kind of cohesion across the many narratives that have been published about being a librarian in a carceral facility. There are many memoirs that specifically focus on the time that librarians and library staff have spent providing services to people in carceral facilities. These types of books tend to highlight the more theatrical elements of the work, while offering little perspective on how what happens in the prison is shaped by diffuse and competing policies and perspectives. Privilege and power work together to allow some people to have their ideological positions validated and accepted at the expense of other perspectives. Conceptualizing library services to people who are incarcerated and people most impacted by incarceration might also include prioritizing the ways in which people who are or have been incarcerated discuss their own reading and the value of information over some of the published accounts of information professionals. Yet many published accounts of reading or accessing information while incarcerated have not been brought into the conversation of library services for people most impacted by incarceration. Beyond this, there is a history of carceral facilities foreclosing or challenging the publication of accounts written by people who are incarcerated. People who are incarcerated are under some pressure to be perceived as engaging in good behavior in order to avoid more punitive conditions, and this may further limit the possibility that they will publicly share accounts of their access (or lack of access) to information and books. In this light, LIS professionals can recognize that the power to describe a situation is something that is both distributed, negotiated, and accumulated around the surveillance and self-management of people inside of carceral facilities (Foucault, 1995). People who are incarcerated are also positioned within categories constructed through carceral logics, and are then repositioned as information sources about types of criminality or criminal belonging (Foucault, 1995). While Foucault did not engage with the Black and anticolonial theory of his period, as Fanon did in his work, Black and anticolonial theory provides a means to see carceral systems as self-sustaining, reconfiguring over time, reproduced through racial logics of confinement and control, and as extending from practices of surveillance and enslavement to the modern carceral system (James, 2016).

Due to the sheer reach of the carceral system as it structures American life, almost any aspect of society and resource provision ultimately connects back, in some way, to incarceration. Important to this work is that even mass literacy in the United States was likely proliferated through and encouraged by early voluntary or compulsory literacy practices in penitentiaries (Schorb, 2014). More specific information on the intertwined histories of incarceration and information is provided in the next chapter. To ground that review, the theorists profiled here have been selected for their contributions to knowledge of the historical foundations of incarceration in the United States, understanding of how policing and incarceration differently impact groups along lines of race and other intersecting identities, and recognition of the unique role that the power to control information and technology has in structuring the experiences of people who are imprisoned or detained in our current moment of mass incarceration.

Gaining perspective on the current period of incarceration in the United States requires looking back at the historical role of incarceration in the country. As the next chapter shows, the control of information access has always been an aspect of the carceral experience in America. In order to better understand how this is true, and how it has shaped the narratives of providing information to people who are incarcerated, this book draws upon prominent histories of incarceration in the United States. Among these are Hernández's *City of Inmates* and Bauer's exposé of private prisons. Hernández (2017) describes how the urban center of Los Angeles, which is now at the carceral forefront of reach and scope in the world, was founded through and built upon the forced removal of Indigenous people and the physical labor of people incarcerated in local jails. Hernández's research not only illustrates who is most likely to be positioned as suspect or criminal in the eyes of the law, but also shows that there has been quite a bit of intention put into structuring carceral systems along the lines of intersecting identities (Million Dollar Hoods, 2019). Bauer's exposé (2018) of his experiences as an undercover prison guard at a private prison in the South traces the histories of slavery and servitude up to the modern prison.

Hernández and Bauer illustrate the racialized foundations of American incarceration, tracing it, alternatively, from colonialism and slavery to present day. Their work aligns with and extends Davis's reflections (2003) on processes of racialized, and especially anti-Black, criminalization throughout enslavement, the penitentiary system, and de facto and de jure racist instantiations. Chavez-Garcia (2012) takes a similar approach in examining juvenile detention, and departs from the traditional notion that juvenile detention was developed under the idea of the state-as-parent (legally, *parens patria*) to describe the role of juvenile containment through the forced removal of Indigenous children from their parents, the curtailment of homosexuality and gender enactments that were viewed as inconsistent with assigned sex, and the eugenicist beliefs that shaped incarceration and containment from the turn of the twentieth century through the 1950s. Together, these and other histories of the role of incarceration in American society provide a frame for understanding how policing and incarceration occur today, both in the United States and on a global scale (Scott, 2013).

The practical aspects of this book are informed by the work of Alexander, Gilmore, and Davis to understand the current state of incarceration in the Unites States. Alexander's *The New Jim Crow* (2010) utilizes statistics similar to those provided in this chapter as a basis for expanding upon what the numbers cannot show—the focused policing and incarceration of Black men as a formal and informal policy. Alexander draws from experience as a lawyer and an examination of more recent history to illustrate how this is not a chance occurrence. The ability to incarcerate large numbers of people, which began in the late 1970s and early 1980s and has continued to the present day, required a massive expansion of prison facilities, many of which were built in rural areas and were promised as economic boons for small towns. Gilmore (2007) describes this expansion as it took place in California and charts its effect on communities from which people were physically removed, thus providing a frame for disrupting the way in which the proliferation of prisons across the American rural landscape has been normalized.[3] Davis's ongoing project is to examine incarceration in the United States and to imagine other possible systems that might better support people who are incarcerated, as is evidenced in her book *Are Prisons Obsolete?* (2003).

Many of the materials that inform this book draw from traditions that denaturalize incarceration in the United States and invite readers to reassess their own perceptions of, investments in, and connections to incarceration. In part, this is because few intellectual traditions concern themselves with dynamics outside of the punitive-rehabilitative spectrum, and because, outside of some religious groups, the majority of formalized groups that exist to provide information to incarcerated people tend to entail some level of rethinking of the role of incarceration in American society. As a field concerned with information access and the function of information in social and political life, library and information science will need to grapple with the role of information regulation as an ongoing practice in carceral facilities. Limiting and controlling access to many types of information is part of the regular operations of carceral facilities. Rethinking incarceration is one way to gain a toolset that sets the stage to effectively advocate for increased information access.

Along these lines, it makes sense to also discuss the process by which groups of people are positioned socially, legally, and politically to be perceived as more likely to be criminal. Bernstein (2014), Kwon (2013), Morris (2016), and others have researched the ways in which youth from specific areas or who are identified along racial lines experience ongoing forms of dispossession, harassment, and policing and incarceration due to criminalized racialization. Notably, Kwon has also documented how youth resist these characterizations and stand with one another to reduce high levels of policing and counter stereotypes. McDonald (O'Hara, 2014), Spade (2011), and Stanley and Smith (2011) have all focused on the ways that LGBTQIA+ people, and specifically transgender Black, Indigenous, and people of color, are often positioned as suspect by the public and police when they are identified by their sexuality or as being transgender. McDonald has repeatedly shared her life story, in which protecting herself from a transphobic attacker led to a prison sentence and a nationwide activist campaign to refute the terms of her sentence (Gares, 2016). Cacho (2012) has specifically focused on how political and legal structures work to preclude certain groups of people from being seen as existing beyond categories of criminality. It stands to reason that how librarians and information professionals view their patrons—as always and already criminal, as soon-to-be criminal, or, alternatively, as capable of complex human experiences, failure, growth, harm, and kindness—will shape whether and how they advocate for people who are incarcerated, and for their communities to have increased access to information that is relevant, meaningful, and desired.

An additional category of research that informs this work centers specifically on the role of technology and information in thinking through information access and incarceration. Access to technology and to information are closely intertwined in American society, but these become conspicuously untied in the context of the carceral facility. Most people who are incarcerated in the United States have limited or no access to modern technologies, much less to the interconnected information worlds of the internet. Information access via the internet is another aspect of the social landscape that has become normalized but stands to be examined in the context of library and information services to people who are incarcerated. Incarcerated people's limited access to technologies does not mean that those technologies are absent, however. In order to understand the role of technology in incarceration, this text is informed by scholars who have examined how certain groups of people, due to racial criminalization, are most likely to experience policing and incarceration and are subject to everyday surveillance and new forms of technologically-mediated surveillance (Kaba, 2021). This follows from a long history in which Black people in America have at once been subject to heavy surveillance, viewed as suspect, and have simultaneously been erased from the dominant social and political landscape (Browne, 2015). This tradition has resulted in the hyper-surveillance of people who are most often positioned as criminal in America.

Some of the earliest tools for facial recognition were trained through the American National Standards Institute's datasets of photographs taken of people who were incarcerated, including those not convicted of any criminal acts (Paglen, 2019; Rouvalis, 2020). Technologies increasingly structure the prison, the community, and the American border and are used to reaffirm existing ideas of who is criminal and who is at risk of being harmed by criminal activity (Benjamin, 2019; Newell, Gomez, and Guajardo, 2017; Sweeney and Villa-Nicholas, 2019; Vukov, 2016; Vukov and Sheller, 2013; Wang, 2018). Racial criminalization shapes what information is positioned as legitimate and available, and saturates algorithmically informed encounters with information (Noble, 2018) and the data gathering practices that people are subject to across the perceived barriers of carceral facilities.

CONCLUSION

How LIS professionals conceptualize systems of incarceration, and what they know about the conditions in carceral institutions, will shape the ways in which they advocate for information access for people who are incarcerated. Fortunately, many theorists have critically engaged with these topics, providing insight into the role that libraries and information access have in addressing the information needs of people who are incarcerated. The heightened surveillance and policing of Black, Indigenous, and people of color, LGBTQIA+ people, people with disabilities, and people living in poverty ties in directly to higher rates of incarceration and sits alongside an assessment of the environmental limitations of carceral facilities to underscore how information access has been used as a form of control along lines of social and political oppression. Connecting systems of incarceration to information control and regulation within carceral facilities reveals the necessity of advocating for increased information access for people who are incarcerated.

As future chapters illustrate, the conditions of carceral facilities shape the information needs and desires of people who are incarcerated. Looking outside of carceral institutions, LIS professionals can open conversations about how systems of incarceration occur in the United States, and the information needs and desires that are aftereffects of systems of incarceration. Knowledge of the scale of incarceration, and its differential impact, can inform how academic, public, and special libraries better assess their services.

The historical implementation of library services overlaps with the histories and philosophies that have structured and legitimated the various incarnations of carceral systems in the United States. The next chapter outlines a few of those points of connection. It moves from a discussion of carceral systems to a broader discussion of library services to people who are incarcerated as they have developed from, reflected, and pushed against structuring carceral logics.

NOTES

1. For example, technologies advertised under the auspices of personal safety and avoidance of the risk of victimization, such as Amazon's Ring or the local area networking app NextDoor, are tools to surveil racial belonging and are used by police departments to further the reach of policing and incarceration (Kurwa, 2019).
2. As noted in the introduction, it is likely that COVID-19–related releases will not lead to a massive reduction of the number of people who are incarcerated with any lasting effects. Some people who were released, including those released from federal prison to home confinement under the CARES Act, are required to return and complete the remainder of their sentences.
3. A number of the texts cited here focus specifically on California as an exemplary state. At present, California detains around 10 percent of the 2.3 million people incarcerated in jails and prisons nationwide. Scholarship has focused on California because of policies there that have pushed rapid prison expansion, increased prison sentences (three strikes laws), and criminalized communities (gang enhancements). The numbers for California were accessed using the Sentencing Project's statistical comparison tool, which includes information on all fifty states. The tool is available at www.sentencingproject.org/the-facts.

REFERENCES

Alexander, M. 2010. *The New Jim Crow: Mass Incarceration in the Age of Colorblindness.* New York: New Press.

American Library Association. 2019. "Prisoners' Right to Read." www.ala.org/advocacy/intfreedom/librarybill/interpretations/prisonersrightoread.

Arford, T. 2016. "Prisons as Sites of Power/Resistance." In *The SAGE Handbook of Resistance,* ed. D. Coupasson and S. Vallas, 224–43. London: Sage.

Bauer, S. 2018. *American Prison: A Reporter's Undercover Journey into the Business of Punishment.* New York: Penguin.

Benjamin, R. 2019. *Race after Technology: Abolitionist Tools for the New Jim Code.* Cambridge, UK: Polity.

Ben-Moshe, L. 2020. "Introduction: Intersecting Disability, Imprisonment, and Deinstitutionalization." In *Decarcerating Disability: Deinstitutionalization and Prison Abolition,* 1–35. Minneapolis: University of Minnesota Press.

Bernstein, N. 2014. *Burning Down the House: The End of Juvenile Prison.* New York: New Press.

Bonczar, T. P. 2003. "Prevalence of Imprisonment in the U.S. Population, 1974–2001." Washington, DC: Bureau of Justice Statistics. www.bjs.gov/content/pub/pdf/piusp01.pdf.

Bouchard, J., and A. Winnicki. 2000. "'You Found What in a Book?' Contraband Control in the Prison Library." *Library & Archival Security* 16, no. 1: 47–61.

Browne, S. 2015. *Dark Matters: On the Surveillance of Blackness.* Durham, NC: Duke University Press.

Cacho, L. M. 2012. *Social Death: Racialized Rightlessness and the Criminalization of the Unprotected.* New York: New York University Press.

Chavez-Garcia, M. 2012. *States of Delinquency: Race and Science in the Making of California's Juvenile Justice System.* Berkeley: University of California Press.

Collins, P. H. 2008. *Black Feminist Thought: Knowledge, Consciousness, and the Politics of Empowerment.* Boston: Unwin Hyman.

Coyle, W. 1987. *Libraries in Prisons: A Blending of Institutions.* New Directions in Information Management 15. Westport, CT: Greenwood.

Crenshaw, K. 1991. "Mapping the Margins: Intersectionality, Identity Politics, and Violence against Women of Color." *Stanford Law Review* 43: 1241-99.

Davis, A. 2003. *Are Prisons Obsolete?* New York: Seven Stories.

Davis, A., and G. Dent. 2001. "Prison as a Border: A Conversation on Gender, Globalization, and Punishment." *Signs* 26, no. 4: 1235-41.

Foucault, M. 1995. *Discipline and Punish: The Birth of the Prison.* 2nd edition. New York: Vintage Books.

Gares, J. (Director). 2016. *Free CeCe!* (Motion picture). Jac Gares Media.

Garland, D. 2001. *The Culture of Control: Crime and Social Order in Contemporary Society.* Chicago: University of Chicago Press.

Gilmore, R. W. 2007. *Golden Gulag: Prisons, Surplus, Crisis, and Opposition in Globalizing California.* Berkeley: University of California Press.

Grasso, A. 2017. "Broken beyond Repair: Rehabilitative Penology and American Political Development." *Political Research Quarterly* 70, no. 2: 394-407.

Green, D. A. 2015. "US Penal-Reform Catalysts, Drivers, and Prospects." *Punishment & Society* 17, no. 3: 271-98.

Hernández, K. 2017. *City of Inmates: Conquest, Rebellion, and the Rise of Human Caging in Los Angeles, 1771-1965.* Chapel Hill: University of North Carolina Press.

Higgins, N. 2017. *Get Inside: Responsible Jail and Prison Library Service.* Quick Reads for Busy Librarians. Chicago: Public Library Association.

Institute for the Development of Human Arts (IDHA). 2020. "Decarcerating Care." www.idha-nyc.org/decarcerating-care.

James, J. 2016. "III. Progeny Theory, Exclusivity, and Elusive Freedom." In "The Womb of Western Theory: Trauma, Time Theft, and the Captive Maternal." *Carceral Notebooks*, vol. 12: 266-77. https://sites.williams.edu/jjames/files/2019/05/WombofWesternTheory2016.pdf.

Kaba, M. 2021. "I Live in a Place Where Everybody Watches You Everywhere You Go" In *We do This 'Till We Free Us: Abolitionist Organizing and Transforming Justice* (88-92). Chicago: Haymarket Books.

Kajstura, A. 2019. "Women's Mass Incarceration: The Whole Pie 2019." Prison Policy Initiative. www.prisonpolicy.org/reports/pie2019women.html.

Kaufman-Mthimkhulu, S. L., and D. Gibson. 2020. "Carceral Ableism: Connecting Freedom Struggles." (Workshop).

Kurwa, R. 2019. "Building the Digitally Gated Community: The Case of Nextdoor." *Surveillance & Society* 17, no. 1/2: 111-17.

Kwon, S. A. 2013. *Uncivil Youth: Race, Activism, and Affirmative Governmentality.* Durham, NC: Duke University Press.

Lerman, A. E, & Page, J. 2012. "The State of the Job: An Embedded Work Role Perspective on Prison Officer Attitudes." *Punishment & Society* 14, no. 5: 503-29.

Lydon, J., K. Carrington, H. Low, R. Miller, and M. Yazdy. 2015. "Coming Out of Concrete Closets: A Report on Black & Pink's National LGBTQ Prisoner Survey." Black & Pink.

McDowell, D. E., C. N. Harold, and J. Battle. 2013. Introduction to *The Punitive Turn: New Approaches to Race and Incarceration,* ed. McDowell, Harold, and Battle, 1-25. Charlottesville: University of Virginia Press.

Meyer, I. H., A. R. Flores, L. Stemple, A. P. Romero, B. D. M. Wilson, and J. L. Herman. 2017. "Incarceration Rates and Traits of Sexual Minorities in the United States: National Inmate Survey, 2011-2012." *American Journal of Public Health* 107, no. 2: 267-73.

Million Dollar Hoods. 2019. https://milliondollarhoods.org/.

Morris, M. W. 2016. *Pushout: The Criminalization of Black Girls in Schools.* New York: New Press.

Newell, B. C., R. Gomez, and V. E. Guajardo. 2017. "Sensors, Cameras, and the New 'Normal' in Clandestine Migration: How Undocumented Migrants Experience Surveillance at the U.S.-Mexico Border. *Surveillance and Society* 15, no. 1: 21–41.

Noble, S. U. 2018. *Algorithms of Oppression: How Search Engines Reinforce Racism.* New York University Press.

O'Hara, M. E. 2014. "'My Struggle Started When I Entered This World': VICE News Interviews CeCe McDonald." VICE News. www.vice.com/en_us/article/d3j5vy/my-struggle-started-when-i-entered-this-world-vice-news-interviews-cece-mcdonald.

Paglen, T. 2019. "They Took the Faces from the Accused and the Dead . . . (SD18)." De Young Museum, San Francisco. https://deyoung.famsf.org/trevor-paglen-they-took-faces-accused-and-dead-sd18.

Phelps, M. S. 2011. "Rehabilitation in the Punitive Era: The Gap between Rhetoric and Reality in U.S. Prison Programs." *Law & Society Review* 45, no. 1: 33–68.

———. 2012. "The Place of Punishment: Variation in the Provision of Inmate Services Staff across the Punitive Turn." *Journal of Criminal Justice* 40: 348–57.

Ritchie, A. J., and L. Craske. 2019. "Unraveling Criminalizing Webs: Building Police-Free Futures." (Special issue). *Scholar and Feminist Online* 15, no. 3. http://sfonline.barnard.edu/unraveling-criminalizing-webs-building-police-free-futures/.

Rouvalis, C. 2020. "How Machines See Us—and Why." *Carnegie Magazine*. https://carnegiemuseums.org/carnegie-magazine/fall-2020/how-machines-see-us-and-why/.

Sawyer, W., and P. Wagner. 2020. "Mass Incarceration: The Whole Pie 2019." Prison Policy Initiative. www.prisonpolicy.org/reports/pie2020.html.

Schorb, J. 2014. *Reading Prisoners: Literature, Literacy, and the Transformation of American Punishment, 1700–1845.* New Brunswick, NJ: Rutgers University Press.

Scott, D. 2013. "Why Prison? Posing the Question." In *Why Prison?* ed. D. Scott, 1–22. Cambridge, UK: Cambridge University Press.

Sentencing Project. 2019. "The Facts: State-by-State Data." www.sentencingproject.org/the-facts/#map.

Simon, J. 2007. "Rise of the Carceral State." *Social Research* 74, no. 2: 471–508.

Spade, D. 2011. *Normal Life: Administrative Violence, Critical Trans Politics, and the Limits of Law.* Cambridge, MA: South End.

Stanley, E., and N. Smith, eds. 2011. *Captive Genders: Trans Embodiment and the Prison Industrial Complex.* Oakland, CA: AK Press.

Stemen, D. 2017. "The Prison Paradox: More Incarceration Will Not Make Us Safe." Vera Institute of Justice. www.vera.org/downloads/publications/for-the-record-prison-paradox_02.pdf.

Sweeney, M., and M. Villa-Nicholas. 2019. "Cultural Affordances of 'Emma,' USCIS's Latina Virtual Assistant." (Recorded lecture). Digital HKS lecture series: Harvard Kennedy School. https://vimeo.com/331443862.

Vukov, T. 2016. "Target Practice: The Algorithmics and Biopolitics of Race in Emerging Smart Border Practices and Technologies." *Transfers* 6, no. 1: 80–97.

Vukov, T., and M. Sheller. 2013. "Border Work: Surveillant Assemblages, Virtual Fences, and Tactical Counter-Media." *Social Semiotics* 23, no. 2: 225–41.

Wang, J. 2018. *Carceral Capitalism.* Semiotext(e) Intervention Series 21. South Pasadena, CA: Semiotext(e).

CHAPTER 2

Carceral Histories
in the United States

The previous chapter discussed the limitations presented when conceptualizing trends in carceral philosophies as swinging between punitive and rehabilitative logics (and being limited to these two poles). Fortunately, researchers have examined the constraints of these two models, mapping out connections between the control of specific groups of people in the historical formation of American incarceration and current forms and practices of incarceration in the United States. In order to better understand the current state of library services and information access to and with people who are incarcerated, this chapter traces direct and indirect lines through the philosophies that informed carceral practices and librarianship, highlighting a history of library services to incarcerated people.

The purpose of this endeavor is twofold. First, specific tools are needed to reassess the nature and impetus of incarceration in the United States. There is arguably a different ethos in imagining prison as a necessary part of the social fabric and recognizing that incarceration in the United State mimicked and enlarged practices similar to those during slavery, and that the high rates of incarceration for Black and Indigenous people and people of color reflect colonial and other logics of control, assimilation, containment, and disposability. These urgently needed histories are placed first and foremost in this chapter in part to maintain a timeline. Through historical research and critical examination, they also provide a framework for assessing how information, and the control of information, has always been a central aspect of incarceration in the United States.

It may seem that turning to critical theories of incarceration is quite far afield from the everyday practice of library and information science. Research into the history of library services to incarcerated people reveals that many of the practical aspects of service have been repeated over time, with little structural change toward examining information access for incarcerated people at a larger scale. The repetition of themes in the library literature for incarcerated people from the early twentieth century to the present stands as a testament to the inefficacy of focusing only on the immediately practical aspects of information provision. Time and time again librarians have repeated the need for funds, reiterated ideas of the library's role as aligning with either punitive or rehabilitative logics of carceral institutions, and have cited the particularities of library services in carceral facilities. Despite the ongoing efforts of librarians to open a larger discussion of library services to incarcerated people within the field (no matter the argument made) and with the general public (LeDonne, 1974), there has been little ground gained in positioning library services to incarcerated people as a defining aspect of library and information science (LIS).

Examining histories of incarceration alongside histories of library services to incarcerated people provides a method to identify and work against the biases within the LIS field that have further reinforced systems of oppression. The control of information and of access to specific types of information comes into focus when identifying the points of overlap between philosophies that have informed types of incarceration in the United States and library services. Information is integral to current practices of incarceration just as it is to librarianship. To this end, the uses of information as a tool of control, as a means for rewriting behavior, and as a threat are included in this chapter.

In an attempt to identify ways to move beyond the narratives of punishment and rehabilitation, this chapter also highlights the efforts of communities, incarcerated people, and librarians who have pushed against the control of information, have advocated for increased information access, and have facilitated the exchange of information between people who are incarcerated and people who are not. These examples of change, negotiation, and advocacy can inform how LIS professionals might develop new rubrics for assessing the need for increased information access among the incarcerated.

Of course, no one historical perspective is complete, and no manifestation of one point in history directly echoes in the next shape it takes. Historical practices may not necessarily reveal the ways in which information control currently manifests itself. This chapter closes by turning to current practices of information access and containment as they take place within carceral systems. This final turn reveals a stark reality in our current moment—that the prison wall is also a barrier between individuals and the information that might sustain them.

A HISTORICAL PERSPECTIVE ON INCARCERATION IN THE UNITED STATES

Looking at the history of incarceration in the United States requires an assessment of the reach and scope of incarceration and an examination of who gets to make, or keep, the true record of the purposes and conduct of carceral facilities (Curtin, 2013). Historians, critical race scholars, investigative journalists, and incarcerated and formerly incarcerated people have repeatedly called for an urgently needed reassessment of incarceration. These philosophical and real-world problems arise in holding individual accounts up against state accounts and are muddied by the way that power, situated in the hands of the state, allows for a very specific telling and retelling of the role of incarceration in American life. To speak against the official narrative, which normalizes incarceration as either a form of punishment or an opportunity for personal transformation, requires an ethical stake in assessing how, who, and why certain individuals, groups, and acts have come to be viewed as criminal over time. As Curtin states, histories of incarceration that deviate from the official account are often not valued because incarcerated people "are still stigmatized, even by their own families, and prison reformers—and historians—and can easily be mischaracterized as the naive defendants of guilty criminals" (2013, 33). Stepping back with a wide view of what constitutes a carceral practice opens the possibility that criminality itself can be a suspect category, even when "crimes" involve harms against individuals and communities. The disambiguation of an act from an identity is responsive to the ways that categories of crime have changed over time and by place, and gives means to work against the entanglement of racial criminalization.

Interrogating criminality involves examining the enduring connections between power and oppression and moving into the murkier depths of everyday acts that constitute the enforcement of, resistance to, or effects of the constraints put in place through institutional forces. The historical review of power, control, and containment in the United States in this chapter does not necessarily reveal straight lines of cause and effect. Rather, it delineates some of the exemplar forces that have shaped incarceration as it now exists, revealing a multitude of maneuvers, goals, and effects that are shored up within the current system.

While some criminologists have cautioned against giving too much attention to racism and racialized oppression in carceral logics (Gottschalk, 2015), a review of where, when, and how racism and racial criminalization emerge within the history of carceral systems in the United States provides insight into its reach. While race and racism are evidenced in, and reconstituted by, the histories briefly noted here, they are also tools used to further the effects of austerity, neoliberalism, scarcity, and the marketability of and capitalization upon the sheer scale of incarceration at the present moment. In other words, racism and white supremacy are often viewed as the reason for disparities between the numbers of Black, Indigenous, and people of color and white people who are incarcerated, but this approach does not always include analyses about the reiteration of historical forces in systems of incarceration, people's lived experience of incarceration, the conditions of carceral facilities, and the systems in place that prioritize or minimize the value of specific individuals or communities (Davis, 2003; Gottschalk, 2015; Kushner, 2019). Incorporating this history in order to develop a more expansive critical approach leads to questions that are of heightened import to librarians and information professionals. More specifically, it can show how forms of incarceration have shaped and continue to structure the composition of the public that is able to easily access information, and how a continuous barrier between individuals and the information they desire might further skew information to best suit a group of people who have easy access, bolstering an idea of the public that is quietly defined by forced removal, containment, and absence.

It is no shock to find that a discussion of the historical antecedents to the current carceral system involves a discussion of violence, categorization, legal mandate, knowledge, and exclusion (Foucault, 1995). Cacho describes this ongoing process as rooted in "the ways in which the law works to affix assumptions of behavior onto bodies. Historically, law has criminalized the recreational activities, survival economies, and intimate relationships of people of color so that the status of 'being of color' was inseparable from conduct assumed to be 'criminal'" (2012, 40). This chapter examines some of the historical precedents for racial criminalization as they were constructed through processes that served to further privilege whiteness.

While much of the historical review in this chapter will focus on the Progressive Era's ideological conceptions of incarceration, the uses of information and categorization, and early library science's own alignment with Progressive Era ideologies, it should be noted that the processes of racializing groups, practicing containment, and establishing institutionalization as a mode of control were already evident in early colonial practices in North America. Prior to colonization in California, "by all accounts, Native peoples in California rarely used corporal punishment or other means of physical force to socialize or reprimand the young for breaking rules" (Chavez-Garcia, 2012, 21). Spanish colonization in the area depended on disrupting forms of social cohesion through forced relocation, removal from families, and the use of carceral facilities. As Hernández notes, "one of the first structures these colonists built was a jail," which was then used to incarcerate

Indigenous people (of the Tongva-Gabrielino tribe, in what is now known as Los Angeles) (2017, 4). Soon, information use and access became a tool used by colonizers to divide the Native people from themselves. Native people's clothing, comportment, religion, and language were all wielded by colonizers as signifiers that justified their violent treatment toward Indigenous peoples. Simultaneously, they situated their own knowledges and ways of being as morally right and legally righteous. During this period the jail existed in California, but corporal punishment prevailed. It was at the close of Spanish colonialism and the onset of Mexican rule in the area that incarceration became a form of control utilized to both contain racialized groups and groups viewed as a threat to the ordering social structure. In the 1820s in Los Angeles, as now throughout America, "public order charges, such as vagrancy, disorderly conduct, and public drunkenness, systematically penalize the landless, homeless, and underemployed. Those who live their lives in public—sleeping, eating, arguing, loving, drinking, playing, etc.—are the most vulnerable to public order arrests, which effectively imprison them for living, as so much of their lives are lived in public" (Hernández, 2017, 30).

The American conquest of California involved a particular variant of containment and control. In 1850, white adults were granted the legal right to own young Native people, with the supposed permission of the Native adults in their lives. This legal right to access the bodies and labor of Native children led to forced relocations, kidnappings, and other forms of containment (Chavez-Garcia, 2012). While not centralized within a physical institution, these practices stand alongside practices of enslavement to attest to the fact that carceral systems have long existed not only in buildings but as dispersed systems of control that are rooted in white supremacy, racism, and racialization.

Across the country, similar actions against Native peoples took place in the early American colonization of the eastern part of the continent, as evidenced in other forms of forced removal, relocation, cultural assimilation, and violence. In this same period, the control of information proliferated throughout American practices of slavery. Literacy laws and regulations were put in place in reaction to uprisings and acts of resistance to enslavement. These laws hinged on the racist ideology that African people who were enslaved, and their descendants, were unequipped to handle the influence of reading, and on the possibility that enslaved people would utilize their literacy to escape (by forging documents and similar methods). The literacy practices of African-born people who were enslaved and their descendants were heavily policed, feared, and punished by white people in the United States (Cornelius, 1983; Rasmussen, 2010; Sweeney, 2010). The inability of white people to maintain control over information through the regulation of literacy points to differences between the North and the South in the maintenance of access to literacy as a means of maintaining power and continuing oppression (Bly, 2008).

As with colonization in California, the bodies of people who were enslaved were also read *as* information, with whiteness maintained through regulations related to movement and gestures, gender, and dress, and through physical violence (Browne, 2015; Snorton, 2017). Information about race was instantiated not only in the bodies of individuals, but was also traced through their familial lines in legal discourse that declared racialized status through blood quantum and similar vagaries. This argument is central to the early roots of critical race theory, where Cheryl Harris (1993) examined how race and racialization became codified into American law in ways that bolstered the economic well-being of white people and legally protected whiteness as a category.[1]

This brief historical review concerns logics of incarceration that may take myriad forms, from colonization to enslavement to systems of surveillance, which have limited people's movement or placed them into publics where they are more and more likely to experience regulation, policing, and other forms of punishment. Here, it makes sense to turn to some of the actual historical practices of information regulation in American instantiations of formal incarceration. The early processes of containment within the American colonies used disciplinary reading practices in order to judge individuals' tendency toward or willingness to engage in (explicitly Christian and tacitly white) reformation (Schorb, 2014). In the early 1700s, ministry projects focused on the literacy development of people who were incarcerated, interpreting the progress of their engagement with biblical texts and sermons as evidence of meaningful conversion, often prior to their public execution. People who were perceived as reading for penitence and who engaged in confession were lauded as examples of the power of both the biblical word and of literacy. These literacy practices were often put on display by clergy prior to and following executions, published and distributed not only to serve as tales of moral failure and the possibility of spiritual redemption, but also to provide examples of literary practices that were socially and spiritually correct (Schorb, 2014). These practices were primarily undertaken with incarcerated people who were white (because Black and Indigenous people were more often subject to other forms of subjugation and physical brutality), but there are examples in this period of attempted enculturation into white spirituality and attendant literacy practices. Those subject to these processes were sometimes lionized as successful examples, though they often privately confessed to isolation due to the loss of their language and cultural belonging, and their communal ways of understanding the world. The case of Joseph Hanno—a Black incarcerated person who could read but was not deemed by Cotton Mather as properly reformed—and others like him were presented as cautionary tales that reinforced racist beliefs about literacy, knowledge, and information access (Schorb, 2014). These racializing admonitions were also drivers of contemporary literacy practice.

Black and Indigenous people, imprisoned or not, were made subject to the colonial impulse of literacy as a way of regulating their behavior through spiritual endeavor. Missionaries and educators actively reduced any access to information that maintained their social ties, and introduced Christianity and Western frames of knowledge with the goal of regulating their behavior. The focus of these efforts was often both racialized and gendered (Sweeney, 2010). Colonizers held the disciplinary power of literacy and information access as part of their appeal. By the end of the eighteenth century, "the concept of early childhood literacy instruction as a deterrent to crime soon became a common refrain, as would the danger of reading novels or other diversionary materials" (Schorb, 2014, 31). The American middle class believed that "reading honed the capacity to moderate temperament, constrain destructive passions, and facilitate the exercise of reason—provided, of course, the right texts were read in the right way" (Schorb, 2014, 45). Reading in the right way not only concerned reading in order to engage in appropriate spiritual practice, but literacy as an act that "worked to legitimate racial exclusion" (Pendergast, 2003, 56).

The management and monitoring of information access and the surveillance of how information was utilized have been aspects of American incarceration over time. The two prominent American models for the early penitentiary—the Pennsylvania and Auburn models—prioritized the control of information through regulating the amount of contact between people who were detained. This was done by enforcing continuous silence, the monitoring of interactions between people who were incarcerated, and the prioritization of the type of literacy that led to adherence to Christian values (Schorb, 2014). Individuals who were incarcerated were seen as producers and purveyors of criminal information. They were largely viewed by the penitentiary and dominant society as either in need of cultivation through performative literacy practices (that occurred under diligent guidance) or as producers of information that encouraged a milieu of criminality and violence, and thus in need of censorship. These conceptions were often tied to beliefs in the individual's capacity to learn and thus to be (quite literally) redeemed.

In the early penitentiaries, faith in the reformative aspects of literacy was often coupled with a belief in the redemptive nature of physical toil. It is important to note here that the enslavement and penitentiary models, which preceded current American systems of incarceration, often intersected. In a history of privately run prisons that extends to a historical review of labor and incarceration, Bauer states that "part of what saved the penitentiary system was the phasing out of slavery in the Northeast. Whites feared a large number of free black men, and the penitentiary offered a way to enforce the compliance and obedience of freed African Americans. As a model of forced labor, it was more efficient than slavery, and unlike slavery, prison labor directly benefited the state" (2018, 59). Bauer's historical analysis links these early precedents of containment and control to the present, examining how modern disciplinary practices reflect racist fears and tropes that have been maintained over time despite social permutations and political shifts. Incarceration is central to the maintenance of these narratives.

These are brief and incomplete examples of the role of information in early and diffuse systems of control and incarceration. Before turning to a history of established, formalized library services in carceral facilities, it makes sense to look to one more recent moment in American history—the Progressive Era.

Progressive Era ideologies of scientific rationality combined with narratives about the racial superiority of whiteness to create new forms of information and knowledge production that furthered the reach of incarceration in the United States. Early in the period, exclusion took place through established practices of de facto and de jure segregation (under Jim Crow), forced removal and compulsory, and often violent, education (as with Native American boarding schools), the control of information about Mexican revolutionary movements and confinement of revolutionaries (Hernández, 2017), and new, legally mandated, forms of immigration control, assessment, and refusal (such as the Page Act and the Chinese Exclusion Act). By the early 1910s, claims to white superiority as a scientific fact took form as eugenics, not only as an ideology that prioritized white, financially established belonging above other ways of being, but as a practice that was actively enacted by white women who were trained to use eugenic assessment to determine the quality of youths' lives and to make determinations about youths' social and genetic viability. These workers were part of a system of surveillance that led to the regulation of youths' behaviors, their removal from their homes, and ultimately often led to the incarceration and at times the forced sterilization of Black, Indigenous, and youth of color and youth living in poverty (Chavez-Garcia, 2012). In this nationwide project, Black, Indigenous, and young men of color were sorted into typologies that were heavily associated with deviance and delinquency. Youth who were believed to engage in what was viewed as non-normative gendered behavior, including homosexuality, were removed from their homes and sent for reformation. Young women were placed in institutional settings and "trained" into proper domesticity, with white women viewed as more likely to be reformed and Black, Indigenous, and young women of color, when not subject to forms of harsher physical discipline, forced into domestic labor.

Young men deemed "defective" under the rubrics of eugenicist social outreach and the new science of social ordering were often institutionalized and sterilized. Nowhere was this procedure more common or enduring than in California, where 20,000 people were subjected to compulsory sterilization in the period between 1910 and the late 1970s (Chavez-Garcia, 2012). It is important to note the endurance of this practice because this length of time illustrates that, once instantiated, the racialization and racial categorization that were shaped by eugenics as field of knowledge continued even as eugenics was rejected as science.[2]

Adults were also subjected to evaluation under eugenicist logics, often under entwined narratives about disability, viability, and race and sexuality (Chapman, Carey, and Ben-Moshe, 2014). White people deemed "feeble-minded" or otherwise disabled were increasingly institutionalized during this period (due to segregation, people who were not white were not likely to be formally institutionalized). Eugenicists also called for the immediate social removal or elimination of people labeled as "defective," a term which included a range of identities and forms of disabilities, during this time. Chapman, Carey, and Ben-Moshe are clear that disability, as defined today, was ever present in and outside of formal institutions and carceral facilities; they state that "although people of color could be kept out of closed institutions through segregation, racially segregated spaces were never free from disability" (2014, 9). They draw from Davis's corpus to show that the influx of disabled Black people into carceral facilities and similar institutions only occurred during the end of formalized practices of enslavement and similar forms of exploitation, in part because eugenicists and their contemporaries heavily materially benefited from these practices (2014).

The Progressive Era is particularly important when looking at the overlap between library services in general and American incarceration. During the late 1800s and early 1900s, a number of disciplines of study became professionalized and began to take on aspects of the sciences. By the 1920s, this included library science as a field of study that informed, but was differentiated from, librarianship (Richardson, 2009). This turn to science and professionalism occurred at a time when librarians had recently begun to organize their efforts to focus on library services for people who were incarcerated. Moves on the part of carceral associations, such as the New York Prison Association's book recommendations and rules for prison libraries issued in 1876, reflected a continuing impulse toward information regulation and control within prison systems (Sullivan, 1998). This early librarian-led focus on materials access came to a head in 1910 when librarians formed the Committee on Libraries in Federal Prisons. This was followed by the 1916 publication of the *Manual for Institution Libraries* by librarians affiliated with the ALA's Committee on Library Work in Hospitals and Charitable and Correctional Institutions (Bailey, 1972). More information about these developments is available later in the chapter.

Throughout the Progressive Era, white women acted as colonial agents under the guise of providing more scientific, regulated, and meaningful social and political education. Schlesselman-Tarango (2016) has traced this tradition within the field of librarianship to the archetype of the White Lady Bountiful. Progressive Era white, middle-class women were positioned near the apex of cultural evolution under eugenicist constructions. They were also viewed as particularly skilled at maintaining the role of the library as a site of cultural assimilation, knowledge regulation, and the moral uprightness or civility that had come to be associated with certain types of reading. No doubt, the specifically gendered whiteness that shaped the practice of librarianship influenced how services for people who were incarcerated were conceived and implemented.

The move toward library science involved a more thorough examination of books' role in society and the ways in which readers engaged with them. Library science began to focus on the internal process of reading as it aligned with the fields of sociology, psychology, and other social sciences (Richardson, 2009). During this period, publications on library services to people who were incarcerated began to move from prescriptive bibliographies designed to fit the environment of the institution and information about book processing to more formalized practices of assessing how library services might occur in carceral facilities. Throughout the 1900s, publications on this topic began to reflect the histories that had shaped them, at times focusing on the belief that books were central to reformation and at other times positioning the library as an extension of carceral facilities. The next section outlines how services to incarcerated people were discussed in library and information science publications throughout the 1900s, revealing that there were other narratives that rose out of community activism and the self-advocacy of incarcerated people. Tracing this history reveals that the philosophies of library services to people who are incarcerated have risen out of racializing histories, and begins to identify points of departure that might allow for new, and much needed, approaches to these services—in carceral facilities and within the library.

A HISTORY OF LIBRARY SERVICES TO PEOPLE WHO ARE INCARCERATED

Library services to incarcerated people tend to be discussed within the field of LIS as newly minted or as particularly of interest in a specific context or social moment. Reviewing the history of publications on this topic reveals that library services to people who are incarcerated have been a concern since soon after the 1870 National Prison Congress, as was reflected in the New York Prison Association's publication on collection development and prison libraries in 1876 (Sullivan, 1998).[3] This area of interest solidified within librarianship following the 1907 meeting of the American Library Association (Richardson, 2009). State library associations formed committees on prison libraries as early as 1909 (specifically, the New York Library Association; Curtis, 1918). Publications throughout the 1900s reflect the developing fields of study and concerns related to reading, information access, and incarceration within the field, as well as the biases of their time. The publications reveal certain themes that have shaped how library services in carceral facilities have been conceptualized, prioritized, or neglected within library science and (later) LIS. They also reflect the social and political concerns of American society and the ways in which people who were incarcerated have advocated for their own access to information.[4]

The early publications on library services to incarcerated people reflected the tensions between the practical and the theoretical that arose during a time of professionalization in the field of library science. Throughout the 1910s, services to incarcerated people became formalized through the Committee on Libraries in Federal Prisons (1910-11) and the ALA Committee on Library Work in Hospitals and Charitable and Correctional Organizations publication of the *Manual for Institution Libraries* (compiled by Carrie Emma Scott, 1916). The Committee on Libraries in Federal Prisons expressed concern about the lack of funds available to acquire printed materials for people in federal prisons, and the committee communicated directly with the U.S. attorney-general to advocate for increased resources and the presence of librarians in the prisons (Curtis, 1918).

Members of the committee urged librarians to visit federal prisons and witness the state of the library services there for themselves. Their efforts led to increased concern about access, but not without certain qualifications. A report in 1911 documenting a visit to the newly established Leavenworth Penitentiary clearly shows that librarians saw themselves as able to determine the appropriateness of materials in the correctional setting—one of the visiting librarians' first acts was to remove "objectionable books" from the scant materials available in the prison (Curtis, 1918). Published communications between the attorney-general and the committee reflect the committee's insistence on the need for libraries, appealing to narratives of American nationalism and the curating (and possibly disciplinary) role of librarians. For instance, a 1911 report stated, "it is a disgrace that a wealthy nation should limit the reading even of its prisoners to books that are filthy and in rags which are largely chance contributions by visitors" (cited in Curtis, 1918, 50). The committee tried to increase financial support for prison libraries, discussed creating a bill to Congress for funds, and approached the American Prison Association in an effort to coordinate their advocacy. But the committee's final report, in 1913, revealed little success in these efforts.

The ALA's *Manual for Institution Libraries* (1916) also positioned the librarian as a cultural and disciplinary curator of information. The prison librarian's role, according to the *Manual*, was to base book collections "on the class of inmates and the functions of the institution" (American Library Association, 1916, 5). Regarding the role of fiction reading, the authors of the *Manual* consider censorship to be a necessary role of the librarian. "Fiction for prisons and reform schools should be censored carefully. Nothing should be accepted which represents vice attractively, contains sensual suggestions, or deals with crime and punishment" (1916, 7). The collection development guidelines also reflect librarians' perceptions of themselves as a civilizing force, and advocate that priority in materials selection be given to the needs of "the exceptional man among the convicts" (1916, 7). Early penitentiary models of reading as a means toward redemption are also reflected in the document, though these shift from the need for spiritual piety to the idea of literacy as a means of ensuring social cohesion. Curtis's *Libraries of the American State and National Institutions for Defectives, Dependents, and Delinquents* (1918) reiterated the role of the library in the reformation of the incarcerated person (Sullivan, 1998). No doubt, these attitudes reflected trends toward enculturation, assimilation, and the disallowance of non-white forms of being or belonging present in the larger field during this moment.

These early, formative documents can serve another function for librarians looking back on the history of library services to people who are incarcerated. Narratives of the need for greater financial resources, the institutional philosophy as shaping collection decisions, and of the librarian as a savior, guide, or at least as facilitator of a "higher" way of being resurface time and again in the hundred years that have passed since these documents were published. While an argument can be made that professionals in the field of library science (and later, LIS) have either engaged in critical discourse of these perspectives or have created new forms of libraries in coordination with community groups or other, non-state affiliated organizations, looking to how individuals in the profession have discussed library services to people who are incarcerated reveals that much of the founding philosophies of these types of services have persevered and been reiterated over time.

The structure of incarceration in the United States, and the groups targeted for surveillance and policing, began to shift over the period of the 1920s through the 1930s, accelerating in the wake of the Great Depression and as Jim Crow practices shaped the social and political landscape. New laws proliferated (Cahalan, 1979; Delaney et al., 2018). Sites of tightening criminal regulation included substance use and access (alcohol and marijuana, primarily) and the regulation of public space, which affected itinerant workers and people who were homeless. The violent repression of Black people continued to be met with indifference or even official endorsement by police forces throughout this period. New laws and practices heavily impacted Black, Indigenous, and people of color, as well as people deemed "foreign-born" by carceral facilities (Cahalan, 1979; Delaney et al., 2018). The publications on library services for incarcerated people during this period reflect the logics that facilitated increased rates of incarceration, as well as the tensions of a profession that was still finding its footing as a science.

The turn toward scientific evaluation probably informed the 1927 National Survey of Prison Libraries, the first survey on the topic of library services in carceral facilities in the United States (Greenway, 2007). Practical models for creating and implementing library services for incarcerated people were developed in 1932 in *The Prison Library Handbook* (Jones). The *Handbook*, created by the ALA's Committee on Libraries in Correctional Institutions, which was partially funded by the Rockefellers' Bureau of Social Hygiene, aimed to promote library work in prisons and to modify existing ALA standards and adapt them to the prison setting. Multiple booklists specifically tailored to services in prisons were also published at this time, including Jones's *2500 Books for the Prison Library* (1933) and *1000 Books for Prison Libraries, 1936-1939* (Methven, 1939), created by the American Prison Association's Committee on Institution Libraries. Access to literacy and information worked along the lines of enculturation and exclusion in these lists. Black interests and authors were not often reflected, even though these lists were created in the wake of the Harlem Renaissance (Sweeney, 2010). Instructions on services to the "foreign born" were primarily concerned with groups of people who would later be considered white, a process Sweeney describes as "trying to bring idealized immigrant readers into the American fold" (Sweeney, 2010, 26). There was a marked increase in library services in federal prisons from the 1920s through the 1940s, and this was accompanied by the 1938 creation of the American Prison Association's Committee on Institutional Libraries (MacCormick, 1950). Bibliotherapy—the belief that orchestrated and constrained practices of reflective, disciplinary reading could have internal psychological and reformative effects—became popular among prison librarians in the 1930s (Sweeney, 2010).

The standards for library services for incarcerated people were prioritized from the 1940s and into the 1950s. Librarians and other professionals developed the "Objectives and Standards for Libraries in Adult Prisons and Reformatories" in 1939 (Coyle, 1987). These standards were approved by the American Prison Association in 1943 and by the American Library Association in 1944. The "Objectives and Standards" document situated the prison library as an educational space (Coyle, 1987) but also emphasized the need for institutional security in the development of library services within prisons (Bailey, 1972). The "Objectives and Standards" were published as a chapter of the *Manual of Suggested Standards for a State Correctional System* by the American Prison Association (Bailey, 1972). A set of the "Objectives and Standards" was also included as an appendix to the *Library Manual for Correctional Institutions*, which was published in 1950 by the American Prison Association. That manual included chapters on the rationale for providing library services in prisons. The authors argued for the role of libraries in rehabilitation, as well as practical information regarding book purchasing, processing, and maintaining statistics (Freedman, 1950). The idea that libraries, or at least reading, played a role in individual rehabilitation was further evidenced by the advocacy of bibliotherapeutic approaches among prison administration and literature throughout the 1940s and into the 1970s, though this advocacy often manifested as "monitoring prisoners' reading and treating them as passive recipients of literary medicine" (Sweeney, 2010, 35).

An emphasis on bibliotherapy may have aligned with goals to enculturate and Americanize people increasingly criminalized throughout this period. Four examples of large-scale social and political events in the 1940s and 1950s support this possibility. The House Committee on Un-American Activities, formed in 1938, actively surveilled people within the United States and their information practices. This Committee fueled racial tensions by positioning Japanese born and people of Japanese descent in the United States as saboteurs and spies (Densho, 2020), fueling anti-immigrant sentiment in this period. Japanese and Japanese American people were removed from the general public and incarcerated in internment camps throughout the early 1940s. A wave of violence against Mexican people and Mexican Americans occurred across the U.S. in 1943; this violence was justified through nativist perspectives (Del Castillo, 2000). Following World War II, narratives of juvenile delinquency and juvenile crime revealed mounting anxieties around (often white) youths' activities as a threat to white, financially stable social formations (Cohen, 1997).

On-the-ground efforts and literary critique flourished in this period. Mexican, Mexican American, and immigrant groups organized for worker's rights from the late 1930s into the 1940s and 1950s. Books, essays, and plays by prominent literary figures offered trenchant analyses of racism and inequality. These would influence and inform the Civil Rights movement and later social and political formations (Araiza, 2009). The social and political tensions of this period played out in library services, in- and outside of carceral facilities.

Writing in 1972, Bailey recounted the development and implementation of standards for prison libraries from the 1940s through the 1960s, tracing the trajectory of the "Objectives and Standards" and the steps that eventually led to their revision. The standards were maintained and revised through the work of the ALA's Association of Hospital and Institution Libraries (AHIL), which formed in the mid-1950s. Cooperation between the American Correctional Association (formerly the American Prison Association) and ALA (specifically AHIL) was formalized in the 1960s through the creation of the Joint Committee on Institution Libraries. In 1962, this Joint Committee overhauled the existing standards and included revisions that were more restrained in their tone and format than the previous standards. The 1962 revisions were published in the 1966 *Manual of Correctional Standards*. It was Bailey's assessment that this version of the standards, when followed, represented "quality library service in an institution on par with a public library" (1972, 262).

Here, it is important to qualify what "on par with a public library" might not entail. Until the late 1950s, the American Library Association actively enforced segregation at its conferences and within the association (Wiegand, 2017).[5] This was despite a long history of Black librarianship that predated the creation of libraries at historically Black colleges and universities and the Hampton Institute Library School (founded in 1925) (Hunt, 2013; Knott, 2015; Jordan and Josey, 1977). Notable Black librarians moved the profession forward, resisted segregation in libraries, and maintained community-based information centers (Hunt, 2013; Knott, 2015; Jordan and Josey, 1977; Wiegand, 2017; Wiegand and Wiegand, 2018). As the Civil Rights movement gained momentum in the South, the ALA's role in library integration was hotly debated, especially with regard to the question of whether or not, and when, the association would issue an official statement in support of integration (Wiegand, 2017). The ALA officially added a statement that libraries should not be segregated by race to the Library Bill of Rights in 1961 (Wiegand, 2017). Black librarians called for more action, pointing to the brutality directed at civil rights protestors. Though initially slow to respond in any meaningful manner, the American Library Association issued more concerted and concise directives and imposed more sanctions throughout the period from 1961 to 1963 (Wiegand, 2017). A 1963 report found that formal and informal discrimination persisted in American libraries (Jordan and Josey, 1977). Segregation was legally ended with the passing of the 1964 Civil Rights Act, but white passivity or resistance to integration, which were pronounced in the South, persisted after this legislation. Wiegand (2017) notes that many white librarians in this period "spoke from the periphery of desegregation activities" and did not experience the visceral and psychic violence that was often meted out against Black librarians and the public as they fought for desegregation.[6]

Other knowledges or ways of being were not recognized within the field at this time. Formal Indigenous (tribal) libraries that were centered in cultural knowledge and information practices are present in the historical record by the late 1950s, and "major grassroots movement to improve tribal libraries began in the 1960s and 70s" (Littletree, 2018, 67).[7] These were not incorporated into larger professional discussions. LGBTQIA+ print materials were legally censored by the U.S. Postal Service, and under the surveillance of the FBI, the receipt of these materials could lead to loss of employment or to public exposure (Burroway, 2008). This censorship was justified under laws that criminalized depictions of homosexuality and gender nonconformity under the Comstock Act of 1873 (Burroway, 2008). For the most part, materials deemed sexually perverse or otherwise offensive for their homosexual content could not be legally sent through the mail until the *ONE, Inc. vs. Olesen* Supreme Court ruling in 1958. Access to publications and freer information-sharing facilitated the collective awareness that undergirded the gay rights and liberation movement, even as LGBTQIA+ people were still being criminalized and institutionalized (George, 2015; Lewis, 2016). The women's liberation movement that gained ground in the late 1960s prioritized information-sharing as a way of building collective consciousness, with Black and other feminists of color organizing around and publishing to re-center their experiences within the movement as it continued (Combahee River Collective, 1977; Evans, 2015). While the number of people detained in state mental health facilities had been declining since 1955—a year when it was "as large, on a per capita basis, as the prison population today"—the rate of institutionalized people with intellectual disabilities grew to its height in 1967 (Ben-Moshe, 2020, 40). These histories all overlap, entwine, and diverge from one another through social and political practices and contexts, all well as through experiences of repression and individual and state violence.

Participants in movements for desegregation and civil rights experienced direct state repression through incarceration, and incarcerated people from these movements engaged in literacy practices while incarcerated. Famous among these is Martin Luther King, Jr.'s 1963 *Letter from Birmingham Jail* written from "the full monotony of a narrow jail cell" (King, 1994). Also widely referenced is Malcolm X's description of his "homemade education" in language, literacy, and reading while incarcerated, as recorded in his 1965 autobiography with Alex Haley, where he recounts the formative role that access to culturally relevant and politically insightful books played in his development as an intellectual (257). Across the nation, incarcerated people documented, and at times published, stories and exposés of their experiences while incarcerated. These records were rarely noted in the articles and books about library services to people who were incarcerated written during this period, but they helped shape these services throughout the late 1960s and 1970s, a long decade in which library services to incarcerated people would receive increased attention, funding, and support.

Returning to Bailey, this review of librarianship and the Civil Rights movement is not to overstate that library services occurring inside of library facilities always or only reflected the practices of segregation. Bailey's words were offered as a testament to the *Standards* and not to services that were actually occurring. The ACA/ALA AHIL Joint Committee surveyed institutional libraries in 1965 and 1966 in order to evaluate their adherence to the guidelines outlined in the recent set of standards. The survey's results revealed that most institutions did not adhere to the standards for library service and did not otherwise prioritize library or materials access for people who were incarcerated (Bailey, 1972; LeDonne, 1974). In light of these findings, and in recognition of the changes occurring in incarceration as practiced in the United States, Bailey made a case for both a revised set of standards and for public libraries "to participate more actively in the service provided to correctional institutions" (1972, 264). This advocacy was tempered by the AHIL's own embrace of bibliotherapeutic approaches to library services in carceral facilities. The AHIL publication *Bibliotherapy Methods and Materials* (1971) positioned librarians as intercessors in the psychological process and as healers of the unconscious realms of incarcerated people (Sweeney, 2010).

The late 1960s and early 1970s were defined by the organizing efforts of Black, Indigenous, and people of color, as well as people living in poverty, women, LGBTQIA+ people, antiwar advocates, students, environmentalists, and more. This organizing did not cease after movements experienced state repression and movement leaders were imprisoned. Within prisons, groups and individuals engaged in large- and small-scale forms of agitation and resistance, organizing uprisings, prison breaks, and prison occupations (Bernstein, 2010; Bissonnette, 2008). The aftereffects of violent policing, the repression of political figures, the surveillance and intelligence-gathering practices under COINTELPRO, the conditions of incarceration, and the cooperation between people who were incarcerated and people outside of prisons changed American awareness about how, and in what ways, incarceration structured society.

Among librarians, the repression of social and political movements led to calls to reconfigure how libraries in carceral facilities functioned to support incarcerated people. To some extent, this shift depended on increased funding for libraries in carceral facilities. Title IV of the 1966 Library Services and Construction Act (LSCA) explicitly provided funding for libraries in carceral institutions. Two years after funds were made available, Wang published the results of a survey of state-affiliated libraries. Wang's findings revealed that few carceral institutions had library services coordinated under the purview of librarians (1969). For many librarians, Wang's study, coupled with results from surveys that showed little adherence to library standards in prisons, acted as glaring reminders of the need for increased library services in carceral facilities. This was made more possible by a revision to Title I of the LSCA in 1971, which extended the funding for public libraries. These funding shifts laid the ground for creating robust, statewide library systems within juvenile detention centers and adult prisons. The establishment of LSCA funds was at least partially influenced by the work of the civil rights organizers and movements in the 1960s.

The increased attention paid to library services for incarcerated people, the augmented funding of them, and the resulting improvements in the services in the 1970s were notable for the variety of approaches that librarians undertook. Several histories and bibliographies that provided some context for these library services were published in the early 1970s. Among these was MacCormick's "Brief History of Libraries in American Correctional Centers," which was presented to the American Correctional Association in 1970 and published as a chapter in 1973. Gillespie also contributed to the field by creating an extensive (485-entry) bibliography on prison libraries, which included publications from 1802 up to the time of publication in 1970.

During this period, new committees were formed and ALA-affiliated groups issued calls for greater services to people who were incarcerated. Members of the ALA's Intellectual Freedom Committee expressed concerns about incarcerated people's' rights to read in the 1970s. The Social Responsibilities Round Table issued a request for the ALA to attend to the needs of people who were incarcerated in 1972, and also formed a Task Force on Services to Prisoners. An ad hoc committee for Library Services to Young Adults in Institutions was formed that same year. These and other ALA-affiliated groups provided trainings for librarians, including a joint workshop on legal resources that was held in coordination with UC-Berkeley and a two-day workshop that the AHIL held in San Jose, California, in 1973.

The goal of the AHIL workshop was to raise critical awareness and to create new library services inside of prisons. The workshop's leaders were clear in their intent. They created a reading list that prioritized the social and political aspects of library services to incarcerated people. Phyllis Dalton, one of the workshop's organizers, opened the session with a statement that the success of the workshop depended on the development of new library services in carceral facilities. Gesturing to a long history of conversations about increasing services in carceral facilities that had brought little results, Dalton wrote, "should there not be library service to those within prison walls just as for those without—or even better, because the prisoners have only those services that are brought to them and have little choice?" (1973, 1). This spirit was tempered by calls for the rehabilitative nature of reading and education. Dalton openly recognized that ideologies embracing rehabilitation and reform facilitated the opportunity to create new programs: "Now is the time to consider library service, for there is an interest in prisons that is unprecedented by the public and by the government for improving the correctional system" (1973, 2).

Jail and prison libraries and research on library services to incarcerated people proliferated in the 1970s. Marjorie LeDonne, with the UC-Berkeley Institute on Library Research, conducted a *Survey of Library and Information Problems in Correctional Institutions* between 1972 and 1974. This project was probably the most recent comprehensive research into library services for incarcerated people. Published in four sections, it presented survey results that revealed the unequal and inconsistent provision of library services in carceral facilities. The report contained information about the availability and need for legal resources and an overview of relevant legislation regarding legal information access, a state-by-state breakdown of library services in carceral facilities, and a bibliography of resources that positioned library services in carceral facilities within their contemporaneous social and political context. LeDonne's work reflected a trend that became apparent in the 1970s, in its multiple points of overlap with the organizing work that was being conducted by people who were incarcerated at the time—including increased agitation for legal resources that ultimately led to a federal mandate for meaningful access to the law. It was during this period that librarians first started to publicly resist the narrative that the library in a carceral facility should align with either a perspective of rehabilitation (often in the form of bibliotherapy) or of punishment. In this regard, LeDonne's work reflected a turn toward recognizing incarcerated people as capable of identifying their own information needs and interests.

Other surveys were conducted during this period. In 1973, the ALA's Social Responsibilities Round Table on Services to Prisoners conducted research on library services in jails. A similar nationwide survey of library services in local jails was conducted in 1975 by the Maine State Library (Angelides and Berg). The Maine State Library study, influenced by a 1974 issue of *Illinois Libraries* described later in this chapter, found inconsistent access to libraries or books (and in some cases, no libraries at all). The authors of that report urged for more, and more frequent, information-gathering on the scope and type of services available in local jails and clearly stated that these services were necessary.

Nowhere was the desire to align library services with the information needs and requests of people who are incarcerated more apparent than in the unaffiliated publication *Inside-Outside*. This newsletter, edited by Stout and Turitz Perolman, ran from 1974 through 1978. *Inside-Outside* acted as a mode of communication between librarians and people who were incarcerated. It contained calls for support, book reviews, librarians' missives, critical examinations of carceral facilities and of the function of incarceration in America, critiques of American imperialism, and more. It also included explicitly anti-incarceration illustrations that served to communicate its philosophical approach to readers, including quotes from Eugene Debs and images of cell bars being pushed open (Austin, 2017; Stout and Turitz Perolman, 1972). Stout, one of the editors of *Inside-Outside*, was noted as a contributor to the bibliography section of LeDonne's substantial research project. Stout's efforts to communicate and act in coordination with people who were incarcerated conveyed librarians' desire to position library services to incarcerated people within a larger frame of their historical, political, and social context.

Expanded funding, growing professional interest in library services for incarcerated people, and the organizing efforts of people who were incarcerated and people working with them outside of the prisons led to an increase in research on these types of services. Three special issues on library services to incarcerated people were published in the 1970s. These were the 1974 special issue of *Illinois Libraries*, published in a response to a recent ACA/ALA joint conference; a 1977 special issue of the *Wilson Library Bulletin* titled "Breaking In: Library Services to Prisoners"; and a 1977 special issue of *Library Trends* titled "Library Services to Correctional Facilities." These issues also addressed the incarceration of youth and adults in the United States, and outlined the overlaps and divergences in how juvenile detentions and prisons shaped their library services.[8] While some articles in these special issues contained hints of philosophical approaches outside of the rehabilitation-or-punishment logic of American carceral institutions, most of the articles did not question the function of incarceration in American society and its role in continuing existing forms of oppression.

The 1970s and 1980s were marked by "tough on crime" and "war on drugs" policies that further criminalized groups that had been actively seeking to resist their oppression throughout the 1970s. While the history of incarceration as a form of racial control, ideological management, and colonization in the United States can be traced back to the systems of slavery and colonialism, scholars have pointed to this more recent period as the origin of modern mass incarceration (Alexander, 2010). Tough on crime and anti-drug policies overlapped with de facto modes of segregation, such as redlining, and made the increased surveillance and policing of Black, Indigenous, and people of color, people living in poverty, people who were disabled, LGBTQIA+ people, and people who lived their lives in public part of a legal process of policing, criminalization, and incarceration. This occurred as newer drugs, specifically crack cocaine, were introduced into and circulated through communities that were experiencing ongoing oppression.

Use and possession of crack cocaine was criminalized at rates exorbitantly higher than cocaine powder, a drug associated at the time with white, predominantly middle-class users (Alexander, 2010). Due to policing, incarceration, and the high costs of bail (which grants the ability to pay to leave the jail with the promise to return for all state-mandated proceedings and sentencing), the structure of the public underwent swift changes. As more people, primarily young Black men and men of color, were incarcerated, communities were drained of their support systems and forced into dependence on rapidly depleting state services. Media reports and official state policies also worked to reinforce narratives and ideologies that enacted racial criminalization, equating being Black, specifically, or a person of color, more broadly, with being (always or always potentially) criminal (Cacho, 2012).

Librarians were not removed from these social and political shifts. Where in the past white public librarians had, at times, enforced the segregation of public libraries (choosing in some cases to close libraries rather than to desegregate), librarians in the 1980s were faced with a public whose composition was continuously being whitewashed through processes of criminalization and incarceration. Activity in the 1970s had generated momentum for new projects and organizing among librarians, but the tenor of librarians' passion for working with incarcerated people shifted, as did librarians' professed trend toward more rehabilitative approaches to carceral systems. Policing also impacted people at the local level, and jail populations swiftly increased. As more and more people were placed in jail prior to sentencing, and prison libraries had become somewhat more established in the 1970s, some librarians turned their focus to how public libraries might provide library services to people in local jails.

The ALA's Association of Specialized and Cooperative Library Agencies (ASCLA) began the Jail Library Services Project in 1979. This project represented a major collaboration between carceral services staff and librarians. The partners on the Higher Education Act II-B-funded grant included the American Correctional Association, the National Jail Association, the National Sheriffs' Association, the Fortune Society, and Sam Houston University. The two-year project resulted in one workshop and two published guides. The goal of the Jail Library Services Project was reflected in the grant title ("Improving Jail Library Services"). The two-day workshop, coordinated by Connie House, the project's director, was preceded by an extensive information-gathering project. House contacted state library systems and local-level providers to ascertain the extent of services being provided within jails and with requests to duplicate awareness-raising projects (in one instance, a scenario in which attendees would participate in a jail simulation) (correspondence, Connie House to Mary Zoller, 1979). The 1980 two-day workshop in Huntsville, Texas, drew attendees from across the United States.

The Jail Library Services Project published two guides in 1981. These guides positioned jail staff and administrators and librarians as partners in providing "the overall education and rehabilitation of inmates and improved jail conditions and services" (Bayley, Greenfield, and Nogueira, 1981, v). One of the guides, *Jail Library Service: A Guide for Librarians and Jail Administrators*, opens with a statement of the groups' belief in the mutually beneficial nature of library services in local jails:

> Inmates have the right to read, and quality jail library service can help them exercise this right. Simultaneously, it aids the jail administrator and jail staff with security by giving inmates a constructive way to use their time. It provides jail staff ready access to educational and professional materials, and gives the public library the opportunity

to meet the needs of a great part of its community. And it gives the public library and the city or county jail the opportunity to work together and hopefully evolve as support groups for each other. (Bayley, Greenfield, and Nogueira, 1981, 1)

The other guide produced by the Jail Library Services Project continued to expound on the need for coordination between the same groups involved in the grant, but it reflected the notion that the goal of both correctional staff and librarians was the coordinated and controlled rehabilitation of people who were incarcerated (Schexnaydre and Robbins, 1981).

The "Library Standards for Adult Correctional Institutions" were again revised in 1981. Librarians' faith in the possibility of carceral institutions as rehabilitative agents probably lasted beyond the punitive turn that occurred during political and legal maneuvers that proposed to be tough on crime, but, following the publication of the *Standards*, their formal publications on this topic tapered off. This change may have been accelerated by the 1982 split between the ALA and the American Correctional Association (ACA) over the newly revised "Library Standards," and particularly by the ALA's inclusion of the "Resolution on Prisoners' Right to Read" statement that accompanied the revision (Conrad, 2017; Sweeney, 2010). The Resolution called for emulations of a California policy—California Penal Code Section 2601(c)—that allowed access to any reading materials permissible to be mailed, with restrictions only on instructions for making weapons and the number of materials a person kept in their cell or other locations. This rift reflected both the social and political stance that librarians advocating for library services in carceral facilities developed during the 1970s and the ACA's increasingly punitive approach, which mirrored the actions of the American government and courts.

Despite a lessening of documented activity, the ASCLA's Library Services to Prisoners group formed a Speaker's Bureau on Jails and Prisons in 1983, and asserted that "overcrowding in U.S. prisons threatens to rule out the establishment of libraries in many facilities, making the effort timely" (ASCLA, 1983). This brief statement indirectly reflected the punitive turn that would enlarge the U.S. prison population from 158,000 people in 1978 (Bayley, Greenfield, and Nogueira, 1981) to the 2.3 million people incarcerated in 2020.

International interest in libraries in carceral facilities was formalized in the mid-1980s through the IFLA's Working Group on Prison Libraries. The Working Group conducted an international survey of libraries in prisons in 1985 and 1986. The group found that "in the United States, prison libraries are used more by prisoners than public libraries are used by the general public," but that many U.S. prisons still did not provide any form of library access (Dalton, 1988, 160).

In the United States, the philosophy of the punitive turn was reflected in publications about library services in prisons, including Hartz and Hartz's *The Library in the Correctional Setting* (1984) and Coyle's *Libraries in Prisons* (1987). Frederick and Emilie Hartz's book is an annotated bibliography and analysis of library publications on prison libraries from the period 1958 to 1983. In this book, the authors offered a scathing critique of the lack of attention given to library services to people in prison, denigrated the faith librarians had professed in the library's role in rehabilitation, and panned librarians' calls to increase access to information for people inside of prisons. Hartz's work reflects the effects of ongoing processes of criminalization. Nowhere is this more apparent than when he discusses library patrons in the prison. Hartz asks: "Did it ever occur to anyone working in corrections that maybe the criminal doesn't want to be reformed . . . these people function as true outlaws who will continue their criminal roles until the day they die, either by natural causes or other terminal misadventures" (Hartz, 1984, viii).[9]

Whereas Hartz's "law and order"-influenced book, which was published by a small press, may not have reached many librarians, William Coyle's book *Libraries in Prisons* (1987) was widely received (and simultaneously criticized by librarians who had called for library services in carceral facilities throughout the 1970s). Coyle openly chastised librarians for advocating for library services in prisons that would be like those in a public library, delineating prison librarianship from other forms of library service on account of its alignment with the punitive function of the prison. In Coyle's conceptual framework, the prison library was an extension of the prison. To this effect, he wrote:

> The state itself . . . is the legitimizer of prison library service. Therefore, it is the state's interests and goals, and not the interests of inmates, that should determine the kind and extent of library service to be made available in prisons. This leads directly to the question: What are the state's interests, and to what extent does the rationale of the public library reflect those interests? (Coyle, 1987, 80).

It may not be difficult to discern that Coyle's answer to the question he asks here is that the public library ethos does not align with the state's interests.

The 1980s closed with two publications reflecting on changes in how library services to incarcerated people had been implemented over the decade. Rubin and Souza reproached Coyle's view of the role of library services in carceral facilities and outlined its alignment with inconsistent and punitive practices of incarceration. Vogel, acting as editor of the *Wilson Library Bulletin*'s special issue on prison libraries in 1989, made similar critiques. These authors described how changes to carceral practices, social and political understandings of the role and function of incarceration, and the increasing numbers of people incarcerated had impacted the possibilities for library services in prisons. Suvak, in that same issue of the *Bulletin*, made a specific case against the foundational assumptions in Coyle's work, noting its impact as one of the few books on prison librarianship published at the time. Suvak's assessment of the book was straightforward—people who were incarcerated would know that a prison library designed according to Coyle's model was an unprofessional farce. Beyond this, "the most fatal flaw in the development of this ill-suited model is the assumption that prisoners are a separate breed, the bottom rung, the true outcasts who have serious flaws that must be corrected for the safety of a society they may reenter" (Suvak, 1989, 33). Together, these critics ended the decade with an urgent request for librarians to reconsider services to incarcerated people as part of the ongoing function of libraries, rather than as a niche area of interest.

CONCLUSION

The historical overview of carceral histories and libraries presented in this chapter (and outlined in figure 2.1) offers many points of entry for further exploration. Tracing the histories of incarceration, literacy practices, and librarianship reveals ongoing overlaps between carceral facilities and libraries. It provides perspective on how librarians' philosophical approaches to carceral systems informed library services, how librarians have aligned with or deviated from the polar conceptions of carceral systems as punitive or rehabilitative, and provides some insight into how contemporary forms of incarceration have shaped the ways in which the "public" served by the library is conceptualized in library discourse.

Within librarianship, a 1990 survey of library services in prisons preceded the ASCLA's publication of the revised "Library Standards for Adult Correctional Institutions" in 1992 (Greenway, 2007), the most recent version of the standards. The early 1990s, when the "Library Standards" were published, were a time of major changes in information access and a period in which racial criminalization was further instantiated. Racialized and stereotyped narratives gained further traction among people with power as communities impacted by the war on drugs were reconfigured by state practices of surveillance, policing, and incarceration. Throughout this period information technologies proliferated and access to developing technologies began to equate to access to information worlds. These events proceeded, informed, and were accelerated by the 1994 Violent Crime Control and Law Enforcement Act. Carceral facilities broke new ground across the nation. In the political vacillation between rehabilitation and punitive incarceration, punishment took hold.

Many of the trends that were examined in this chapter remain present in librarianship today. Some of these are practical—such as calls for funding libraries in carceral facilities, the need for librarians, and descriptions of the role of libraries in carceral facilities—and have been present for more than a century. The more theoretical themes—how patrons are conceptualized along the lines of criminality, the role of the library within a carceral facility, the tools used to lay claim to the information needs and rights of people who are incarcerated—have been and continue to be debated in the field.

The next chapter, "Forms of Incarceration," disambiguates some of the institutions named in this chapter. It draws from Ruth Wilson Gilmore's (2007) utilization of "carceral geographies" to describe their contemporary functions and the ways in which incarceration occurs in American society and between carceral institutions. This situates an analysis of contemporary publications and services that begins in chapter 4.

FIGURE 2.1

Library Services to Incarcerated People: 1870–1992

National Prison Congress

1870

Discussion of library services in prisons.

Catalog and Rules for Prison Libraries

1876

New York Prison Association.

ALA Committee Formed

1911

Committee on Libraries in Federal Prisons.

Manual for Institution Libraries

1916

ALA Committee on Library Work in Hospitals and in Charitable and Correctional Institutions.

Libraries and Personal Reformation

1918

Curtis publishes *Libraries of the American State and National Institutions for Defectives, Dependents and Delinquents.*

Bibliotherapy Gains Traction

1930s

The Prison Library Handbook

1932

ALA Committee on Libraries in Correctional Institutions/American Prison Association Committee on Education.

2500 Books for the Prison Library

1933

ALA Committee on Libraries in Correctional Institutions/American Prison Association Committee on Education.

1000 Books for Prison Libraries

1939

American Prison Association Committee on Institution Libraries.

Standards Approved

1944

Objectives and Standards for Libraries in Adult Prisons and Reformatories. Approved by American Prison Association in 1943/ALA in 1944.

Name Change

1954

American Prison Association becomes American Correctional Association (ACA).

Joint Committee on Institution Libraries

1956 and 1957

ACA and the ALA Association of Hospital and Institution Libraries (AHIL) form joint committee.

Standards Revised

1962

ACA/ALA AHIL Joint Committee on Institutional Libraries.

Survey of Institutional Libraries

1965 and 1966

Conducted by ACA and ALA AHIL Joint Committee.

Library Services and Construction Act

1966

Title IV funds institutional libraries when matched with state funds.

Institutional Library Service Programs in U.S.A

1966

Wang. Indiana State Library. Survey of state-affiliated institutional libraries.

Prison Libraries—Bibliography

1968

Gillespie. "A Citation-Entry Analysis of the Literature on Prison Libraries."

Historical Review
1970
MacCormick presents "Brief History of Libraries in American Correctional Centers" to ACA.

Right to Read While Incarcerated
1970
ALA Office for Intellectual Freedom expresses concern.

Library Services and Construction Act
1971
Title I funds public libraries, with option for funds to be designated for institutional libraries.

Bibliotherapy: Methods and Materials
1971
ALA Association of Hospital and Institution Libraries.

Request to Prioritize Services
1972
ALA Social Responsibilities Round Table Task Force on Service to Prisoners issues general request to ALA members.

Survey of Institutional Libraries
1972
Survey of Library and Information Problems in Correctional Institutions begins under LeDonne's supervision.

Young Adults
1973
Library Service to Young Adults in Institutions ad hoc committee of the ALA Young Adult Services Division formed.

Workshop
1973
ALA AHIL and others hold two-day workshop in California on "Library and Information Service for Prison Populations."

Survey Results
1974
LeDonne. Correctional institution survey results published in four sections through the Institute of Library Research at UC Berkeley.

Inside-Outside
1974
An unaffiliated newsletter between librarians and incarcerated people. Publication continued until 1978.

Illinois Libraries
1974
Special journal issue in response to ALA/ACA joint conference.

Young Adult Standards
1975
Library Standards for Juvenile Correctional Institutions created by ACA/ALA.

Library Trends
1977
Special issue on "Library Services to Correctional Facilities."

Wilson Library Bulletin
1977
Special issue on "Breaking In: Library Service to Prisoners."

Jail Library Services Project
1979 and 1980
ALA Association of Specialized and Cooperative Library Agencies (ASCLA), ACA, and others. Funded by Higher Education Act IIB grant.

Institute
1980
House and ALA ASCLA hold five-day institute in Texas on jail library services.

(continued)

FIGURE 2.1 *(continued)*

Prisoners' Right to Read
1982

ALA includes "Resolution on Prisoners' Right to Read," modeled on California Penal Code Section 2601(c), with updated standards for adult institutions.

The Library in the Correctional Setting
1984

Hartz and Hartz. Rue Chien. Small press publication of a bibliography that reflected the punitive turn.

"The Challenge Continues: Prison Librarianship in the 1980s."
1989

Rubin and Souza address the increasing rate of incarceration in the United States. *Library Journal.*

Survey of Correctional Institutions
1990

Conducted by ALA ASCLA to inform forthcoming revision of the standards.

ALA Standards Revised
1992

ALA ASCLA publishes the current version of *Library Standards for Correctional Institutions.*

ACA Disbands Collaboration
1982

ACA disbands collaboration with ALA in response to "Resolution on Prisoners' Right to Read." ACA forms own standards for prison libraries.

Libraries in Prisons: A Blending of Institutions
1987

Coyle. Greenwood Press. Considered controversial by Coyle's peers.

Wilson Library Bulletin
1989

Vogel is editor of special section on prison libraries. Issue describes changes in incarceration.

IFLA Guidelines
1992

International Federation of Library Associations (IFLA) publishes first edition of *Guidelines for Library Services to Prisoners.*

NOTES

1. See *Knowledge Justice: Disrupting Library and Information Studies through Critical Race Theory* (2021), edited by Sofia Y. Leung and Jorge R. López-McKnight, for a deep engagement on critical race theory and LIS.
2. Forced sterilization, often conducted after a person received limited or false information, continued into the 2010s (Beam, 2021).
3. Sullivan and Vogel (2003) discuss localized efforts to create library services, including prison- and state-level services in the nineteenth century, in their book chapter "Reachin' through the Bars." Their chapter interrogates the punitive/rehabilitative split among librarians in carceral facilities (and librarians' faith in the functions of prisons, in general) by emphasizing how each approach leads to censorship.
4. Sullivan provides a model for historical review that utilizes three categories: "reform rhetoric," which is the way society perceives and justifies incarceration; "the reality of the prison," which includes what books are available and what people who were incarcerated actually read or wanted to read; and "the discourse of articulate convicts," or the ways in which literate people describe and enact literacy practices around their incarceration (1998, 114).
5. Jordan and Josey note that the first "completely desegregated Association meeting was held in the South" in 1956 (1977, 19).

6. Carceral facilities were segregated during this time, and practices of racial segregation in at least some prisons formally persisted until 2005,when the Supreme Court ordered an end to the practice except in extraordinary circumstances (Trulson et al., 2008).

7. Littletree (2018) draws a sharp distinction between the enculturating information practices forced upon Native peoples through Indian boarding schools, on the one hand, and the role of self-determination in the history of tribal libraries on the other.

8. The inclusion of research on juvenile detention center libraries was probably influenced by the creation of the ACA/ALA's 1975 "Library Standards for Juvenile Correctional Institutions."

9. Hartz and Hartz, along with another author extended the bibliography, and its attendant argument, in the publication of a 1987 work (Hartz, Krimmel, and Hartz). The general approach of librarians to incarcerated people during this time might be encapsulated in Koons's review of the 1987 work for *Library Journal*, which recommended the book as "helpful for public libraries," despite being "caustic" (100).

REFERENCES

Alexander, M. 2010. *The New Jim Crow: Mass Incarceration in the Age of Colorblindness*. New York: New Press.

American Library Association, Committee on Library Work in Hospitals and Charitable and Correctional Institutions. 1916. *Manual for Institution Libraries*. Chicago: American Library Association Publishing Board.

Angelides, C., and K. Berg. 1975. *Library Service in County Jails*. Augusta, ME: Maine State Library.

Araiza, L. 2009. "'In Common Struggle against a Common Oppression': The United Farm Workers and the Black Panther Party, 1968-1973." *Journal of African American History* 94, no. 2: 200-223.

Association on Specialized and Cooperative Library Agencies (ASCLA). 1983. "Speakers on Prison Libraries Organized by ALA's ASCLA." *Library Journal* 108, no. 9: 858.

Austin, J. 2017. "Reform and Revolution: Juvenile Detention Center Libraries in the 1970s." *Libraries: Culture, History, and Society* 1, no. 2: 240-66.

Bailey, A. 1972. "Standards for Library Service in Institutions: A. In the Correctional Setting." *Library Trends* 21: 261-66.

Bauer, S. 2018. *American Prison: A Reporter's Undercover Journey into the Business of Punishment*. New York: Penguin.

Bayley, L., L. Greenfield, and F. Nogueira. Association of Specialized and Cooperative Library Agencies. 1981. *Jail Library Service: A Guide for Librarians and Jail Administrators*. Chicago: American Library Association.

Beam, A. 2021. "California to Pay Victims of Forced, Coerced Sterilizations." *Associated Press* (July 7). https://apnews.com/article/california-business-science-health-government-and-politics-bb019f426cd bb839790ac98d420a0224.

Ben-Moshe, L. 2020. *Decarcerating Disability: Deinstitutionalization and Prison Abolition*. Minneapolis: University of Minnesota Press.

Bernstein, L. 2010. *America Is the Prison: Arts and Politics in Prison in the 1970s*. Chapel Hill: University of North Carolina Press.

Bissonnette, J. 2008. *When the Prisoners Ran Walpole: A True Story in the Movement for Prison Abolition*. Cambridge, MA: South End.

Bly, A. 2008. "'Pretends He Can Read': Runaways and Literacy in Colonial America, 1730-1776." *Early American Studies* 6, no. 2: 261-94.

Browne, S. 2015. *Dark Matters: On the Surveillance of Blackness*. Durham, NC: Duke University Press.

Burroway, J. 2008. "Fifty Years Ago, a Supreme Court Victory." *Gay & Lesbian Review* 15, no. 2: 6-7.

Cacho, L. M. 2012. *Social Death: Racialized Rightlessness and the Criminalization of the Unprotected*. New York: New York University Press.

Cahalan, M. 1979. "Trends in Incarceration in the United States since 1880: A Summary of Reported Rates and the Distribution of Offenses." *Crime & Delinquency* 25, no. 1: 9-41.

Chapman, C., A. C. Carey, and L. Ben-Moshe. 2014. "Reconsidering Confinement: Interlocking Locations and Logics of Incarceration." In *Disability Incarcerated: Imprisonment and Disability in the United States and Canada*, ed. Chapman, Carey, and Ben-Moshe, 3-23. Palgrave Macmillan.

Chavez-Garcia, M. 2012. *States of Delinquency: Race and Science in the Making of California's Juvenile Justice System*. Berkeley: University of California Press.

Cohen, R. D. 1997. "'The Delinquents': Censorship and Youth Culture in Recent U.S. History." *History of Education Quarterly* 37, no. 3: 251-70.

Combahee River Collective. 1977. "The Combahee River Collective Statement." BlackPast. www.blackpast .org/african-american-history/combahee-river-collective-statement-1977/.

Conrad, S. 2017. Prison librarianship: Policy and practice. Jefferson, N.C.: McFarland & Company, Inc.

Cornelius, J. 1983. "'We Slipped and Learned to Read': Slave Accounts of the Literacy Process, 1830-1865." *Phylon* 44, no. 3: 171-86.

Coyle, W. 1987. *Libraries in Prisons: A Blending of Institutions*. New Directions in Information Management 15. Westport, CT: Greenwood.

Curtin, M. E. 2013. "The Hidden History of Black Prisoners." In *The Punitive Turn: New Approaches to Race and Incarceration*, ed. D. E. McDowell, C. N. Harold, and J. Battle, 29-44. Charlottesville: University of Virginia Press.

Curtis, F. R. 1918. *The Libraries of the American State and National Institutions for Defectives, Dependents, and Delinquents*. Minneapolis: Bulletin of the University of Minnesota.

Dalton, K. C. 1991. "'The Alphabet Is an Abolitionist': Literacy and African Americans in the Emancipation Era." *Massachusetts Review* 32, no. 4: 545-80.

Dalton, P. I. 1973. "Library and Information Services for Prison Populations." In P. I. Dalton, Workshop on Library and Information Services for Prison Populations, March 2-3, 1973. Santa Cruz, University of California Extension.

———. 1988. "Prison Library Service from an International Viewpoint." *IFLA Journal* 14, no. 2: 155-60.

Davis, A. 2003. *Are Prisons Obsolete?* New York: Seven Stories.

Del Castillo, R. 2000. "The Los Angeles 'Zoot Suit Riots' Revisited: Mexican and Latin American Perspectives." *Mexican Studies/Estudios Mexicanos* 16, no. 2: 36-91.

Delaney, R., R. Subramanian, A. Shames, and N. Turner. 2018. "American History, Race, and Prison." Reimagining Prison, Vera Institute of Justice.

Densho. 2020. "Dies Committee." https://encyclopedia.densho.org/Dies_Committee/.

Evans, S. M. 2015. "Women's Liberation: Seeing the Revolution Clearly." *Feminist Studies* 41, no. 1: 138-49.

Foucault, M. 1995. *Discipline and Punish: The Birth of the Prison*. 2nd edition. New York: Vintage Books.

Freedman, E. I. (ed.), and Committee on Institution Libraries of the American Prison Association. 1950. *Library Manual for Correctional Institutions: A Handbook of Library Standards and Procedures for Prisons, Reformatories, for Men and Women and Other Adult Correctional Institutions*. New York: American Prison Association.

George, M.A. 2015. "The Harmless Psychopath: Legal Debates Promoting the Decriminalization of Sodomy in the United States." *Journal of the History of Sexuality* 24, no. 2: 225-61.

Gilmore, R. W. 2007. *Golden Gulag: Prisons, Surplus, Crisis, and Opposition in Globalizing California*. Berkeley: University of California Press.

Gottschalk, M. 2015. "Is Mass Incarceration the 'New Jim Crow'? Racial Disparities and the Carceral State." In *Caught: The Prison State and the Lockdown of American Politics*, 119-38. Princeton, NJ: Princeton University Press.

Greenway, S. A. 2007. "Library Services behind Bars." *Bookmobiles and Outreach Services* 10, no. 2: 43-64.

Harris, C. 1993. "Whiteness as Property." *Harvard Law Review* 106, no. 8: 1707-91.

Hartz, F. R. and Hartz, E. K. 1984. *The Library in the Correctional Setting: A Selective, Annotated, Classified Bibliography of the Literature of Prison Librarianship, 1958-1983*. Lyons, GA: Rue Chien.

Hartz, F. R., M. B. Krimmel, and E. K. Hartz. 1987. *Prison Librarianship: A Selective, Annotated, Classified Bibliography, 1945-1985*. Jefferson, NC: McFarland.

Hernández, K. L. 2017. *City of Inmates: Conquest, Rebellion, and the Rise of Human Caging in Los Angeles, 1771-1965*. Chapel Hill: University of North Carolina Press.

House, C. 1979. "Correspondence, 1979-1980." Record Series 23/11/76, American Library Association Archives at the University of Illinois at Urbana-Champaign.

Hunt, R. 2013. "African American Leaders in the Library Profession: Little Known History." *Black History Bulletin* 76, no. 1: 14-19.

Jones, E. K., and American Library Association, Committee on Libraries in Correctional Institutions. 1932. *The Prison Library Handbook: Prepared for the Committee on Libraries in Correctional Institutions of the American Library Association and the Committee on Education of the American Prison Association*. Chicago: American Library Association.

Jones, P. 1933. *2500 Books for the Prison Library*. American Library Association, Committee on Libraries in Correctional Institutions, and American Prison Association. Minneapolis, MN: Harrison and Smith.

Jordan, C. L., and E. J. Josey. 1977. "A Chronology of Events in Black Librarianship." In *Handbook of Black Librarianship*, ed. E. J. Josey and A. A. Shockley, 15-24. Littleton, CO: Libraries Unlimited.

King, M. L., Jr., 1994. *Letter from Birmingham Jail*. San Francisco: Harper San Francisco.

Knott, C. 2015. *Not Free, Not for All: Public Libraries in the Age of Jim Crow*. Amherst: University of Massachusetts Press.

Koons, P. 1987. "Prison Librarianship Bibliog." *Library Journal* 112, no. 13: 100.

Kushner, R. 2019. "Is Prison Necessary? Ruth Wilson Gilmore Might Change Your Mind." *New York Times Magazine*, April 17. www.nytimes.com/2019/04/17/magazine/prison-abolition-ruth-wilson-gilmore.html.

LeDonne, M. 1974. "Survey of Library and Information Problems in Correctional Institutions." U.S. Department of Health, Education, and Welfare.

Leung, S., and J. R. López-McKnight, eds. 2021. Knowledge Justice: Disrupting Library and Information Studies through Critical Race Theory. Cambridge, MA: MIT Press.

Lewis, A. J. 2016. "'We Are Certain of Our Own Insanity': Antipsychiatry and the Gay Liberation Movement, 1968-1980." *Journal of the History of Sexuality* 25, no. 1: 83-113.

Littletree, S. D. 2018. "'Let Me Tell You about Indian Libraries': Self-Determination, Leadership, and Vision—The Basis of Tribal Library Development in the United States." Doctoral dissertation, University of Washington. https://digital.lib.washington.edu/researchworks/handle/1773/42418.

MacCormick, A. H. 1950. "Purposes and Needs of the Prison Library." In *Library Manual for Correctional Institutions: A Handbook of Library Standards and Procedures for Prisons, Reformatories, for Men and Women and Other Adult Correctional Institutions*, by E. I. Freedman (ed.) and Committee on Institution Libraries of the American Prison Association. New York: American Prison Association.

———. 1973. "A Brief History of Libraries in Correctional Institutions." In *Readings in Prison Education*, ed. A. R. Roberts, 317-36. Springfield, IL: Charles C. Thomas.

Methven, M. L., and American Prison Association, Committee on Institution Libraries. 1939. *1000 Books for Prison Libraries, 1936-1939*. St. Paul, MN: Dawson-Patterson.

Pendergast, C. 2003. *Literacy and Racial Justice: The Politics of Learning after Brown v. Board of Education*. Carbondale: Southern Illinois University Press.

Rasmussen, B. B. 2010. "'Attended with Great Inconveniences': Slave Literacy and the 1740 South Carolina Negro Act." *PMLA* 125, no. 1: 201-3.

Richardson, J. V. 2009. "Library Science in the United States: Early History." In *Encyclopedia of Library and Information Sciences,* 3rd edition, ed. M. J. Bates and M. N. Maack, 3440-48. New York: Taylor & Francis.

Rubin, R. J., and S. J. Souza. 1989. "The Challenge Continues: Prison Librarianship in the 1980s." *Library Journal* 114, no. 4: 47-51.

Schexnaydre, L., and K. Robbins. 1981. *Workshops for Jail Library Service: A Planning Manual*. Chicago: American Library Association.

Schlesselman-Tarango, G. 2016. "The Legacy of Lady Bountiful: White Women in the Library." *Library Trends* 64, no. 4: 667-86.

Schorb, J. 2014. *Reading Prisoners: Literature, Literacy, and the Transformation of American Punishment, 1700-1845*. New Brunswick, NJ: Rutgers University Press.

Snorton, C. R. 2017. *Black on Both Sides*. Minneapolis: University of Minnesota Press.

Stout, J. A., and G. Turitz Perolman. 1972. *Inside-Outside: A Newsletter on Library Services to Youth and Adults in Prisons, Jails, and Detention Centers*. https://archive.org/details/insideoutside1421unse.

Sullivan, L. 1998. "Reading in American Prisons: Structures and Strictures." *Libraries & Culture* 33, no. 1: 113-19.

Sullivan, L. E., and B. Vogel. 2003. "Reachin' through the Bars: Library Outreach to Prisoners, 1798-2000." In *Libraries to the People: Histories of Outreach*, ed. R. S. Freeman and D. M. Hovde. Jefferson, NC: McFarland.

Suvak, D. 1989. "'Throw the Book at 'Em': The Change-Based Model for Prison Libraries." *Wilson Library Bulletin* 64: 31-33.

Sweeney, M. 2010. *Reading Is My Window: Books and the Art of Reading in Women's Prisons*. Chapel Hill: University of North Carolina Press.

Trulson, C. R., J. W. Marquart, C. Hemmens, and L. Carroll. 2008. "Racial Desegregation in Prisons." *The Prison Journal* 88, no. 2: 270-99.

Vogel, B. 1989. "Prison Libraries—Escaping the Stereotype—An Introduction." *Wilson Library Bulletin* 64, no. 2: 25.

Wang, R. 1969. *Institutional Library Service Programs in the U.S.A.* Indianapolis, IN: Extension Division, Indiana State Library.

Wiegand, W. 2017. "'Any Ideas?': The American Library Association and the Desegregation of Public Libraries in the American South." *Libraries: Culture, History, and Society* 1, no. 1: 1-22.

Wiegand, W. A., and S. A. Wiegand. 2018. *The Desegregation of Public Libraries in the Jim Crow South: Civil Rights and Local Activism*. Baton Rouge: Louisiana State University Press.

X, M., and A. Haley. 1965. *The Autobiography of Malcolm X*. New York: Grove.

CHAPTER 3

Forms of Incarceration

I t is one thing to discuss incarceration at a national scale, and another to begin to differentiate between the operation of types of facilities and their various practices. Turning to the differences and similarities between types of carceral facilities provides some insight into how carceral systems function in relation to one another. Types of carceral facilities in the United States, the structure of incarceration and reentry, and official and diffuse practices of policing and incarceration are outlined in this chapter. It provides a point of entry into understanding and differentiating between carceral institutions. It is, at heart, a chapter about carceral geography (Gilmore, 2007), the terrain of incarceration in the United States.

Conceptualizing the various manifestations of carceral institutions and practices in the United States creates opportunities to locate points of entry for the implementation of services, to locate when narratives of rehabilitation or punishment attach to actual practices, and to disrupt some of the prominent portrayals of recidivism (being re-incarcerated after release) as a measure of the viability or failure of incarceration. This chapter offers descriptions of types of institutions, demographic information about the people incarcerated in those institutions, and some information about the carceral systems at the local, state, and federal levels. It also describes some of the processes and materials that surround incarceration, such as bail and risk assessment measures. It then turns to government-administered practices of continued assessment and surveillance post-release, including the official and dispersed forms of surveillance that people experience during the process of immigration, reentry, and post-incarceration.

Some of the information in this chapter will probably be familiar to readers. The carceral system in the United States is so large, and so widely distributed, that few locations do not contain a local jail, prison, or some other carceral facility. Differentiating between institutions while showing their connections reveals that the general public, when widely defined to include people incarcerated near libraries, stands to be reconceptualized in light of the impact of incarceration across the United States. Given that public libraries are positioned to provide services to 96 percent of the U.S. population, and that people who are incarcerated need access to academic, legal, medical, and other specialized information, this chapter helps librarians and information professionals to identify how their conceptions of their scope of services might change if their patron base is defined as including people who are detained or incarcerated (Institute of Museum and Library Services, 2013, 7).

PRISONS

Prisons are carceral facilities designed with the intention of being used for long-term incarceration. Prison systems tend to permeate each other—people in custody might be held in a type of prison other than the jurisdiction that holds power over them (local, state, or federal), and some local jails have cells reserved for people with state or federal convictions. For the sake of clarity, though, this section covers three types of facilities: state prisons, federal prisons, and privately run prisons (or "private prisons"). People are typically incarcerated in state prisons when they have been convicted of breaking local or state laws and have over a yearlong sentence, and are incarcerated in facilities of the Federal Bureau of Prisons when convicted of federal crimes. Privately run prisons are contracted at either the state or federal level and are run by private (nongovernment) entities.

As an aftereffect of mass incarceration, many state prisons have held much larger numbers of people than they were designed to contain. This practice, known as overcrowding, has led a few states to create legislation that seeks to reduce the number of people in state prisons. In some instances, the overcrowding of prisons has led to legislation that has redirected some people into local jails, which were not designed for long-term incarceration. In states with extremely large prison populations, such as California and Texas, state and federal legislation has been passed in attempts to reduce overcrowding. California has been federally mandated to reduce the population in its state prisons to within 137.5 percent of the capacity for which they were originally designed (Burns, 2019). Texas has implemented parole systems that have reduced the number of incarcerated people in the state while maintaining ongoing surveillance of the individuals who were released (Barnes, 2019).

Despite the efforts undertaken in Texas and California, overcrowding has continued to be an issue in American prisons in general. Thirty-three states had overcrowded prisons in 2000. Overcrowding has been identified as a source of mental and physical harm to incarcerated people (Ghiorzo and Blount-Hill, 2019). Presently, Mississippi, Louisiana, and Oklahoma have the highest rates of per-capita incarceration in the United States, and also some of the most overcrowded prisons (Barnes, 2019). Per-capita imprisonment is lowest in Vermont and Massachusetts, but these rates still exceed the per-capita incarceration rates of most countries in the world (Wagner and Sawyer, 2018). Patterns of incarceration vary somewhat between states, but all reflect the national statistics discussed in chapter 1 and testify to the ways that racism has informed the implementation of incarceration in the United States.[1]

People are incarcerated in federal prisons after they are convicted of violations of federal law. As of February 2021, the most prominent convictions were for drug offenses, which constitute 46.4 percent of the offenses that led to federal conviction (Bureau of Prisons, 2021). Recall here that the racialized policing of drug offenses has been listed as one of the ways in which Black, Indigenous, and people of color are continuously subjected to incarceration even as rates of drug use hold across race (Alexander, 2010; Burns, 2019). Federal prisons comprise "the largest prisons system in the country," and around 13 percent of all incarcerated people were located in federal facilities in 2014 (Barnes, 2019, 492).

There are 7 contracted (privately managed) prisons utilized by the Federal Bureau of Prisons (Bureau of Prisons, 2021), and the number of federally contracted private prisons has been reduced from 12 in 2019. The use of private prisons varies by state system—22 states do not utilize private prisons, while around 53 percent of the people incarcerated in New Mexico are located in private facilities (Sentencing Project, 2019). Private carceral facilities are notorious for having limited or no oversight and for operating at the lowest cost possible in order to yield a profit for their owners (Bauer, 2018). Their operating practices result in severely limited medical care, limited training or requirements for staff, and egregiously inhumane practices of containment (Bauer, 2018; Dodson and Brown, 2019).

Prison architecture commonly falls into five categories. These types are the telephone pole (designed around a central corridor), radial (cell blocks or units around a central point), courtyard (buildings arranged around an outdoor space), campus-style (buildings are generally near one another, but the facilities are in separate buildings), and high-rise (skyscraper) (St. John, 2019). People who are incarcerated are assigned a risk level that determines what type of facility, or where in a facility, they will be located. (Many systems have an intake facility, sometimes known as a Reception and Diagnostic Center, where people undergo evaluation and then are assigned to a specific prison, often distant from their families and social support networks.) The three main facility types are minimum, medium, and maximum security (some prisons include more than one security level), and the special classifications within a facility can include psych, medical, or administrative segregation (solitary confinement) or protective custody (which can also be solitary confinement). People who are incarcerated in medical or psych areas of the prison, those who are in administrative segregation, and those who will be executed by the state typically have the least access to resources and the most restrictions on their movement and access to information. Medical and psychological diagnoses obviously tie directly to an information need, as does the lack of mental stimulation available to people in administrative segregation or on what is colloquially known as death row. Restrictive housing means that people who are incarcerated may have limited or no access to physical libraries, even if a library is available, well-stocked, and administered by a librarian.

People who are sentenced to life without the possibility of parole (LWOP) are also typically housed in highly restricted areas of the prison, with few resources. LWOP sentences have increased in the United States at accelerating levels since the 1970s, and people with these sentences are often viewed by the prison as disposable and are made vulnerable to violence within prison systems (American Civil Liberties Union, 2013). The conditions of incarceration for people sentenced to life without the possibility of parole are emphasized here because, as of 2017, 1 in 7 people incarcerated in state and federal prisons was serving a life or a "virtual life" (over 50-year) sentence (Nellis, 2017). There are some instances where states have reduced LWOP sentences, as occurred in California regarding juvenile conviction to life without the possibility of parole, and some individuals' LWOP sentences have been commuted (Drop LWOP, 2019; Equal Justice Initiative, 2017).

There are, of course, more disciplinary and intentionally punitive types of facilities and sentences. The Federal Bureau of Prisons has entire facilities that are designed to hold people in administrative segregation or other restrictive conditions. These prisons are known as "supermax" sites. Moreover, certain extralegal detention facilities continue in operation, despite allegations of and indictments for torture (as is the case at Guantanamo). The federal and state governments continue to sentence some people to execution, although this is persistently contested. These sites and practices are often positioned as outside of the normative function of carceral institutions like jails or prisons, but can be alternately viewed as indicators of the reach and scope of contemporary carceral practices. It should be noted, though, that almost half of the states in the United States either do not sentence people to death or are under a governors' moratorium that bars state execution (Death Penalty Information Center, 2021).

Systemic racism and other biases in sentencing shape the populations of state and federal prisons. Across the United States, Black and Latinx people receive longer sentences (and thus spend more time in prison) than their white counterparts (research on the incarceration of Indigenous people indicates similar trends, but is somewhat inconclusive). This is the case even when controlling for conviction histories and other life circumstances (Havis, 2019). Anti-Blackness in sentencing is evidenced in the higher likelihood that Black men will be sentenced to spend the remainder of their lives in the prison system. Racism in sentencing is evident across age groups for people sentenced to life without the possibility of parole in cases where they receive convictions for activities the court holds to be nonviolent (Havis, 2019). Manifestations of bias in sentencing are also gendered—women, and especially Black women, are more likely to receive prison sentences than men who are accused of engaging in similar activities, probably due to a perception (systemic or individual) that women have failed to act within normative (and normatively white) gender roles (Havis, 2019; Ritchie, 2017). LGBTQIA+ people of all ages, and specifically LGBTQIA+ Black, Indigenous, and people of color, are especially impacted by policing and incarceration (Prison Policy Initiative, 2021). Black trans women in particular, and Black and Indigenous transgender, two-spirit, and gender non-conforming people and transgender and gender-nonconforming people of color more broadly, routinely experience sexual and physical violence from other people, during encounters with police, and while incarcerated (Prison Policy Initiative, 2021; Ritchie, 2017).

JAILS

Jails are facilities defined by their intended use for short-term incarceration. Jails differ from prisons in that people may be detained in them prior to being sentenced by a court; they are often (but not always) designed to contain smaller numbers of incarcerated people than prisons; and they are regularly described as sites of detention for people who are sentenced but convicted to serve less than a year in incarceration. In the United States, about 630,000 of the 2.3 million people who are incarcerated are kept in jails. A subset of that group, 470,000 people, have not been convicted of a crime (Sawyer and Wagner, 2020). The number of people incarcerated in local jails increased substantially throughout the 2000s, with a slight decrease in the 2010s. One out of every 20 people is likely to have experienced or will experience incarceration in a local jail facility (Kilgore, 2015).

Jails differ from prison in a few other significant ways. They are local, and they are typically operated by, or operate in coordination with, the same agencies that conduct policing in the community. Some people in jails are being incarcerated for other agencies, including Immigration and Customs Enforcement, the Federal Bureau of Prisons, and the U.S. Marshalls (Sawyer and Wagner, 2020). The design of jails as short-term facilities means that they often lack architectural features (libraries and classrooms, for example) that might be built into longer-term facilities. The time allowed for visiting with people from outside of the jail is often restricted and is sometimes only available by video (this is also sometimes the case in prisons). Solitary confinement or administrative segregation housing, both forms of incarceration that require people to remain in their cells for around twenty-three hours a day, may be more prominent in jails than in prisons (Kilgore, 2015). Due to their limited services and reduced overhead costs for programming, many jails operate at a lower per-person cost than prisons (Kilgore, 2015). Jails are rarely designed to include housing that adequately accommodates people who are ill or require ongoing medical care, people who are under duress or experiencing mental health crises, and people who would typically be kept segregated in a prison due to their perceived, claimed, or imposed affiliations with formalized gangs or their prior knowledge of one another (Harpster, 2019). This increases the psychological, physical health, and general risks that people may encounter when they are incarcerated in local jails.

The people who are detained in jails prior to receiving a conviction are often held there for financial reasons. Depending on many circumstances of their case, the local precedents for bail, and the court's decision, people may be held until they can pay bail. Bail ostensibly provides a financial guarantee that people who have ongoing court cases will appear for future court dates. In practice, the amounts of bail money required and the application of bail to a variety of charges which previously did not require a financial guarantee of appearance have meant that many people are incarcerated prior to being convicted (Kilgore, 2015). According to the Prison Policy Initiative, "the median bail amount for felonies is $10,000, which represents 8 months' income for a typical person detained because they can't pay bail" (Sawyer, 2019).[2] Some states and local jurisdictions have placed restrictions on the use of bail, and states are increasingly reassessing whether to retain cash bail.

Prohibitively expensive bail, which is sometimes a result of multiple charges being "stacked" against a person when they are arrested (stacking is when charges are added by the police but will later most likely be dismissed in the courtroom), results in people being incarcerated in local jails throughout their court proceedings, which may take years to complete. Even the financial impact of a few days of incarceration can have a cumulative effect—a person may lose their job, may not have access to child care, or may experience reduced housing security. These effects mount up over time, pushing people who are incarcerated further and further into the oversight of government agencies, where they are made more vulnerable to policing and surveillance. This effect is noted in narratives of recidivism that often use tracking information about when and how often individuals are subsequently incarcerated after their release to justify arguments that people are individually responsible for their actions or to account for the failure of the philosophical approaches of carceral facilities. Looking at the social and fiscal effects of incarcerating people because they cannot afford to pay to be released reveals that bail policies, the increasing requirement for bail to be posted, and unachievable bail amounts all play a role in perpetuating the forced movement of people into jails and prisons.

Even without the ability to afford bail as a factor, pretrial detention (incarceration before being sentenced) can have lasting consequences on a person's life and immediate social support network. People held in pretrial detention are more likely to accept plea deals or to plead guilty in order to receive a sentence and have a clearer idea of how long they might be incarcerated, even when they have not actually engaged in the behaviors of which they are accused (Heaton, Mayson, and Stevenson, 2017). Bail is often required or increased due to risk assessment procedures that courts use to determine how people will conduct themselves in relation to the court. Like other technologies currently being advertised and implemented in carceral systems, the purveyors of risk assessment tools make claims to reduce bias and create neutral forms of assessment. However, on closer examination, risk assessment tools evaluate circumstantial information through a specific lens, incorporating (depending on the tool) ratings of housing stability, association with people who have a history of convictions or incarceration, and other factors that are, for the most part, unavoidable in communities that are continuously surveilled and policed (Bechtel et al., 2017). Risk assessment criteria have been found to be faulty in other contexts as well; specifically as applied in policing, because they reiterate and reflect ongoing bias. For example, in the Chicago Police Department's use of a now-decommissioned risk assessment model, the frequency of stops and encounters with police for mundane activities (which have been popularized under the phrase of "*activity* while Black" or "*activity* while trans") was fed into models of predictive policing and possibilities for risk (City of Chicago, Office of Inspector General, 2020). Sutherland refers to the collection, accumulation, and enduring records of these tools as the "carceral archive" (2019). Sutherland clearly connects the data practices of policing and incarceration to their antecedents, and succinctly states that "data cultures in contemporary policing have not been inaugurated by new technologies; instead, these ongoing practices are built on the violent history of chattel slavery and appeals to white panic constructed around notions of order and 'safety'" (Sutherland, 2019).

YOUTH INCARCERATION

Juvenile detention centers are utilized to incarcerate youth under the age of 18. Juvenile detention statistics are typically gathered using one-day census-taking measures. According to the Office of Juvenile Justice and Delinquency Prevention (OJJDP), a one-day survey (the Juvenile Residential Facility Census) in 2016 revealed that, on that day, "45,567 juvenile offenders were held in 1,772 residential placement facilities" (Hockenberry and Sladky, 2018). In 2018, the OJJDP data showed that 1,510 juvenile facilities in the United States detained or incarcerated 37,529 youth (Puzzanchera et al., 2020). This number includes information for both privately run (607) and government-administered (local- and state-level, 903) facilities, and youth in pre- and post-adjudication. Despite the fact that many states are changing their models of youth detention and incarceration to be primarily locally based, youth are still being sentenced to the almost 80 state-run, high-population institutions for youth which are sometimes referred to as "youth prisons" (Youth First, 2019).

The number of youth who are detained or incarcerated increases if the definition of carceral facilities for young people is broadened to include all locations where youth are detained as they undergo the process of adjudication or as sites for confinement following a conviction, such as group homes, residential treatment centers, ranches and wilderness camps, boot camps, and shelters. Under that definition, there are nearly 2,000 juvenile facilities across the United States (Sawyer, 2019). These facilities are designated to contain youth under the age of eighteen, though there are instances when youth are tried as adults and will be processed through adult institutions. In California, there are pilot programs for transitional-age youth (typically defined as 18–25, though there is some shift in the age bracket) to be incarcerated in juvenile detention facilities. This change relies on research on the brain development of young people (Chief Probation Officers of California, 2016).

Two-thirds of the youth who are detained or incarcerated are held for nonviolent crimes, probation violations (including incomplete community service), and status offenses (such as truancy) that are charges due to age, rather than because the youth were involved in activities deemed criminal (Bolin, 2019). One in ten youth who are incarcerated are located within adult jails and prisons (Sawyer, 2019). The ages at which people under 18 are tried in adult courts and sentenced to adult institutions vary across states, and in some states, such as Oklahoma, some violent acts are used as justification for young people (as young as 13) to be tried in adult court systems (10A OK Stat § 10A-2-5-205, 2018). Although it is condemned by international rights groups, youth in the United

States can be sentenced to life without parole (Rovner, 2021). Many states have banned or not recently utilized the practice, but it remains in use in nearly 20 states (Rovner, 2021).

As with adult carceral systems, Black, Indigenous, and youth of color are more likely to experience encounters with police, to be more surveilled in compulsory environments (such as school), and to receive longer sentences when convicted of the same crimes as white youth (W. Haywood Burns Institute, 2016). Due to social and political stratification and the instantiation of power through reduced material resources, Black, Indigenous, and youth of color are more likely to attend schools in high-surveillance environments and to bear the brunt of "logics of dispossession" (Fine and Ruglis, 2009). Youth are policed, detained, and incarcerated along the intersections of race, gender, and sexuality in ways that reflect biases and stereotypes that derive from the long histories that have shaped incarceration in the United States (Meiners, 2007). For instance, Morris (2016) outlines the ways in which young Black women are simultaneously positioned as uneducated and unable to make informed decisions about their lives, on the one hand, and categorized (and sexualized) as adults, despite their age, on the other hand. LGBTQIA+ youth, and especially LGBTQIA+ Black, Indigenous, and youth of color and youth who are living in poverty, experience discrimination and oppression that pushes them further and further into the public, where they are more likely to be surveilled and subject to policing and incarceration. LGBTQIA+ youth are estimated to be incarcerated at twice the rate at which they compose the general population of youth in the United States (Movement Advancement Project et al., 2017).

Rates of youth incarceration have been declining in recent years (Bolin, 2019; Sawyer, 2019). In early 2020, they were at a low equivalent to the rates of incarceration in the 1970s. This decrease may be due to an ongoing decline in arrests of young people (Puzzanchera, 2020). Advocates for youth emphasize that despite this decrease, youth incarceration continues to have a profound impact on Black, Indigenous, and youth of color. "With 72 percent of all youth locked up for non-violent offenses, the U.S does not have an alarming crime problem; we have an alarming incarceration problem—one that harms primarily youth of color" (W. Haywood Burns Institute, 2020). This was exacerbated by the COVID-19 pandemic. In the early months of the pandemic, the number of youth held in juvenile detention facilities appeared to be diminishing, primarily because there was a decline in the number of new admissions (this was also true for adults, as was mentioned in the introduction) (Annie E. Casey Foundation, 2020). By late 2020, this course had reversed. According to the Annie E. Casey Foundation, which conducted regular surveys of juvenile detention centers throughout this period, "the number of young people in detention grew by 8% in the second half of 2020." "Black and Latino youth are slower to be released than their white peers (10% and 8% slower, respectively, in the month of November), and the gap favoring white youth has grown larger than it was before the pandemic began" (2021).

Youth have organized to work for the closure of detention facilities and to identify their needs and desires for their communities, which largely do not align with carceral concerns (Melendrez and Young Women's Freedom Center, 2019). As young women and transgender and gender-nonconforming youth have identified their points of entry into the juvenile detention center and juvenile courts—points that include status crimes, survival behaviors, and increased policing in their communities—they have also provided instructions that adults can follow to reduce the risks that youth face through policing and incarceration (Melendrez and Young Women's Freedom Center, 2019). Undoubtedly, libraries have a role to play in facilitating the public's access to information about youths' campaigns, including providing opportunities for youth to speak about their experiences and for public engagement with the ways in which youth are regulated and policed.

STATE (COMMUNITY) SUPERVISION

Probation, supervised release, and parole, forms of state-enacted community supervision, structure the conditions of life for an extremely large number of people and their families. Including those sentenced to community supervision in the number of people under carceral control has a startling effect—it enlarges the frame of mass incarceration to show its extremely broad reach. Effectively, "56 percent of the 6.7 million adults under criminal justice control" were under some form of community supervision in 2015 (Phelps, 2018, 124). Slightly over 60 percent of cases seen by juvenile courts result in probation, and the juvenile court system orders out-of-home placements around 25 percent of the time (Hockenberry & Puzzanchera, 2020). The implementation of community surveillance is stratified along lines of privilege, with wealthier (and often white) individuals more likely to receive community supervision sentences that are truly a diversion from prison, while young Black men are most likely to have some experience of probation in their lifetime (Phelps, 2018).

The terms of implementation for probation, supervised release, and parole vary—probation is typically considered by the court to be a sentence that defers incarceration by setting tasks and community supervision, parole is a set of requirements for behavior and supervision after release from prison and is "required as a mandatory condition of prison release," and supervised release is state-supervision post-imprisonment in the federal system that is ordered by the court as part of sentencing (Phelps, 2018, 127; Steiner, 2019)—but they share many similarities in practice. No matter the overseeing agency, which may be at the local or state level or, increasingly, a private entity, the conditions of community supervision are likely to include all or some of the following:

- Completing multiple classes or programs
- Living in community-based or transitional housing
- Maintaining employment
- Not associating with specific people, including, at times, friends or family
- Paying fines and fees
- Reporting any and all financial activity
- Reporting to an overseeing officer or entity on a frequent basis
- Restricted movement and electronic monitoring
- Showing up on time for all classes and appointments
- Submitting all required documentation and payments on time
- Submitting regular alcohol and drug tests

The requirements that individuals are expected to meet are set by individual caseworkers, courts, or local, state, and federal agencies. Research has shown these requirements to be inconsistently implemented, arbitrarily created, and often unrealistic, given the conditions of people's lives prior to community supervision (Klingele, 2013). In part, this is because community supervision has often been touted as a more humane alternative to incarceration. In practice, community supervision swings between a "progressive alternative sanction and an additional mode of punitive state control" (Phelps, 2018, 128). While courts view community supervision, under any conditions, to be a less punitive alternative than incarceration (Klingele, 2013), people who have experienced intensive forms of community supervision report that it is nearly or often equivalent, in many ways, to formal incarceration (Martin, Hanrahan, and Bowers, 2009).

Private prison industries are increasingly focusing on community supervision and its requirements, including transitional housing, as sites of financial growth. The research on private interests in community supervision and reentry-based services notes that it is a "boom industry" for companies known for their role in private prisons (such as GEO Group, CoreCivic, and Management and Training Corporation), and even some high-ranking staff at large-scale nonprofits involved in community supervision and reentry have an economic stake in this work (Latessa and Lovins, 2019, 324). A range of state-re-quired interventions, therapies, behavior monitoring, job development programs, day reporting centers, housing, education (sometimes required for drug-related convictions and often for convictions related to driving while intoxicated), special programs (often required for people with sex offender or domestic violence convictions), and similar activ-ities and enterprises are overseen by "companies and individuals" that derive "both their clients and their incomes from contracts with local governments or a 'fee for services' model in which the client pays either directly or through insurance" (Latessa and Lovins, 2019, 325). Young people and adults under community supervision or in the process of reentry are likely to have encountered some form of private industry as they seek to fulfill their supervision requirements. These are compulsory contracts and fees; chapter 7 shows that not meeting these requirements and costs often leads to reincarceration.

Despite limited oversight of these companies, their services and products are expanding, as is the scale at which they are implemented (Latessa and Lovins, 2019). In April 2020, BI International, a subsidiary of GEO Group, entered into a five-year contract with U.S. Immigration and Customs Enforcement to expand its existing super-vision of people in the process of immigration (BusinessWire, 2020). Billed as a diversion from physical detention in immigration centers and as a requirement following deten-tion for an immigration violation, the newest iteration of the Intensive Supervision and Appearance Program (ISAP IV) contract includes electronic monitoring, GPS tracking, telephone reporting with voice recognition, biometric reporting (facial recognition), and case management that involves assessment and home visits (Immigration and Customs Enforcement, 2020).

State supervision regulations can be difficult to meet for a myriad of reasons, and not meeting these requirements can have life-altering consequences. While immigration is largely a civil matter, not meeting the ISAP IV community supervision requirements can lead to detention or potential deportation. People who have been sentenced through the criminal court system or are otherwise obligated to community supervision experience the process as arbitrarily designed, and often have their community supervision revoked due to an inability to meet unreasonable regulations. Revocation is often responsible for what has popularly been termed "recidivism." Examining the impact and complexi-ties of community supervision complicates the narrative of personal responsibility that is inherent in discussions of recidivism, which is often described as a person's likelihood to engage in continuing criminal behavior (or to "reoffend"). Given that Black, Indige-nous, and people of color, LGBTQIA+ and especially transgender people, and people who are living in poverty or live their lives in public are always positioned as criminal or likely to be criminal by the state, and thus more likely to be surveilled, policed, and incarcer-ated, the rates at which community supervision is revoked due to (what are often) minor infractions is astounding. Looking to community supervision as a direct line into carceral facilities reveals some of the interlocking mechanisms that support incarceration as an American institution.

For instance, "estimates suggest that half of the people admitted to U.S. jails and more than one-third of those admitted to prison arrive there as a result of revocation from community supervision" (Klingele, 2013). These numbers may be complicated by individual supervisors' decisions to enforce a community supervision violation rather than reporting something that may lead to an additional conviction (Phelps, 2018), but the instances of this type of softer reporting are likely rare. In fact, research into community supervisors' perceptions and their enforcement of often unreasonable sanctions means that "any mistake can result in revocation" (Klingele, 2013, 1059). The people most likely to be policed and incarcerated are often the people most likely to receive more restrictive, difficult to meet, or intolerable conditions of community supervision. This may be why there is a higher likelihood that people who experience high levels of policing are more likely to prefer a "short stint in jail or prison to a longer period of probation supervision" (Phelps, 2018, 131), especially given that "in many cases community supervision is not an alternative to imprisonment, but only a delayed form of it" (Klingele, 2013, 1015).

Community supervision and monitoring also take place in ways that are more difficult to trace. These include monitoring through other agencies, including hospitals, when requested by community supervision officers or the police; bans on access to food stamps or other forms of government assistance, which occur in some states when people have a felony conviction history (Born, 2018; Hager, 2016); and ankle bracelets and house arrest (also known as GPS or electronic monitoring). These forms of control shape the lives of people who are subject to them and are likely to shape the future of incarceration. While there were about 125,000 people on some form of electronic monitoring in 2019 (Bagaric, Hunter, and Loberg), scholars are increasingly suggesting that technologies provide a viable alternative to mass incarceration. Some argue that constant surveillance is a necessary element in reducing what they see as the personal responsibility for crime that leads to recidivism (Bagaric, Hunter, and Loberg, 2019), thus shaping new forms of surveillance that will potentially be developed off of data accumulated from people who are most negatively impacted by incarceration. Others argue that continued monitoring and surveillance through technologies kept in the home and on the body is not a sustainable solution to mass incarceration, but is a lesser evil compared to experiences of incarceration, especially incarceration that occurs prior to a conviction (Wiseman, 2014). In either instance, these technological narratives tend to sidestep people's actual experiences under state surveillance. Some supporters of these technologies argue that people who were otherwise imprisoned would not have a right to privacy that is revoked by the comprehensive monitoring systems that have been proposed as alternatives to incarceration. Others justify the use of electronic monitoring, house arrest, and other types of state supervision as a reform that will reduce the number of people who are incarcerated by removing them from physical facilities (Schenwar and Law, 2020 refute this claim). Each of these approaches needs to be critiqued as a reflection of carceral practices and as evidence of how these technologies facilitate carceral incursions into everyday life. The proponents of a system that could monitor "every movement . . . in real time for the entire duration of the sanction" also anticipate the normalization of that system's use as a mundane facet of state supervision and, consequently, of public life (Bagaric, Hunter, and Loberg, 2019, 1268).

State supervision is extensive and far-reaching, and probably affects how librarians and information professionals conceptualize the general public that is served by their libraries. An examination of community supervision reveals that the distinctions made between people who are incarcerated (who are often considered to be separate from the public served by libraries and other information providers) and those who are "free" to constitute the public are flawed. When considering that "one in thirty-eight adults in the United States is undergoing correctional supervision" (Bagaric, Hunter, and Loberg, 2019, 1227), it becomes obvious that the public is not only affected by absences due to incarceration but is also infused with carceral realities.

Thinking about the requirements of community supervision can also offer insight into how it disrupts or reduces information access. People under house arrest or on electronic monitoring may have only limited access to physical libraries. Librarians and other information professionals can approach supervising entities or advocacy groups focused on post-incarceration practices in order to determine how to best serve patrons who are under state supervision. This service may entail requesting that libraries be added as access sites for people under community supervision, providing outreach at transitional housing, identifying groups that oversee required classes, and offering story times when and where these classes occur, or otherwise creatively thinking through the difficulty of navigating community supervision, family and social connections, and the burden of being under what is often arbitrary surveillance.

IMMIGRATION AND CUSTOMS ENFORCEMENT (ICE) DETENTION

There are 137 ICE facilities located in the United States (Immigration and Customs Enforcement, n.d.). ICE detention facilities are often maintained through contracts with private prisons or local jails (National Immigrant Justice Center, 2019). While being detained in ICE facilities is supposed to be considered "strictly civil" in character, "many aspects of immigration detention make that detention indistinguishable from criminal incarceration" (Ryo and Peacock, 2018, 5). Active ICE detention centers and private juvenile detention centers span the country, and have been the focus of digital librarians and data scientists who have charted the pervasiveness of practices of detaining people in the process of immigration (Dreyfus, 2018; Torn Apart, n.d.).

Almost 50,000 people are held in ICE detention centers on any given day. The majority of people detained in 2015 were from Mexico and Central America (43 percent and 46 percent, respectively), and small percentages of those detained were from other Latin American countries, Europe and North America, Asia, or countries in the African continent (Ryo and Peacock, 2018). Most people detained were under thirty years old, and most were men (Ryo and Peacock, 2018). The gendered dynamics of immigration may speak to the difficulty of traveling to the United States, but reports of violence against cisgender and transgender women reflect the dangers that they face inside of ICE facilities. Women have reported sexual assault and other forms of abuse while detained (MALDEF, 2014) and transgender women have experienced violence or died while in ICE custody (Wade, 2019). Young people are also detained in large numbers—almost 70,000 young people were detained in 2019 (Sherman, Mendoza, and Burke, 2019). It is possible that the numbers of youth in ICE custody are higher, as recent investigations have revealed that some youth are held in juvenile detention centers but under the authority of ICE, often at a great distance from their families (Ellis and Hicken, 2019).[3]

In 2017, around 70 percent of the people in ICE custody were detained in private, contracted facilities (National Immigrant Justice Center, 2019; Sentencing Project,

2019). Private facilities are not only beholden to profits—they also sidestep many forms of oversight that are supposed to occur in jails and prisons that are government property (Alvarado et al., 2019; Bauer, 2018). Poor conditions in ICE facilities have been widely publicized, as have detainees' limited access to resources, including access to legal materials and the court—some people detained in ICE facilities will only ever have interactions with courts through remote video (American Civil Liberties Union, 2019; Myslinska, 2019).

NOT ON THE MAP

Everywhere there is a carceral facility, there is also a library somewhere nearby. But not all carceral facilities in the United States are easily seen (Begley, 2012). Diffuse forms of surveillance and community supervision, described above, permeate society. There are also cases of facilities in the United States that have been intentionally obscured by local, state, or federal bodies. An exposé in 2015 revealed that the Chicago Police Department had been running a facility, called Homan Square, outside of the purview of the law or public knowledge (Ackerman, 2015). Investigations about Homan Square found that people detained there, even if temporarily, had little legal recourse and that incarceration in the nondescript warehouse was structured by racism in the practice of policing (Ackerman, 2015). It is possible that similar institutions exist in other locations.

CONCLUSION

Several reports suggest that what seem to be excessively punitive situations in jails and prisons are commonplace. Among these are the consistent reports of abuse issued by transgender people who are incarcerated (Leitsinger, 2020), the invasive searching of family members and friends, including young children, when they visit people who are incarcerated (Cramer, 2019), and the high rates of suicide in carceral facilities (Fazel, Ramesh, and Hawton, 2017; MacFarlane, 2019). In addition to these, the ongoing advocacy on the part of people who are incarcerated, from hunger strikes to union organizing, are stark reactions to the everyday conditions of incarceration in the United States.

Understanding the different types and functions of carceral facilities not only provides a context for thinking about practical library and information services, it also provides a frame of reference for why these services are necessary in those facilities. This review of types of facilities, and information about how people are detained and about the strictures of community supervision, makes clear that there are many sites in which to initiate or increase library and information services for people who are detained, incarcerated, or under state supervision. Beyond this, it provides library and information professionals with background knowledge that can facilitate larger conversations and programs about raising awareness of carceral practices, their consequences, and alternatives.

The policies and practices in carceral facilities determine how and what information may be available to the people held in them. The next chapter, "Information and Incarceration," covers this topic in depth. Beginning with a review of library and information science literature from 1992 to the present, it reveals the overlaps and disconnects between how librarians and information professionals discuss information access for incarcerated people, the role of information access in the lives of people who are incarcerated, and how the particularities of specific types of confinement shape incarcerated people's information needs.

NOTES

1. The Sentencing Project maintains state-by-state data on rates of incarceration at www.sentencing project.org/the-facts/ (2020).
2. Felony definitions vary by state but, for the most part, felonies are defined as any action or set of actions that leads to a conviction of more than one year of imprisonment.
3. The Center for Migration Studies documented ICE detention response to the COVID-19 pandemic, finding that while reductions occurred, the number of releases was not adequate to meet health requirements, and staff and transfers were transmission points for the disease (Kerwin, 2020). As in other carceral facilities across the United States, people who were detained were placed at heightened levels of risk of infection due to unsanitary conditions, the inability to socially distance, and lack of access to the materials needed to take health precautions.

REFERENCES

10A OK Stat § 10A-2-5-205 (2018). 2018 Oklahoma Statutes. Title 10A. Children and Juvenile Code §10A-2-5-205. Certification as youthful offender or juvenile. https://law.justia.com/codes/oklahoma/2018/title-10a/section-10a-2-5-205/.

Ackerman, S. 2015. "Homan Square Revealed: How Chicago 'Disappeared' 7,000 People." *The Guardian*. www.theguardian.com/us-news/2015/oct/19/homan-square-chicago-police-disappeared-thousands.

Alexander, M. 2010. *The New Jim Crow: Mass Incarceration in the Age of Colorblindness*. New York: New Press.

Alvarado, M., A. Balcerzak, S. Barchenger, J. Campbell, R. Carranza, M. Clark, A. Gomez, D. Gonzalez, T. Hughes, R. Jervis, D. Keemahill, R. Plevin, J. Schwartz, S. Taddeo, L. Villagran, D. Wagner, E. Weise, and A. Zhu. 2019. "'These People Are Profitable': Under Trump Private Prisons Are Cashing in on Detainees." *USA TODAY Network*. www.usatoday.com/in-depth/news/nation/2019/12/19/ice -detention-private-prisons-expands-under-trump-administration/4393366002/.

American Civil Liberties Union. 2013. "A Living Death: Life without Parole for Nonviolent Offenses." www.aclu.org/report/living-death-life-without-parole-nonviolent-offenses.

———. 2019. "Immigration Detention Conditions." www.aclu.org/issues/immigrants-rights/immigrants -rights-and-detention/immigration-detention-conditions.

Annie E. Casey Foundation. 2020. "COVID-19 Youth Detention Population Survey." www.aecf.org/m/ blogdoc/aecf-covid19youthdetentionpolutionsurvey-2020.pdf.

———. 2021. "Survey: More Youth in Secure Detention despite Rise of COVID-19." www.aecf.org/blog/ survey-more-youth-in-secure-detention-despite-rise-of-covid-19/.

Bagaric, M., D. Hunter, and C. Loberg. 2019. "Introducing Disruptive Technology to Criminal Sanctions: Punishment by Computer Monitoring to Enhance Sentencing Fairness and Efficiency." *Brooklyn Law Review* 84, no. 4: 1227–86.

Barnes, L. M. 2019. "Prison Populations, Trends in." In *American Prisons and Jails: An Encyclopedia of Controversies and Trends*, ed. V. B. Worley and R. B. Worley, 491–94. Santa Barbara, CA: ABC-CLIO.

Bauer, S. 2018. *American Prison: A Reporter's Undercover Journey into the Business of Punishment*. New York: Penguin.

Bechtel, K., A. M. Holsinger, C. T. Lowenkamp, and M. J. Warren. 2017. "A Meta-Analytic Review of Pretrial Research: Risk Assessment, Bond Type, and Interventions." *American Journal of Criminal Justice* 42: 443–67.

Begley, J. 2012. "What Does the Geography of Incarceration in the United States Look Like?" Prison Map. http://prisonmap.com/about.

Bolin, R. M. 2019. "Juvenile Detention Centers." In *American Prisons and Jails: An Encyclopedia of Controversies and Trends*, ed. V. B. Worley and R. B. Worley, 357–61. Santa Barbara, CA: ABC-CLIO.

Born, M. 2018. "In Some States, Drug Felons Still Face Lifetime Ban on SNAP Benefits." National Public Radio. www.npr.org/sections/thesalt/2018/06/20/621391895/in-some-states-drug-felons-still-face -lifetime-ban-on-snap-benefits.

Bureau of Prisons. 2021. "Statistics: Offenses." www.bop.gov/about/statistics/statistics_inmate_offenses .jsp.

———. 2021. "About Our Facilities: Contract Prisons." www.bop.gov/about/facilities/contract_facilities.jsp.

Burns, J. L. 2019. "Prison Populations, Downsizing of." In *American Prisons and Jails: An Encyclopedia of Controversies and Trends,* ed. V. B. Worley and R. B. Worley, 487–91. Santa Barbara, CA: ABC-CLIO.

BusinessWire. 2020. "The GEO Group Announces Five-Year Contract with U.S. Immigration and Customs Enforcement for Intensive Supervision and Appearance Program (ISAP)." www.businesswire.com/ news/home/20200324005145/en/The-GEO-Group-Announces-Five-Year-Contract-With-U.S. -Immigration-and-Customs-Enforcement-for-Intensive-Supervision-and-Appearance-Program-ISAP.

Chief Probation Officers of California (CPOC). 2016. "Governor Brown Signs Transitional Age Youth Pilot Program Legislation Relying on Mounting Brain Research of Treatment Options for Youthful Offenders Age 18–21." www.cpoc.org/post/governor-brown-signs-transitional-age-youth-pilot-program -legislation-relying-mounting-brain.

City of Chicago, Office of Inspector General. 2020. "Advisory Concerning the Chicago Police Department's Predictive Risk Models." https://igchicago.org/wp-content/uploads/2020/01/OIG-Advisory-Concerning -CPDs-Predictive-Risk-Models-.pdf.

Cramer, M. 2019. "Strip-Searching of 8-Year-Old at Prison Leads Virginia to Halt the Practice." *New York Times.* www.nytimes.com/2019/12/06/us/strip-search-buckingham-correctional-center.html.

Death Penalty Information Center. 2021. "State by State." https://deathpenaltyinfo.org/state-and-federal -info/state-by-state.

Dodson, K. D., and J. Brown. 2019. "Privatization." In *American Prisons and Jails: An Encyclopedia of Controversies and Trends,* ed. V. B. Worley and R. B. Worley, 529–32. Santa Barbara, CA: ABC-CLIO.

Dreisbach, T. 2020. "Exclusive: Video Shows Controversial Use of Force inside an ICE Detention Center." National Public Radio. www.npr.org/2020/02/06/802939294/exclusive-video-shows-controversial -use-of-force-inside-an-ice-detention-center.

Dreyfus, E. 2018. "'ICE Is Everywhere': Using Library Science to Map the Separation Crisis." *WIRED.* www.wired.com/story/ice-is-everywhere-using-library-science-to-map-child-separation/.

Drop LWOP. 2019. "Drop LWOP Fact Sheet." https://droplwop.files.wordpress.com/2019/03/lwop-fact -sheet-2019.pdf.

Ellis, B., and M. Hicken. 2019. "'Secret and Unaccountable': Where Some Immigrant Teens Are Being Taken by ICE." CNN. www.cnn.com/2019/10/24/us/ice-kids-detention-invs/index.html.

Equal Justice Initiative. 2017. "California Abolishes Death in Prison Sentences for Children." https://eji.org/ news/california-abolishes-juvenile-life-without-parole/.

Fazel, S., T. Ramesh, and K. Hawton. 2017. "Suicide in Prisons: An International Study of Prevalence and Contributory Factors." *Lancet Psychiatry* 4, no. 12: 946–52.

Fine, M., and J. Ruglis. 2009. "Circuits and Consequences of Dispossession: The Racialized Realignment of the Public Sphere for U.S. Youth." *Transforming Anthropology* 17, no. 1: 20–33.

Ghiorzo, J. C., and K.-L. Blount-Hill. 2019. "Overcrowding." In *American Prisons and Jails: An Encyclopedia of Controversies and Trends*, ed. V. B. Worley and R. B. Worley, 425–27. Santa Barbara, CA: ABC-CLIO.

Gilmore, R. W. 2007. *Golden Gulag: Prisons, Surplus, Crisis, and Opposition in Globalizing California.* Berkeley: University of California Press.

Hager, E. 2016. "Six States Where Felons Can't Get Food Stamps." The Marshall Project. www.themarshall
    project.org/2016/02/04/six-states-where-felons-can-t-get-food-stamps.

Harpster, N. T. 2019. "Jails Compared to Prisons." In *American Prisons and Jails: An Encyclopedia of
    Controversies and Trends,* ed. V. B. Worley and R. B. Worley, 351–54. Santa Barbara, CA: ABC-CLIO.

Havis, L. 2019. "Sentencing Disparities and Discrimination in Sentencing." In *American Prisons and Jails:
    An Encyclopedia of Controversies and Trends*, ed. V. B. Worley and R. B. Worley, 579–82. Santa Barbara,
    CA: ABC-CLIO.

Heaton, P., S. Mayson, and M. Stevenson. 2017. "The Downstream Consequences of Misdemeanor Pretrial
    Detention." *Stanford Law Review* 69, no. 3: 711–94.

Hockenberry, S., and A. Sladky. 2018. "Juvenile Residential Facility Census, 2016: Selected Findings."
    Washington, DC: Office of Juvenile Justice and Delinquency Prevention.

Hockenberry, S., and Puzzanchera, C. 2020. "Juvenile Court Statistics 2018." Pittsburgh, PA: National
    Center for Juvenile Justice.

Immigration and Customs Enforcement. n.d. "Detention Facility Locator." www.ice.gov/detention
    -facilities.

———. 2020. "Intensive Supervision Appearance Program IV (ISAP IV) Support Services." https://beta.sam
    .gov/opp/df1b63595f19eb5ea8724539ff394f3b/view.

Institute of Museum and Library Services. 2013. "Public Libraries in the United States Survey: Fiscal Year
    2010." Washington, DC: Institute of Museum and Library Services.

Kerwin, D. 2020. "Immigrant Detention and COVID-19: How a Pandemic Exploited and Spread through
    the US Immigrant Detention System." Center for Migration Studies of New York.

Kilgore, J. 2015. "Jail—The Local Face of Mass Incarceration." In *Understanding Mass Incarceration:
    A People's Guide to the Key Civil Rights Struggle of Our Time.* New York: New Press.

Klingele, C. 2013. "Rethinking the Use of Community Supervision." *Journal of Criminal Law and
    Criminology (1973–)* 103, no. 4: 1015–70.

Latessa, E. J., and L. B. Lovins. 2019. "Privatization of Community Corrections." *Criminology and Public
    Policy* 18: 323–41.

Leitsinger, M. 2020. "Transgender Prisoners Say They 'Never Feel Safe': Could a Proposed Law Help?"
    KQED. www.kqed.org/news/11794221/could-changing-how-transgender-inmates-are-housed-make
    -prison-safer-for-them.

Lilly, J. R., and M. Nellis. 2013. "The Limits of Techno-Utopianism: Electronic Monitoring in the United
    States of America." In *Electronically Monitored Punishment: International and Critical Perspectives*, ed.
    M. Nellis, K. Beyens, and D. Kaminski, 21–43. Taylor and Francis.

MacFarlane, S. 2019. "Nearly 300 Inmates Attempt Suicide in America's Prisons Each Year." NBC. www
    .nbcwashington.com/news/local/suicide-in-american-federal-prisons-2019/83062/.

MALDEF. 2014. "Complaints Regarding Sexual Abuse of Women in DHS Custody at Karnes County
    Residential Center." www.maldef.org/assets/pdf/2014-09-30_Karnes_PREA_Letter_Complaint.pdf.

Martin, J. S., K. Hanrahan, and J. H. Bowers, Jr. 2009. "Offenders' Perceptions of House Arrest and
    Electronic Monitoring." *Journal of Offender Rehabilitation* 48, no. 6: 547–70.

Meiners, E. 2007. *Right to Be Hostile: Schools, Prisons, and the Making of Public Enemies.* New York:
    Routledge.

Melendrez, A., and Young Women's Freedom Center. 2019. "Centering the Lives of San Francisco System-
    Involved Women and TGNC People: A Participatory and Decolonizing Model." Young Women's
    Freedom Center.

Morris, M. W. 2016. *Pushout: The Criminalization of Black Girls in Schools.* New York: New Press.

Movement Advancement Project, Youth First, and Center for American Progress. 2017. *Unjust: LGBTQ
    Youth Incarcerated in the Juvenile Justice System.* Denver, CO: Movement Advancement Project.

Myslinska, D. R. 2019. "Living Conditions in Immigration Detention Centers." www.nolo.com/legal
-encyclopedia/living-conditions-immigration-detention-centers.html.

National Immigrant Justice Center. 2019. "Toolkit: Immigration Detention Oversight and Accountability."
www.immigrantjustice.org/research-items/toolkit-immigration-detention-oversight-and-accountability
#faq.

Nellis, A. 2017. "Still Life: America's Increasing Use of Life and Long-Term Sentences." The Sentencing
Project. www.sentencingproject.org/publications/still-life-americas-increasing-use-life-long-term
-sentences/.

Phelps, M. S. 2018. "Ending Mass Probation: Sentencing, Supervision, and Revocation." *Future of Children*
28, no. 1: 124–46.

Prison Policy Initiative. 2021. "Visualizing the Unequal Treatment of LGBTQ People in the Criminal
Justice System." www.prisonpolicy.org/blog/2021/03/02/lgbtq/.

Puzzanchera, C. 2020. "The Decline in Arrests of Juveniles Continued through 2019." Office of Juvenile
Justice and Delinquency Prevention. www.ojjdp.gov/ojstatbb/snapshots/DataSnapshot_UCR2019.pdf.

Puzzanchera, C., S. Hockenberry, T. J. Sladky, and W. Kang. 2020. "Juvenile Residential Facility Census
Databook." Office of Juvenile Justice and Delinquency Prevention. www.ojjdp.gov/ojstatbb/jrfcdb/.

Ritchie, A. 2017. *Invisible No More: Police Violence Against Black Women and Women of Color*. Boston: Beacon.

Rovner, J. 2021. "Juvenile Life Without Parole: An Overview." *The Sentencing Project*. www.sentencing
project.org/publications/juvenile-life-without-parole/.

Ryo, E., and I. Peacock. 2018. "The Landscape of Immigration Detention in the United States." American
Immigration Council. Special Report.

Sawyer, W. 2019. "Youth Confinement: The Whole Pie 2019." Prison Policy Initiative. www.prisonpolicy
.org/reports/youth2019.html.

Sawyer, W., and P. Wagner. 2020. "Mass Incarceration: The Whole Pie 2020." Prison Policy Initiative.
www.prisonpolicy.org/reports/pie2020.html.

Schenwar, M., and V. Law. 2020. *Prison by Any Other Name: The Harmful Consequences of Popular Reforms*.
New York: New Press.

Sentencing Project. 2019. "Private Prisons in the United States." www.sentencingproject.org/publications/
private-prisons-united-states/.

———. 2020. "State-by-State Data." www.sentencingproject.org/the-facts/.

Sherman, C., M. Mendoza, and G. Burke. 2019. "US Held Record Number of Migrant Children in Custody
in 2019." Associated Press. https://apnews.com/015702afdb4d4fbf85cf5070cd2c6824.

St. John, V. 2019. "American Prison Designs." In *American Prisons and Jails: An Encyclopedia of Controversies
and Trends*, ed. V. B. Worley and R. B. Worley, 357–61. Santa Barbara, CA: ABC-CLIO.

Steiner, M. 2019. "What is Federal Supervised Release?" *NOLO*. www.nolo.com/legal-encyclopedia/what
-federal-supervised-release.html .

Sutherland, T. 2019. "The Carceral Archive: Documentary Records, Narrative Construction, and Predictive
Risk Assessment." *Journal of Cultural Analytics* 1, no. 1. https://culturalanalytics.org/article/11047-the
-carceral-archive-documentary-records-narrative-construction-and-predictive-risk-assessment.

Torn Apart. n.d. "Volume 1." http://xpmethod.columbia.edu/torn-apart/volume/1/index.

W. Haywood Burns Institute. 2016. "Stemming the Rising Tide: Racial and Ethnic Disparities in Youth
Incarceration and Strategies for Change." www.burnsinstitute.org/wp-content/uploads/2016/05/
Stemming-the-Rising-Tide_FINAL.pdf.

———. 2020. "United States of Disparities." https://usdata.burnsinstitute.org/#comparison=2&placement
=1&races=2,3,4,5,6&offenses=5,2,8,1,9,11,10&year=2017&view=map.

Wade, P. 2019. "A Trans Woman Died in ICE Custody. Then ICE Deleted Video Footage of Her." *Rolling
Stone*. www.rollingstone.com/politics/politics-news/trans-woman-died-in-ice-custody-deleted-video
-footage-904237/.

Wagner, P., and W. Sawyer. 2018. "States of Incarceration: The Global Context 2018." Prison Policy
    Initiative. www.prisonpolicy.org/global/2018.html.

Wiseman, S. R. 2014. "Pretrial Detention and the Right to Be Monitored." *Yale Law Journal* 123: 1344–1404.

Youth First. 2019. "The Facts Report: The Geography of America's Dysfunctional and Racially Disparate
    Youth Incarceration Complex." www.nokidsinprison.org/the-facts.

CHAPTER 4

Information and Incarceration

H ow librarians have discussed and described their own efforts to provide information within carceral facilities is central to this book. The professional and philosophical approaches that imbue library literature, as well as the concerns that librarians and information professionals highlight, shape the ways in which library services for people who are incarcerated have been portrayed in the period between the publication of the most recent (1992) version of the "Library Standards for Adult Correctional Institutions" and the present. The first section of this chapter is a review of the literature on library services for people who are incarcerated that has been published since 1992, revealing patterns and trends in areas of concern over time.

The carceral facility shapes information access and access to reading materials, determining the ease or difficulty with which people who are incarcerated are able to access information and the types of information they are able to access. The second portion of the chapter places personal stories of people who have been incarcerated alongside analyses of the information requests that library and information professions have received from patrons in jails and prisons. It reveals that many of the types of information that are professedly provided to people who are incarcerated are often difficult to access or to verify—including legal materials, and, following the passage of the Prison Litigation Reform Act (1995) and *Lewis v. Casey* (1996) verdict, legal recourse (Salvatore, 2019). Beyond this, the chapter emphasizes the role of information access in maintaining a sense of self and agency over time, despite conditions that are often dehumanizing and in which choices are deeply constrained.

LIBRARY AND INFORMATION SCIENCE LITERATURE: 1992-2019

Library Services to Adults

The publications from 1992 to 2019 on library services to people who are incarcerated primarily, but don't always, center an approach similar to that undertaken by public libraries. This narrative of public library-style services and access runs counter to the ideas promulgated in Coyle's 1987 text. A review of fifty-six articles about library services to adults in carceral institutions written during this period reveals that there were trends that emerged by decade, that conversation about library services to people in carceral facilities was ongoing, and that at least some public libraries explored their role in providing information to people who are incarcerated during this period of time. The six books, a guide published through the Public Library Association, four chapters on information provision for people who are incarcerated, and the updated ALA statement on "Prisoner's Right to Read" also promote, for the most part, greater information access and encourage library and information science professionals to consider adults who are incarcerated as their current or future patrons.

In order to identify trends over the nearly three decades explored in this section, articles that discussed in-prison library services, library services to people in jails, and partnerships between libraries and programs in adult carceral institutions in the United States were categorized by content. A total of fifty-six articles were included in this analysis, and the majority were published in peer-reviewed journals. Articles in trade publications were also included when they fit with the theme and were published by the American Library Association or in *Corrections Today*. The analysis intentionally skews toward academic articles in order to form a professional-level analysis of the trends in how library and information services were discussed and implemented. State-level or city-level information was not included for this same reason, though these sometimes presented the complexity of services, especially on the topic of censorship.[1] No dissertations were considered in this review, nor were publications that discussed library services to incarcerated people in an international context. These restrictions not only reflect the discourse of library and information science education and theory in the U.S., they also helped to scope the review project. This does mean that alternate discourses may exist from the one shown in this chapter. It is likely that the number of publications on law library access and legal programming in prisons is underrepresented here because of the parameters set for inclusion in this analysis. Conrad's 2017 book on prison policy and librarians' experiences provides a review of prominent legal cases and includes a broader range of popular publications in the review of literature on this topic.

Overall, thirteen articles on library and information services to adults who are incarcerated were identified in the period between 1992 and 1999, twenty-seven (including four in a special issue of *Education Librarian*) in the period between 2000 and 2009, and sixteen (one in a special issue of *Library Trends* on global approaches to library services in prison, with the introduction to that issue omitted from analysis) in the period from 2010 to 2019. (All of the articles and other materials included in this analysis are listed chronologically in Appendix A.) The articles were categorized by focus and intent using a grounded theory approach, which involved creating code categories generated through a review of the articles (Charmaz, 2006; Glaser and Strauss, 1967). Articles that covered multiple topics (i.e., fell into two or more codes) were duplicated in the analysis. This was done in order to better assess the overarching concerns of library and information professionals during each of the three periods described.

Between 1992 and 1999, the most frequently addressed themes were technology in the library, largely due to a three-part series of short articles by Vogel on utilizing CD-ROMs published in *Corrections Today* and discussions of carceral philosophies. Three articles discussed the role of the library in rehabilitation. These were joined by an article on the redemptive qualities of access to a library that was written by a person who was incarcerated (Bratt, 1996). One of the articles (Sullivan, 1998) offered a critique of rehabilitation and its historical antecedents in compulsory religious literary engagement. Other topics addressed included access to legal materials, funding (specifically LSCA), literacy, and the role of academic libraries.

A comparative plethora of articles related to library and information access for people in jails and prisons were published in the period between 2000 and 2009. Of the twenty-seven articles in this period, which include four short pieces in a special issue of *Education Libraries*, 9 addressed carceral philosophies. Four articles centered on the punitive nature of providing library service, including issues of security and the library (security was mentioned in almost all the articles, though sometimes just in passing), staff concerns about access to information, library materials as contraband, and ideas of public safety. Six of the articles that explicitly addressed carceral philosophies discussed rehabilitation, with Sullivan (2000) again offering critical background about rehabilitative models. Eight articles discussed technology (sometimes only touching on the subject), typically underscoring the lack of technology in the day-to-day functions of the library in prisons. Six articles provided an overview of the quotidian practice of librarianship in a carceral facility, covering topics such as funding, staffing, library standards, collections, and, at times, censorship (this topic was also occasionally discussed as an issue of security). Two articles focused on the recruitment of prison librarians and the possibility of incorporating experience in carceral facilities into library education. One article cautioned that the institutionalization of librarians in prisons meant that professional values would be compromised (Geary, 2003). Access to legal materials and the aftereffects of *Lewis v. Casey*, a Supreme Court ruling that lack of "legal research facilities or legal assistance" did not constitutionally violate a right to access to the law "unless prisoners have been substantially harmed by these deficiencies" (Justia, 2021), were stark concerns for legal librarians and librarians in prisons. Other topics addressed included the history of library services to people who are incarcerated, information-seeking behaviors, medical information, reentry, and the role of academic libraries. Three articles in the special issue of *Education Libraries* were written by incarcerated people, who provided portrayals of or reflections on having access to library materials and information.

Many of the articles written in this period cited the high rates of incarceration, and some mentioned how expanded prison populations limited information availability and reduced resources. One article situated information from prison librarians and from two incarcerated people within contemporary research in the social sciences and the history of library services to people who are incarcerated (Greenway, 2007). Greenway's article not only addressed many of the topics listed above, but also incorporated practical information related to language services, applied public library models, and the ways that librarians and incarcerated people expressed the value of information access inside of prisons.

Sixteen articles were published on the topic of library and information services for incarcerated adults between 2010 and 2019. During this period, access to technology, carceral philosophies, incarcerated people's information-seeking behavior, and legal materials and access were the most frequent concerns. (Information-seeking behavior was highlighted in publications about mail-in reference services, which will be discussed later in this chapter, and again in chapter 6.) The three articles that addressed carceral philosophies were again split between punitive approaches and discussions of the library's role in rehabilitation. Articles that covered law library services complicated the definition of meaningful access to the court and presented models for legal information instruction. Articles that highlighted technology emphasized the difficulties of accessing information in prisons as information increasingly became only available online, with one article suggesting that third-party technologies, such as Google Scholar, could provide adequate legal resource access (Kelmor, 2016). One article specifically focused on the meager and inaccessible legal materials available in immigrant detention facilities (Dunaway, 2017). Some articles also addressed the day-to-day functions of the library in a carceral setting, including programs and adherence to the 1992 standards. Other topics broached during this period were the history of libraries in institutions, funding, collections, patron privacy, the legal precedent for libraries in prisons to have their records brought into criminal court proceedings, the role of academic library services to people who are incarcerated, and censorship.

Several books, guides, and book chapters related to library services in carceral facilities and information access for incarcerated people were also published between 1992 and 2019. Vogel (*Down for the Count: A Prison Library Handbook*) and Rubin and Suvak (*Libraries Inside: A Practical Guide for Prison Librarians*) published guides to providing library services in adult correctional facilities in 1995. Vogel's introduction recognizes the effects of the increasingly expansive criteria for incarceration and the social and political status of people who are incarcerated as less than fully human. Vogel refers to the status of people who are incarcerated as "'non-persons' in prison communities across the United States" (1995, v). Vogel's goal is to increase the amount of information access and library services available to people who are incarcerated by positioning these services within the context of the prison (describing the actual day-to-day issues that arise in the practice of library service) and in larger society (recognizing how increasing rates of incarceration overlap with other social and political factors, such as reduced social support systems). Rubin and Suvak's 1995 edited volume presents an overview of reflections and perspectives from current or former librarians in carceral facilities, ranging from discussions of social organization in carceral facilities and the impact of "management philosophy" (Suvak, 1995, 3) through collection development, staffing, and programming. The volume opens with a brief mention of the expanding reach of incarceration in the United States, citing the one million people who were incarcerated in 1994.

In 2003, Sullivan and Vogel published a collaborative overview of historical library services in carceral facilities, which covered the philosophical approaches that informed those services. Their chapter pressures librarians not to conform to a "hegemony that attempted to exclude whole categories of reading as demonic, irrational, heretical, or criminal" in its reliance on narratives of rehabilitation (2003, 114). Alternately, they assert that the result of librarians and library outreach aligning with punitive goals is an approach that leaves "no books allowed" (2003, 114). Their critical coverage of the history of library services, censorship, prison expansion, the dearth of resources and funding, and information access as a form of control informs this book.

Three years later, Clark and MacCreaigh's book (2006) addressed the possibilities and practical concerns that arise when trying to create a prison library that is modeled on public library services. Drawing from their experiences creating a library in the Arapahoe County Detention Facility, as well as conversations with other librarians in carceral facilities, the authors present an overview of day-to-day library services and program implementation that draws upon public library philosophies as these relate to the rights of people who are incarcerated to access information, and their ideas for balancing this against the context of the institution. Clark and MacCreaigh frame their text within the increased number of prisons in the United States and offer a cautionary statement against the belief that the librarian somehow "saves" people who are incarcerated.

Vogel followed Clark and MacCreaigh with an updated guide in 2009. Vogel opens *The Prison Library Primer* by pointing out the interlinked nature of carceral effects and the larger society, stating that "America's staggering prison industry and populace have erased the distinction between the culture of the prison and that of outside communities" (2009, v). Vogel traces changes in practices, political stances, and social conceptions of crime and criminality and their impact on library services in prisons in the period since her earlier work was published. She positions the practical aspects of contemporaneous library services in carceral facilities within a call to the larger library profession to recognize and act on the information needs and desires of people who are incarcerated. This work underscores the impact of mass incarceration and extremely limited access to technologies as areas for advocacy and action, thus returning to a theme at the conclusion of the chapter with Sullivan in 2003.

Shirley's 2016 chapter "In a Place of Monotony and Despair: A Library!," in an edited volume by Barlow and Jaeger, positions library services for people who are incarcerated within the frameworks of diversity, poverty, and information access, and notes facilities' ability to limit information access under the claim that it constitutes a security concern. In a chapter that is part personal reflection and part recounting of an illustrious career, Shirley describes her first interactions with incarcerated patrons, how she incorporated information from community groups, and her work as Maryland's correction education library coordinator. She brings the topics outlined in this analysis to the fore throughout the chapter, highlighting literacy skills, multilingual access, the children of people who are incarcerated, and her own efforts to increase access to technology, including the creation of technology-rich mobile reentry units that were made available to people who were soon to be released from prison.

Conrad's *Prison Librarianship: Policy and Practice* was published the following year. In this text, Conrad assesses the ongoing relevance of the ASCLA's "Library Standards for Adult Correctional Institutions" (1992) against the library services that are actually available in carceral facilities. Through explanatory surveys and interviews, Conrad compares the standards with the actual experiences of librarians in prison settings. Her work emphasizes the need for updated standards, while revealing that punitive philosophies have diminished the funding for libraries in prisons. The legal information that Conrad provides, as well as the information about practitioners' experiences, complement the other information in her book.

Styslinger, Gavigan, and Albright's edited work *Literacy behind Bars* (2017), on literacy for incarcerated adults and youth, situates library programming for incarcerated people within mass incarceration. It justifies literacy-related services by introducing research that shows a correlation between literacy levels and incarceration. It includes contributions on a range of topics, including street literature (also known as urban fiction) (Irvin, 2017) and social justice (Doyle, Bemiss, and Styslinger, 2017), some of which critically engage with the meaning and value of literacy practices.

Higgins's *Get Inside: Responsible Jail and Prison Library Service* (2017) affirms the trend toward a public library model for library services in carceral facilities, and calls for public librarians to provide library services to people who are incarcerated. Released by the Public Library Association and freely available to its members, Higgins's guide positions practical aspects of services within a narrative of the negative impact of mass incarceration. It covers many of the concerns of these services, including interactions with facility staff, responding to censorship, institutional barriers, and programs that connect people inside of prisons to their loved ones on the outside.

Two chapters published at the end of the decade reflect ongoing conversations in librarianship regarding library services. Rayme's chapter promotes increased library services through a lens of the needs of diverse users (2017). Jacobson's chapter on information needs and information access for people who are incarcerated, specifically by a reference service provided through the mail, highlights innovative ways in which public libraries can and do address the institutionally created lack of access to technology and restrictions on general access to information.

Possibly in response to the rise in rates of incarceration, a new, and more comprehensive ALA statement on the "Prisoners Right to Read" was adopted in June of 2010. Eldon Ray James, a formerly incarcerated librarian, and Diane Walden, a longtime institutional librarian, worked with others to create a statement that reflected the profession's goals and values. The statement acknowledged that while legislation about information access in carceral facilities might shape librarian's censorship and selection practices, the ALA advocates for incarcerated people to have the fullest opportunities for intellectual freedom as possible. This includes access to technology and the internet. A small revision of the Statement was approved in 2014. The subsequent 2019 revision incorporates the need for materials to be discoverable. It also includes a statement that "[p]eople who are incarcerated or detained should have the ability to obtain books and materials from outside the prison for their personal use," which reflects the ongoing barriers to access being placed upon people who are incarcerated.

Library Services to Youth

Conrad (2017) notes the dearth of recent publications about library services to people who are incarcerated, comparing the rates of publishing on other types of librarianship to the rates of publishing on topics related to library services for people who are incarcerated. Even when widening the scope of analysis to include trade publications, this trend is dramatically apparent when considering the number and types of publications about library services to incarcerated youth published between 1992 and 2019 (see Appendix B). During this period, a total of 32 articles were published on the topic. Twenty-seven of these articles were popular profiles of services. Most often, the popular articles provided brief summaries of direct services, the day-to-day functioning of specific facilities, the types of programs implemented in the library, public libraries' outreach to youth who are incarcerated, and profiles of librarians providing library services in juvenile detention. Some of the popular publications during this period reflected on aspects of collection development and censorship of materials in juvenile detention center collections, and a few discussed the role of school librarians. Among the articles, there was some limited coverage of reentry and of the possibility that youth will be on probation as an alternative to incarceration or after their release from juvenile detention. Two articles from the 2010s discuss the use of technology in juvenile detention centers.

The majority of publications during this period were issued following the 1999 revision of the "Library Standards for Juvenile Correctional Institutions." Two book chapters profiled specific projects and introduced the possibility of collaboration between public librarians and juvenile detention centers. Sweeney's 2011 chapter set the stage for a book-length work, *Literacy: A Way Out for at-Risk Youth* (2012), that emphasized the role of literacy skill-building as part and parcel of juvenile detention center libraries. Sweeney's text incorporates research with librarians at juvenile detention centers and profiles of programs and libraries to present an array of possible partnerships and collaborations. Styslinger, Gavigan, and Albright's 2017 edited work, mentioned in the section above, also focused on literacy practices. The other book published in this period, Zeman's *Tales of a Jailhouse Librarian: Challenging the Juvenile Justice System One Book at a Time* (2014), is a personal account of working as a librarian in a juvenile detention center. It emphasizes the role of reading in the lives of youth who are incarcerated.

One academic article briefly mentions a program that placed library and information science students as librarians in a juvenile detention center, and describes their role in facilitating connections between the youth there and the community. The three remaining articles (authored by me) focus on philosophical approaches to juvenile detention center librarianship and include historical reviews of services, as well as examinations of the literacy practices of incarcerated youth.

It is important to acknowledge that there was an informal working group focused on library services for youth who were incarcerated that was very active in the early years of the 2010s, though this group is not documented in any of the listed articles. This group of librarians working in juvenile detention centers, known as Library Services for Youth in Custody, met regularly and maintained a web presence that is available in the Internet Archive (2016). It also coordinated the release of the "In the Margins" book award for several years. The award has continued even though the group is no longer extant.

Patterns in Publications

A review of publications over the previous three decades reveals that librarians continue to discuss library services for people who are incarcerated in the same manner as they have since the profession began to take an interest in providing these types of services. Reaching further back in time, the publications over the last 100 years tend toward descriptions of the rote aspects of library services to incarcerated people, emphasizing practices of information categorization and delivery, describing practical aspects of services, and assessing the library's role in the carceral facility. While at times these publications have specifically espoused a philosophical approach to library services, they have more often been shaped by adherence to a certain perspective—most often falling along the lines of either rehabilitation or punishment. These approaches have been normalized as the role of carceral institutions and, hence, the libraries inside them. Within this overarching approach to (or justification for) services, there have been some changes, however. Since the 1970s librarians have more openly, but not consistently, acknowledged the racial demographics of incarceration and have more often promoted access to culturally relevant materials, including the need for language-specific materials. There have also been a few critically needed mentions of how nationalist narratives of inherent criminality have shaped carceral terrains.

Most publications in this period maintain that the library in the carceral facility should align with the implementation and goals of public library service. Along this thread emerge a few important points of deviation and calls for advocacy, however. First are the frequent discussions of censorship as it occurs within libraries in carceral institutions. This holds for both youth in juvenile detention and adults who are incarcerated. Second is the growing distance between accessing information through technologies in the world outside of the juvenile detention, jail, or prison and the impossibility of this access for people who are incarcerated. Finally, the more recent publications increasingly address the effects of rising rates of incarceration and the possibility that people who are incarcerated will return to the community.

The next section incorporates topics that are not often prioritized in the literature on library services to people who are incarcerated. It first provides a review of publications about the role of information for people who are incarcerated. It then incorporates this research in discussing a few published accounts in which people who are or have been incarcerated express the value that access to information holds for them.

INFORMATION AND INCARCERATION

The ideologies that librarians carry into library service for incarcerated people—ideas of incarceration as serving the role of either punishing or rehabilitating people, as well as the "functions" of reading and information access in supporting those aims—are reflected in the ways that librarians have discussed library services during the previous thirty years. When focused on reading as a force for redemption (or, at times, on limiting access to information as a needed form of punishment or as necessary to "reshape" individuals' thoughts), librarians and information professionals have prioritized their ways of knowing over how people who are incarcerated actually describe their practice of accessing information. Turning to research that draws upon the information requests made by people who are incarcerated, as well as their descriptions of the role of texts in their lives, may help to prioritize their experience over librarians' perspectives and to trouble the line that researchers have drawn between the information practices of incarcerated people and the information practices of people who are not detained.

Simultaneously, examining the types of information that are requested by incarcerated people, and describing the importance they place on access to information, yields insight into limited information access as a feature of the ongoing systemic oppression of people that occurs when they are incarcerated. This section attempts to hold two modes of thinking about incarceration and information access side-by-side. The first is Chatman's discussion of "life in the round" (1999). In analyzing the information practices of women who were incarcerated, Chatman found information practices that served to create an internal world inside of the prison—including the sharing of information about how to survive incarceration and how to work toward release—as well as the reinforcement of various roles people might hold in the process of information sharing, production, and regulation. Chatman's work has served as a reminder that approaches to incarceration as a space that is devoid of information access do a disservice to incarcerated people. Mehra encourages people who draw from Chatman's work to incorporate information about power, oppression, and how individuals navigate their positions within these through their information practice (2021).

The second mode of thinking is the recognition that, as information has moved further and further into the digital realm and more and more resources are available solely through the internet and its concomitant technologies, the ability of people who are incarcerated to access information has declined. This has been compounded by a simultaneous increase in the number of people in jails, prisons, and other carceral institutions and a reduction of funding for most libraries in these institutions. Many prison libraries are run on shoestring budgets (often out of an inmate welfare fund, which is funded by the commissary or vending machine purchases made by incarcerated people and visitors—itself an exploitative practice for people who have so little funds to purchase materials and are thus positioned as potentially personally responsible for the lack of resources within the prison). Moreover, the libraries in prisons are consistently understaffed (Conrad, 2017; Sweeney, 2010), and people who are incarcerated have reduced access to materials and information during their incarceration. Simply put, in addition to the many successful efforts on the part of carceral institutions to censor information (PEN America, 2019), limitations of time, location in the facility, and scant material resources are barriers to the information and books that people who are incarcerated are able to access, even in those instances when information is available (or ostensibly available) in the facility.

Recent publications on the types of information requests (i.e., reference questions) from people who are incarcerated provide insight into the ways that limiting access to information is a function of the carceral system. Within the last decade, researchers have turned to an analysis of the types of reference questions generated by people inside. Following Chatman, this research often encourages readers to "consider the ways that requests for information structure a worldview and an information system" (Rabina, Drabinski, and Paradise, 2016, 292). Adding to this, information requests can be analyzed to reveal what information is not, or is only partially or infrequently, available to people in carceral facilities, thereby providing a reflection of ongoing carceral practices (Austin and Villa-Nicholas, 2019; Rabina, Drabinski, and Paradise, 2016).

Through an extended engagement with reference questions from incarcerated people, Drabinksi and Rabina have established three main areas of information needs and desires. These are reentry-related, self-help, and reference. Each of these categories reflects a service that is often assumed to exist in carceral facilities (Drabinski and Rabina, 2015). In utilizing the by-mail reference service as an opportunity for LIS students to respond to real reference questions, the authors found that students could identify the specific types of resources most often requested by incarcerated people. These information sources included "government sources," "traditional reference resources," "miscellaneous websites," a reentry guide, "open access reference/scholarly sources," and information generated by "advocacy groups" (Rabina and Drabinski, 2015, 126). The authors recognize that their work may be used to create a recommended resources list for the materials included in libraries in carceral facilities, but they push against the possibility of interpreting their results only in this manner.

Drabinski, Rabina, and Paradise build from the experience of working with LIS students to answer the information requests from people who were incarcerated to review how "prisons and jails as an environment . . . produce certain kinds of questions . . . that tell us as much about the conditions of confinement as they do about the individuals seeking answers to particular questions" (2016, 293). Their review of nearly 300 information requests sent by people who were incarcerated reveals particular patterns of information needs and desires. They found that most of the requests concerned practical information (around 65 percent), but some requests reflected "curiosity" and a desire to "broaden horizons" (around 34 percent) (2016, 294). The topics most frequently broached in the reference requests involved information that could be found in directories, information about employment (both existing opportunities and possibilities of creating new enterprises), legal information, government information, general reference, entertainment, religious and spiritual information, housing, and professional development. Through requests for feedback from patrons of the service, the researchers found that the service was highly valued by patrons, and they received indications that it would often be incredibly difficult for patrons to otherwise access the information that had been provided through the by-mail service (Drabinski, Rabina, and Paradise, 2016).

Incarceration not only shapes the types of information requests that are made by people who are incarcerated, it also creates requests that must pass through an intermediary service. In the case of the reference by mail services maintained by public libraries, some requests for information—for instance, legal or medical information—may fall outside the realm of the services that public librarians can reliably perform. Scoping in to focus on the types of medical information requests made by people who were incarcerated, Couvillon and Justice (2016) examined over 200 letters sent to a by-mail medical reference service for people incarcerated in Texas. The researchers found that people consistently requested information about specific diseases and medications, reflecting the difficulty of acquiring a second opinion or researching prescription medications while incarcerated. Patrons of the service also shared their concerns about the conditions of their living environment, the health dangers posed by carceral facilities, and their desire to share information with others in the prison in order to be collectively more informed about diseases, medications, and other relevant health information (Couvillon and Justice, 2016). Here, medical librarians acted as intermediaries for people who were incarcerated who needed access to reliable information that could individually and collectively be used to assess their well-being and to advocate for more livable conditions.

Practitioners and LIS educators who have implemented by-mail reference services for incarcerated people note that "the strictures that the State places on information access within carceral institutions" as well as "culturally relevant interests are present within requests from patrons" (Austin and Villa-Nicholas, 2019, 252). Practitioners especially underscore the ways in which the physical and temporal environments of prison shape how and what information is requested. These include issues related to vision and access to reading or prescription glasses, how time spent incarcerated shapes the background knowledge that people use in framing their broad requests for information—specifically in requesting information about technology and technologically mediated processes—and how the time lapse involved in a by-mail program—in which carceral officials potentially spend some time reviewing communications as they leave and arrive in facilities—shapes the process of providing information (Jacobson, 2018). Librarians overseeing by-mail reference services also emphasize the more intimate dimensions of providing information to people who may have only limited access to other sources of reliable information. Jacobson says that the requesters "trust this service with very private, personal, and disparate details," and she prioritizes "their expectation that they will be treated like people and not like inmates" (2018, 156). This involves recognizing that people who are incarcerated do access, share, and construct information worlds, while also acknowledging the intensity with which their information access is actively curtailed.

Given the intentional positioning of carceral facilities as politically, socially, and geographically removed from the public, it is especially imperative to note that information access is regulated and to identify how people who are incarcerated are also positioned within information worlds that, while existing in and maintained by internal dynamics (Chatman, 1999), also potentially represent the porousness of barriers that are imagined to keep specific information out and other information inside. Individual's requests for information are not generated without prior knowledge or experience. There are sometimes requests for specific types of information from people who have had only limited exposure to contemporary information sources—for example, people who received life sentences in the 1990s requesting information about social media platforms with which they have probably never interacted—and these requests indicate the ways in which information flows exist across the barriers of the carceral facility.

Librarians and information professionals need to acknowledge the variety of information sources that do enter and circulate within carceral contexts, and the ways and circumstances in which these information flows become impeded. Among these possible sources of information are television and radio broadcasts; information carried into the carceral facility by people who are newly admitted; information from people outside the prison that is communicated by phone, video visitations, in-person visitations, and technology-based messaging or e-mail, magazine subscriptions, information on tablets (when available, and this information is often only available at a cost); books sent by family members or by volunteer groups that provide free books for incarcerated people; information from carceral staff and the institution; and media resource catalogs. Other, more intentional forms of information transfer have received more attention than library services for incarcerated people, to varying degrees. As carceral facilities have moved toward punishment and policies of greater austerity, religious groups, and particularly Christian groups and missionary programs, have become prominent as information providers to people who are incarcerated.[2] Groups that focus attention on addiction and recovery, such as Alcoholics Anonymous, have created piecemeal distribution systems for their materials in carceral facilities across the country in order to make their programming and support groups available to people who are incarcerated. Educational programs, particularly college education, have created new flows of information between people who are incarcerated and the people (and their campus communities) who provide the coursework. Research also shows that carceral facilities do not frequently demand programs such as these, and in some states educational programs in prisons have been redirected from general education to job development and other, narrower topics (Sweeney, 2010).[3] Despite this, each of these information sources can provide the basis for seeking additional information, thereby laying a foundation for beginning to request information that may be absent within the carceral facility.

Of course, access to these information sources is moderated by oversight within the carceral facility and by the types of confinement to which people are subject. People in psych units, observation units, and similar sections of the carceral facility most likely face increased levels of oversight regarding their reading habits and their attempts to connect to the larger community or to access information (if they are allowed to do so at all). People in disciplinary confinement (i.e., administrative segregation or solitary) are not only subject to increased levels of surveillance and information management by facility staff, but are often prohibited from accessing information and media and communicating with other people. There are legal precedents to justify these types of restrictions. The U.S. Supreme Court's 2006 decision in *Beard v. Banks* allows carceral facilities to deny access to secular media and photographs if they can demonstrate that this restriction is for people held in disciplinary sections of the facility who are deemed recalcitrant (Sweeney, 2008).[4]

PERSONAL ACCOUNTS

It is likely that the strictures imposed on access to materials and information tend to structure the ways in which people who are incarcerated express their own appreciation for and engagement with texts and information. Given this, librarians and information professionals should critically reflect on whether or not they re-create narratives that normalize incarceration by focusing on how incarcerated people's information practices diverge from the various ways in which people use information and books to make meaning, foresee a future, construct selfhood, pass time, escape, fantasize, self-regulate, be entertained, and otherwise engage in the internal worlds that information access and reading provide in a society that is largely structured by literacy (Austin, 2019a). The word *literacy* here must be broadly understood to stretch beyond print texts and information to include various forms of media and the underlying cultural messages within them (Winn, 2011).

In addition to the strictures created by carceral facilities, publishing structures and publicized conceptions of incarceration also shape the narratives available for people who are incarcerated to discuss their reading. The ability people who are incarcerated exhibit in using information and books to navigate their incarceration and possible release is remarkable. Too often, however, this is framed by the obligation to speak in modes that match the function of the carceral system as either punitive or rehabilitative, rather than as acts of personal will. This is probably amplified by how incarceration is portrayed in the larger society that people must navigate upon their release. This results in an easy elision of individuals' accounts of their own reading practice as an aftereffect of reformative incarceration. Recalling that information is more likely to be restricted than made available in carceral environments can help library and information professionals to recognize that the individualized meaning and maneuvers present in the information practices of incarcerated people, no matter the type of facility, are shaped by factors of cultural power in publishing and the privileging of information, prior knowledge and familiarity, and resource availability or scarcity. So, too, are the reading and information practices of all readers and information seekers.

People who are incarcerated have consistently documented the importance that access to information, and especially books, holds for them. Research has tended to focus on the revelatory role of reading for education and enlightenment (Brottman, 2016) or the role of reading and information access in resistance movements and the development of revolutionary consciousness (Cummins, 1994). By contrast, only limited attention has been given in library and information science to the ways in which incarcerated and formerly incarcerated people discuss their own reading and information access. Yet people's experiences of reading while incarcerated abound in their memoirs, in newspapers, and in the knowledge that they hope to communicate to others who are in similar life circumstances. For instance, Shaka Senghor, the author of *Writing My Wrongs: Life, Death, and Redemption in an American Prison*, has publicly promoted a reading list that he drew inspiration and meaning from during his time incarcerated (Senghor, 2014). As in the instance of Malcolm X's *Autobiography*, many incarcerated people's memoirs utilize texts as signposts for forming consciousness, making sense of the writer's own circumstances, and many other modes of maintaining a self in dire and dehumanizing circumstances.[5] Outside of library and information science, Sweeney's work has focused on the collective reading experiences of women who are incarcerated in order to explore how books mediate their understanding of their selves, others, and incarceration (2008, 2010). As with the readers Sweeney describes, it is most common to find accounts that justify the role of reading as redemptive or a tool for self-recognition. This is evidenced in the titles of online, published accounts of reading and incarceration, such as "The book that changed my life . . . in prison," "The books that saved my life in prison," or "The books that kept me from falling apart in county jail" (Gross, 2018; Schwartz, 2018; Wilson, 2018).

Diving into these articles and accounts not only reveals the individual and at times collective power of reading; it also makes clear the breadth of reading interests and activities engaged in by people who are incarcerated, and the urgency that readers who are incarcerated bring to the act of reading (Books to Prisoners, 2019; Gross, 2018; Schwartz, 2018; Wilson, 2018). Even in circumstances where it is increasingly difficult to acquire books from the library, or in which facilities have narrowed book access by restricting the number of approved book vendors, currently and formerly incarcerated people like Chris Wilson put in tremendous effort to access materials (2018). The women in Sweeney's studies developed complex systems of distribution for library books and their own materials, at times referring to the transfer and caretaking of reading materials as the "underground book railroad"—a name that suggests not only the racialized nature of incarceration and censorship, but also the cultural relevance of the books that were shared between them (Sweeney, 2010). Reading and access to books is frequently recorded as life-saving. For instance, Wilson writes: "I didn't just live *for* that library. I lived *because* of that library. The Patuxent prison library saved me from crushing despair. It saved hundreds of other guys, too" (Wilson, 2018). Reflecting on a period of time in jail, Schwartz underscores the value of reading and information access, and positions reading at the apex of pleasure. Schwartz states: "Literature saved me in that place. The arrival of each book was better than anything I had ever known. Better than sex. Better than drugs or alcohol. Better than recovery. Better than daytime. Better than the moon" (2018). In documenting an attempted (and failed) New York statewide ban on print materials being sent into the prison by anyone other than private vendors which had restricted holdings, reporter Gross (2018) turned to people who had been incarcerated to showcase a few of their most poignant reading experiences. Five contributors shared how they came into contact with various materials and the meaning they derived from their reading, documenting the role of books in their ability to endure and to find inspiration while incarcerated.

Sweeney positions her work in the intellectual tradition of Angela Davis, and focuses on how reading might become liberatory. In keeping with this, library and information professionals should ask themselves how their conceptions of the role of reading while incarcerated might actively support the normalization of incarceration rather than prioritizing the experiences, desires, needs, and humanity of people who are incarcerated. In order to avoid regarding reading and information access as valuable for incarcerated people because it is redemptive or rehabilitative—a viewpoint which can easily slip into punitive modes when individuals are deemed as being beyond redemption or are sentenced to life in prison and may not physically return to the larger society—library and information professionals need to cultivate a complex critical awareness of how powerful systemic forces shape publishing as well as incarceration. These forces structure the information landscape, and position some knowledges, literacies, and cultural traditions as outside of the purview of prison libraries.

Culturally relevant materials for Black, Indigenous, and people of color are necessary aspects of collection development in carceral facilities, yet many of these materials are banned throughout the United States (Austin et al., 2020; Conrad, 2017; Sweeney, 2010). LGBTQIA+ materials are also subject to increased scrutiny and censorship (Austin et al., 2020; Sweeney, 2010; Conrad, 2017). Returning to the demographic information provided in earlier chapters reveals the lengths to which carceral facilities use access to information as a way to assert and justify their power on the basis of potentially unfounded claims to the safety and security of their facilities. In some instances, calling attention to culturally specific materials—for example, books written for Black or Latinx audiences by Black or Latinx authors, or that, like urban fiction (Irvin, 2017), feature realistic or fantastic situations about the experience of Black and brown people who are navigating poverty and systemic oppression, and who may at times be portrayed as unabashedly engaged in behaviors that are deemed criminal—has led to increased restrictions on these and other types of materials. (Books to Prisoners, n.d., publishes lists of banned books and updates on these changes online.) Restrictions can be further codified by the selection habits of the librarians themselves in carceral facilities. Librarianship is largely composed through a culture of whiteness as a profession. The value systems that shape cultures of whiteness tend to prioritize books that have received acclaim and are published and reviewed by mainstream publishers. These pitfalls of collection development can be exacerbated by large library vendors that restrict the titles available to order by placing requirements that official publishers have met some qualification to have their materials listed for purchase by libraries. (This may especially affect small-scale presses and publishers of urban fiction.)

A lack of language-specific materials also serves to further isolate people who are incarcerated or detained, and to restrict their access to information. This is true in carceral facilities across the United States, some of which have banned Indigenous language materials under security concerns related to coded communication (Austin et al., 2020). There is a need for materials in languages other than English in all facilities. Due to the patterns of policing and detaining people involved in the act of migration, the need for materials in languages other than English is pronounced in immigrant detention facilities. While it has been notoriously difficult to obtain information about the conditions and resources (or lack thereof) available in immigrant detention facilities, a few actions on the part of people who are detained and their advocates have served to reveal how information is used by the facilities as a mode of control. For instance, a 2020 exposé found that ICE employees responded with physical force following a demonstration staged by people who were requesting information in their own language (Dreisbach, 2020). The complaints by the people detained speak not only to the conditions of the facility, but also to the need for information access. Among their complaints were: "the guards were discriminating against them, they lacked access to clean water, the bonds for their immigration cases were too expensive, and they were receiving information only in English" (Dreisbach, 2020). Language access is a key area of concern for people who are detained in immigrant detention facilities, including access to materials in Indigenous languages and legal information, but these are often unavailable or severely lacking (Dunaway, 2017; Jawetz and Shuchart, 2019).

The placement of immigration detention centers in isolated areas has also diminished detainees' access to legal information, contact with family members, and other forms of information access (Noguchi, 2019). Information professionals have begun to meet the information needs of the public and families who are being separated by documenting the locations of immigration detention facilities and private juvenile detention centers (Dreyfuss, 2018; Torn Apart, n.d.), but this approach is only a start in meeting the vast information needs and desires of people who are detained, their families, and other people impacted by their detainment. The need to provide language-specific materials to children in immigration detention facilities has been acknowledged by the ALA (American Library Association, 2015), but this type of access only begins to reveal the information needs created by forced detention and isolation from resources. Due to the obscurity of information about immigration detention practices, librarians and information professionals will need to connect with existing groups or with currently and formerly detained individuals to determine the information needs of people detained in these facilities and gain insight on how detention shapes their information requests and information access. The starting points for this process may be present in the work of rights and advocacy organizations, the work of on-the-ground groups providing humanitarian aid at the borders, and in the oral and personal archives documented by Ordaz (2020) in an exploration of affective presence as a counter to state narratives of a functioning institution. There are ethical concerns involved in making information about people who are held in immigrant detention publicly available, even when that information reveals the severity of government practices of detainment (Romabiles et al., 2020). This, in addition to government practices that limit information access inside and communication with people outside of immigration detention facilities, may be part of why the publicly available information is so limited.

Critically positioning the reading and information practices of incarcerated people within larger social and political systems is necessary, and this brief review is only a beginning. It does not uncover the breadth of interests or desires expressed by people who are incarcerated. As a gesture to the deep, nuanced, and articulated information practices of people who are incarcerated, this section closes with a short analysis of how transgender women who are incarcerated have pushed against the limitations of publishing to create modes of communication that convey the culture of the prison while also respecting the specific information needs of other transgender women.

The guide "Surviving Prison in California: Advice by and for Transgender Women" was written by transgender women in prison and is distributed by the TGI Justice Project (TGIJP, 2011). TGIJP describes itself as "a group of transgender, gender variant and intersex people—inside and outside of prisons, jails and detention centers—creating a united family in the struggle for survival and freedom" (TGIJP, n.d.). The *Surviving Prison* guide is significant for many reasons, including its realistic approach to incarceration. It describes the maneuvers that transgender women must undertake in order to reduce their exposure to violence in an institution that often denigrates their existence and offers little resources or recourse. Distributed outside of traditional publishing, the guide serves to illustrate what it becomes possible to say when the discussion of the realities of prison, rather than its supposedly rehabilitative effects, is centered. In this guide, transgender women prioritize their own experiences and the overlaps between those experiences in order to show how the carceral system shapes the possibilities available to them. The authors are thus able to show their care and compassion and create community through the act of passing information. This communal document stands in deep contrast to narratives that suggest that reading must fit with the rehabilitative goals of incarceration. The guide provides library and information professionals with a vantage point from which to argue against the conditions of incarceration while also arguing for the necessity of information access for survival, community, and the myriad possibilities that such access offers for making meaning.

CONCLUSION

Library and information services for people who are incarcerated have continued to focus on the role that access to these services plays in the assumed rehabilitative or punitive functions of incarceration. This overview of LIS publications issued between 1992 and 2019 reveals the breadth of types of librarianship that can be involved with services to incarcerated people, and touches on the growing body of information about the rise and continuance of mass incarceration. The publications during this period did not consistently focus on the information requests of people who were incarcerated, how incarcerated people value access to library materials and other information, or how racism and other forces at play in mass incarceration might shape patrons' information needs and desires.

Recent publications, however, suggest that a shift is occurring both within and outside of the field. Tracie D. Hall, the executive director of the ALA, has published several essays encouraging library and information professionals to interrogate and push against racism within the LIS field, especially with regard to community disinvestment, censorship, incarceration, and information and library access (Hall, 2021a, 2021b). Hall links this advocacy to libraries' alignment with ongoing social and political movements for change.

Concerns over information control, censorship, and information access in carceral facilities have also surfaced in recent mainstream publications, including *Vogue* (Prakash, 2020), *Mother Jones* (Michaels, 2020), and the *Washington Post* (Hart, 2018), as well as in a PEN America report on carceral censorship practices (2019). New research is seeking to bypass the lack of transparency about censorship in carceral facilities by creating digital resources that include aggregated information about censored or banned materials (Cauley, 2020). These collective efforts to document and resist censorship in carceral facilities are reflected in the attention recently given to this topic in local newspapers across the country, often written in reaction to abrupt changes in local or state access policies.

Prison librarians continue to publish on the barriers to access to recreational and legal materials, and the possible maneuvers around those barriers. Bingman-Forshey and Gibbons (2020) present the challenges within Pennsylvania prisons, a significant site given recent policy changes that use technology to intercede in how people access or receive information, including through the physical mail.[6] These authors describe how invasive security searches have curtailed prison libraries' ability to engage in the interlibrary loan of hardcover books, and they note that hardcover books are often permanently damaged by the staff when performing contraband searches (2020). Recent publications that concern library services and incarceration at a national level include an overview that centers on the role of public libraries in programming and other services (Bilz, 2020) and a potential method for evaluating library services in prisons (Rosen, 2020). Other relevant publications have focused on policing and safety in libraries and the intersections of librarianship and abolition (Abolitionist Library Association, 2020; Balzer, 2020; Dapier and Knox, 2020; Graham, 2020; Library Freedom Project, 2020).

Two recent publications on library services in juvenile detention centers bookend aspects of youth incarceration. My work on restorative justice practices in library services with youth, which draws upon interviews with librarians in an urban library system, hinges on ways that librarians and library systems can engage in practices to address disruption and harm that do not potentially subject youth to police violence or incarceration (Austin, 2020). My article includes information about a variety of restorative justice approaches and practices, as well as actionable examples of them. Formby and Paynter (2020) look to the possible post-incarceration consequences of a lack of access to library services in juvenile detention centers. Their work situates library services in juvenile detention within the realm of education. They advocate for library media centers and librarians within juvenile detention centers, and emphasize that the literature on youth educational achievement, literacy, and incarceration shows that access to libraries and librarians will facilitate youth rehabilitation and reduce rates of re-incarceration.

Placing a review of library and information science publications alongside information produced by incarcerated people presents a more comprehensive overview of how information is controlled and used to produce control inside of carceral facilities. The statements that incarcerated people make about the value of accessing information must be simultaneously positioned within the attempts of the state to maintain control through information access. Positioning reading and information practices within the context of state regulation and control might connect to how the reading practices of people outside of prisons are also configured by the political and social forces that shape publishing, access to legitimacy, and the many forms of knowledge and information distribution that are affected by factors such as racism, ableism, misogyny, and homo- and transphobia. For people who are incarcerated, this is compounded by almost all-encompassing restrictions to accessing information online.

The first set of chapters in this book has addressed aspects of information and incarceration, including philosophical approaches to incarceration, the history of information control and provision in carceral facilities, an overview of contemporary carceral practices and sites, and a deep engagement with the connections between information and incarceration over the previous three decades. It now turns to the interstitial space of technologies, information access, and incarceration, a burgeoning area of research that contrasts heavily to (and often constrains the possibilities for) existing library services in carceral facilities. The second half of the book is concerned with current practices of information provision as maneuvers through and around the carceral landscape. It includes information about direct and indirect library services, reentry as a process and possible site for library programming, and a few of the on-the-ground concerns related to library services in carceral settings.

NOTES

1. This decision primarily excluded state and local-level assessment or profiles of specific services. It may have erased some of the more critical, political work done by librarians, staff, and volunteers, such as the Window to Freedom library in Chicago, which served women in a Chicago jail (Mantilla and O'Leary, 2001).
2. Sweeney discusses this specifically in relation to Joyce Meyer's missionary provision of her self-help texts to women who are incarcerated (2010).
3. See Bryan and Ginsburg's "Higher Education in Jails and Prisons Programming List" (n.d.) and the Alliance for Higher Education in Prison's directory (2019) for more information about existing programs.
4. Access to religious material is a constitutionally protected right.
5. These are not isolated practices, nor are they always practices developed only while incarcerated. For instance, Anna Malaika Tubbs found that Malcolm X's engagement with the dictionary began as a practice of curiosity around language encouraged by his mother (2021).
6. See Austin, 2019b, for background on the Pennsylvania Department of Corrections' mail policy.

REFERENCES

Abolitionist Library Association. 2020. "Solidarity with Douglas County Public Library." www.change.org/p/solidarity-with-douglas-county-public-library.

Alliance for Higher Education in Prison. 2019. "National Directory of Higher Education in Prison Programs." www.higheredinprison.org/national-directory.

American Library Association. 2015. "Resolution on Improving Access to Spanish, Bilingual, and Books in Various Languages for Children in Detention Centers." www.ala.org/aboutala/sites/ala.org.aboutala/files/content/governance/council/council_documents/2015_annual_council_documents/cd_38_Resol_on_chldrn_n_%20crisis_rev_63015_final.pdf.

———. 2019. "Prisoners' Right to Read: An Interpretation of the Library Bill of Rights." www.ala.org/advocacy/intfreedom/librarybill/interpretations/prisonersrightoread.

———. 2014. "Prisoners' Right to Read: An Interpretation of the Library Bill of Rights." https://web.archive.org/web/20180519142617/http://www.ala.org/advocacy/intfreedom/librarybill/interpretations/prisonersrightoread.

——. 2010. "Prisoners' Right to Read: An Interpretation of the Library Bill of Rights." https://web.archive
.org/web/20141204214039/http://www.ala.org/advocacy/intfreedom/librarybill/interpretations/
prisonersrighttoread

Austin, J. 2019a. "Literacy Practices of Youth Experiencing Incarceration: Reading and Writing as Points
of Regulation and Escape." *Libri: International Journal of Libraries and Information Studies* 69, no. 1:
77-87.

——. 2019b. "Mechanisms of Communicative Control (and Resistance): Carceral Incorporations of ICT
and Communication Policies for Physical Mail." *First Monday* 24, no. 3-4.

——. 2020. "Restorative Justice as a Tool to Address the Role of Policing and Incarceration in the Lives of
Youth in the United States." *Journal of Librarianship and Information Science* 52, no. 1: 106-20.

Austin, J., J. Lincoln, K. C. Briggs, M. Charenko, and M. Dillon. 2020. "Race, Racism, and the Contested
Ground of Information Access for Incarcerated People." *Open Information Science*, 4, no. 1: 169-85.

Austin, J., and M. Villa-Nicholas. 2019. "Information Provision and the Carceral State: Race and Reference
beyond the Idea of the 'Underserved.'" *The Reference Librarian* 60, no. 4: 233-61.

Balzer, C. 2020. "Rethinking Police Presence: Libraries Consider Divesting from Law Enforcement."
American Libraries 51, no. 9/10: 46-49.

Bilz, K. 2020. "Public Library Services for the Incarcerated and Detained." *Kentucky Libraries* 84, no. 2: 16-23.

Bingman-Forshey, H., and P. Gibbons. 2020. "Behind the Wall: Service Challenges at a Prison Library."
Public Services Quarterly 16, no. 1: 65-69.

Books to Prisoners. n.d. "Banned Books Lists." www.bookstoprisoners.net/banned-book-lists/.

Books to Prisoners. 2019. *Dear Books to Prisoners*. Seattle, WA: Left Bank Books.

Brottman, M. 2016. *The Maximum Security Book Club: Reading Literature in a Men's Prison*. New York:
HarperCollins.

Bryan, V., and R. Ginsburg. n.d. "Higher Education in Jails and Prisons Programming List." https://
docs.google.com/spreadsheets/d/1KyAKXEvjacK4nqjFHO5r8Wb0DU3HtRqgeBaCVOlE5aM/
edit#gid=1035278084.

Cauley, K. 2020. "Banned Books behind Bars: Prototyping a Data Repository to Combat Arbitrary
Censorship Practices in U.S. Prisons." *Humanities* 9, no. 4.

Charmaz, Kathy 2006. *Constructing Grounded Theory*. London: Sage.

Chatman, E. 1999. "A Theory of Life in the Round." *Journal of the American Society for Information Science*
50, no. 3: 207-17.

Clark, S., and E. MacCreaigh. 2006. *Library Services to the Incarcerated: Applying the Public Library Model in
Correctional Facilities*. Santa Barbara, CA: Libraries Unlimited.

Conrad, S. 2017. *Prison Librarianship: Policy and Practice*. Jefferson, NC: McFarland.

Couvillon, E., and A. Justice. 2016. "Letters from the Big House: Providing Consumer Health Reference for
Texas Prisons." *Journal of Hospital Librarianship* 16, no. 4: 281-86.

Cummins, E. 1994. "The Rise and Fall of California's Radical Prison Movement." Stanford, CA: Stanford
University Press.

Dapier, J., and E. Knox. 2020. "When Not to Call the Cops." *American Libraries* 51, no. 9/10: 49.

Doyle, J. L., E. M. Bemiss, and M. E. Styslinger. 2017. "The Places We Can Go: Book Clubs for Social Justice."
In *Literacy behind Bars: Successful Reading and Writing Strategies for Use with Incarcerated Youth and
Adults*, ed. M. E. Styslinger, K. Gavigan, and K. Albright, 55-60. Lanham, MD: Rowman and Littlefield.

Drabinski, E., and D. Rabina. 2015. "Reference Services to Incarcerated People: Part I, Themes Emerging
from Answering Reference Questions from Prisons and Jails." *Reference and User Services Quarterly* 55,
no. 1: 42-48.

Dreisbach, T. 2020. "Exclusive: Video Shows Controversial Use of Force inside an ICE Detention Center."
National Public Radio. www.npr.org/2020/02/06/802939294/exclusive-video-shows-controversial
-use-of-force-inside-an-ice-detention-center.

Dreyfuss, E. 2018. "'ICE Is Everywhere': Using Library Science to Map the Separation Crisis." *Wired.* www.wired.com/story/ice-is-everywhere-using-library-science-to-map-child-separation/.

Dunaway, S. E. 2017. "¿Dónde está la biblioteca? It's a Damn Shame: Outdated, Inadequate, and Nonexistent Law Libraries in Immigrant Detention Facilities." *Legal Reference Services Quarterly* 36, no. 1: 1–33.

Formby, A. E., and K. Paynter. 2020. "The Potential of a Library Media Program in Reducing Recidivism Rates among Juvenile Offenders." *National Youth-at-Risk Journal* 4, no. 1: 14–21.

Glaser, B. G., and A. L. Strauss. 1967. *The Discovery of Grounded Theory: Strategies for Qualitative Research.* Chicago: Aldine.

Graham, L. 2020. "Libraries, Prisons, and Abolition." https://scholarworks.iupui.edu/bitstream/handle/1805/24045/Graham2020LibrariesPrisonsAbolition.pdf?sequence=1&isAllowed=y.

Gross, D. A. 2018. "The Book That Saved My Life . . . in Prison." *The Guardian.* www.theguardian.com/culture/2018/jan/19/the-book-that-changed-my-life-in-prison.

Hall, T. D. 2021a. "Defending the Fifth Freedom: Protecting the Right to Read for Incarcerated Individuals." *American Libraries* 52, no. 1: 6.

———. 2021b. "Revolutions Where We Stand: We Must Connect the Fights Against Library and Community Disinvestment." *American Libraries* 52, no. 3-4: 5.

Hart, A. 2018. "Librarians Despise Censorship. How Can Prison Librarians Handle That? It's Complicated." *Washington Post*, January 16. www.washingtonpost.com/news/posteverything/wp/2018/01/16/librarians-despise-censorship-how-can-prison-librarians-handle-that-its-complicated/.

Higgins, N. 2017. *Get Inside: Responsible Jail and Prison Library Service.* Chicago: Public Library Association.

Irvin, V. 2017. "Call-and-Responsive Reading: Street Literature as Agency for Incarcerated Readers." In *Literacy behind bars: Successful Reading and Writing Strategies for Use with Incarcerated Youth and Adults*, ed. M. E. Styslinger, K. Gavigan, and K. Albright, 35–40. Lanham, MD: Rowman and Littlefield.

Jacobson, E. 2018. "Reference by Mail to Incarcerated People." In *Reference Librarianship & Justice: History, Praxis, & Practice,* ed. K. Adler, I. Beilin, and E. Tewell, 151–59. Sacramento, CA: Library Juice.

Jawetz, T., and S. Shuchart. 2019. "Language Access Has Life-or-Death Consequences for Migrants." Center for American Progress. www.americanprogress.org/issues/immigration/reports/2019/02/20/466144/language-access-life-death-consequences-migrants/.

Justia. 2021. *Lewis v. Casey,* 518 U.S. 343 (1996). https://supreme.justia.com/cases/federal/us/518/343/.

Library Freedom Project. 2020. "It's Not Enough to Say Black Lives Matter—Libraries Must Divest from the Police." https://libraryfreedom.medium.com/its-not-enough-to-say-black-lives-matter-libraries-must-divest-from-the-police-2ab4adea58f1.

Library Services for Youth in Custody. 2016. https://web.archive.org/web/20161007092941/http://youthlibraries.org/.

Mantilla, K., and C. O'Leary. 2001. "Windows to Freedom: Radical Feminism at a Jail Library." *Off Our Backs* 31, no. 2: 6–17.

Mehra, B. 2021. Elfreda Annmary Chatman in the 21st century: At the intersection of critical theory and social justice imperatives. In N.A. Cooke and A. Gibson (Eds.), Chatman Revisited (Special issue). *Journal of Critical Library and Information Studies*, 3.

Michaels, S. 2020. "Books Have the Power to Rehabilitate. But Prisons Are Blocking Access to Them." *Mother Jones*, November. www.motherjones.com/crime-justice/2019/11/prison-libraries-book-bans-california-sacramento-reading-rehabilitation/.

Noguchi, Y. 2019. "Unequal Outcomes: Most ICE Detainees Held in Rural Areas Where Deportation Risks Soar." NPR, August 15. www.npr.org/2019/08/15/748764322/unequal-outcomes-most-ice-detainees-held-in-rural-areas-where-deportation-risks.

Ordaz, J. 2020. "Migrant Detention Archives: Histories of Pain and Solidarity." *Southern California Quarterly* 102, no. 3: 250–73.

PEN America. 2019. "Literature Locked Up: How Prison Book Restriction Policies Constitute the Nation's Largest Book Ban." https://pen.org/wp-content/uploads/2019/09/literature-locked-up-report-9.24.19 .pdf.

Prakash, P. 2020. "Liberation Library Is Pushing for Prison Abolition, One Book at a Time." *Vogue*. www .vogue.com/article/liberation-library-prison-abolition.

Rabina, D., and E. Drabinski. 2015. "Reference Services to Incarcerated People: Part II, Sources and Learning Outcomes." *Reference and User Services Quarterly* 55, no. 2: 123-31.

Rabina, D., E. Drabinski, and L. Paradise. 2016. "Information Needs in Prisons and Jails: A Discourse Analysis Approach." *Libri: International Journal of Libraries and Information Studies* 66, no. 4: 291-302.

Rayme, M. 2017. "Prison Libraries: On the Fringe of the Library World." In *Librarians with Spines: Information Agitators in the Age of Stagnation*, ed. Y. S. Cura and M. Macias, 99-110. Los Angeles: Hinchas.

Romabiles, K., A. Lanthorne, A. Lucas, and L. Lamont. 2020. "Ethics, Sustainability and the Challenge of Digital Curation for a Real-Time Archive." *Journal of Digital Media Management*, 9, no. 1: 63-70.

Rosen, J. 2020. "Evaluating Impact in the Forgotten Field of Prison Librarianship." *Serials Librarian* 79, no. 1-2: 38-48.

Rubin, R. J., and D. Suvak. 1995. *Libraries Inside: A Practical Guide for Prison Librarians*. Jefferson, NC: McFarland.

Salvatore, C. 2019. "Are Prison Law Libraries Falling Short on Access Goals?" Law360. www.law360.com/ articles/1195317.

Schwartz, L. 2018. "The Books That Kept Me from Falling Apart in County Jail." Lit Hub. www.lithub.com/ the-10-most-important-books-i-read-in-jail/.

Senghor, S. 2014. "8 Books to Lift You Out of Darkness." TED. https://ideas.ted.com/8-books-to-lift-you-out -of-darkness/.

Styslinger, M. E., K. Gavigan, and K. Albright, eds. 2017. *Literacy behind Bars: Successful Reading and Writing Strategies for Use with Incarcerated Youth and Adults*. Lanham, MD: Rowman and Littlefield.

Sullivan, L. E., and B. Vogel. 2003. "Reachin' through the Bars: Library Outreach to Prisoners, 1798-2000." In *Libraries to the People: Histories of Outreach*, ed. R. S. Freeman and D. M. Hovde. Jefferson, NC: McFarland.

Suvak, D. 1995. "The Prison Community." In *Libraries Inside: A Practical Guide for Prison Librarians*, ed. R. J. Rubin and D. Suvak, 3-22. Jefferson, NC: McFarland.

Sweeney, J. 2011. "Interagency Cooperation in Juvenile Detention Center Library Services: An Introduction to the Issues." In *Advances in Library Administration and Organization 30*, ed. D. Williams and J. Golden, 187-206. Bingley, UK: Emerald Group Publishing.

———. 2012. *Literacy: A Way Out for at-Risk Youth*. Santa Barbara, CA: Libraries Unlimited.

Sweeney, M. 2008. "Reading and Reckoning in a Women's Prison." *Texas Studies in Literature and Language* 50, no. 3: 30-28.

———. 2010. *Reading Is My Window: Books and the Art of Reading in Women's Prisons*. Chapel Hill: University of North Carolina Press.

TGI Justice Project. n.d. "About Us." www.tgijp.org/about.html.

———. 2011. "Surviving Prison in California: Advice by and for Transgender Women." www.tgijp.org/prison -survival-guide.html.

Torn Apart. n.d. "Volume 1." http://xpmethod.columbia.edu/torn-apart/volume/1/index.

Tubbs, A. M. 2021. *The Three Mothers: How the Mothers of Martin Luther King, Jr., Malcolm X, and James Baldwin Shaped a Nation*. New York: Flatiron Books.

Vogel, B. 1995. *Down for the Count: A Prison Library Handbook*. Metuchen, NJ: Scarecrow.

———. 2009. *The Prison Library Primer*. Lanham, MD: Scarecrow.

Wilson, C. 2018. "The Books That Saved My Life in Prison." Medium. https://medium.com/s/library-stories/the-books-that-saved-my-life-in-prison-d0c5b8f86f34.

Winn, M. T. (2011). *Girl Time: Literacy, Justice, and the School-to-Prison Pipeline*. New York: Teachers College Press.

Zeman, M. E. 2014. *Tales of a Jailhouse Librarian: Challenging the Juvenile Justice System One Book at a Time*. Brooklyn, NY: Vinegar Hill.

Technologies and Flows of Power

Print materials are often highlighted in discussions of incarceration because incarcerated people's access to technologies is so limited. Yet, technologies, including information and communications technologies (ICTs), are increasingly ever-present within the carceral environment. Few library and information science (LIS) publications go beyond advocating for increased levels of technological access for incarcerated people. This section pushes against this trend of a one-sided advocacy by examining how access to technologies, and the possibilities they afford, can reveal some of the power structures that shape incarceration in the United States. It draws from computer science, criminology, feminist and gender studies, media and communication studies, race and ethnic studies, sociology, and surveillance studies to review the current implementation of ICTs, often through third-party, contracted vendors, within carceral facilities.

This interstitial section examines the tension between incarcerated people's access to technologies and the proliferation of technologies that are utilized in carceral institutions. It covers technologies in carceral facilities, provides some background information on third-party vendors of technologies specifically designed for carceral facilities, and includes some of the known instances in which the bodies and actions of incarcerated people have been positioned as sources of information for both state and non-state actors, including for digitization projects and for training and refining algorithms. Contrasting the use of technologies in carceral facilities against the examination in the previous chapter of the restrictions on individual's ability to access information while incarcerated reveals that access to (or, conversely, the denial of access to) technologies is used as a form of control in carceral facilities. This builds from and mimics the ongoing mundane police and state surveillance of public and private space that is fueled by anti-Blackness, racism, and other forms of oppression (Kaba, 2021). The difference between access and types of technologies reveals how tracing information access and control allows for a clear line of sight into the flows of power within carceral facilities. This view not only illustrates the porousness of information and incarceration when in the hands of the powerful, it also reveals rampant third-party interests in gathering data through practices of confinement.

TECHNOLOGY AS MEDIATOR

An examination of the ways in which limiting or denying access altogether to the internet (and other technologies) shapes the information worlds of people who are incarcerated does not completely account for the ways that incarceration is often highly technologically mediated. From the introduction of tablets by private corporations to the surveillance of communication, technologies increasingly intermediate interactions between incarcerated people and the world (Johnson and Hail-Jares, 2016). As technologies are touted as an improvement to issues of information access—especially when there are limited books or other print materials in the facility, are restrictions and bans maintained in the mailroom, and there is limited funding for recreational materials or easily readable legal information—they are also positioned as in line with the security-focused claims made by carceral facilities that are utilized to curtail certain types of information access. Critical attention has been paid to the ways in which private companies profit extensively from tablet or kiosk access. Research has also focused on the ethics behind implementing technologies within carceral facilities, specifically as rehabilitative tools. Knight and Van De Steene provide an international literature review on information access and incarceration, and note that some technological interventions "are in danger of masking . . . or reinforcing the use of imprisonment," but alternatively, technologies may also be able to "position the prison and its people as part of a wider community" (2021, 63). Other aspirational and existing uses of technologies are situated in their possibility to foreclose, such as biometric surveillance and complete technological intervention as an alternative form of detention or incarceration (Bagaric, Hunter, and Loberg, 2019; Center for Media Justice, 2019; Immigration and Customs Enforcement, 2020; Nellis, 2019; Schenwar and Law, 2020).

These approaches rely on the notion that these technologies cannot fail, despite research that has shown the discriminatory functions and flawed techno-utopian approaches of these technologies (Benjamin, 2019; Lilly and Nellis, 2013). Moreover, ankle monitors and other electronic surveillance technologies often must be financed or rented by the person who is subject to them, which creates insurmountable costs and drives people subject to these technologies into debt (Equal Justice Initiative, 2019; Pittman, 2020). The biometric functionality of technologies currently ordered for some people in deterrence, parole, probation, and federal supervised release have documented failures that can lead to increased state sanctions or create false violations, which have resulted in job loss and re-incarceration (Nellis, 2019; Osberg and Mehrotra, 2020).

Focusing primarily on the technologies that people who are incarcerated may be allowed to access and positioning them as digital consumers fails to decipher the technologically mediated environment of the carceral facility as a way in which flows of power can be parsed and traced. It also sidesteps the histories of racial criminalization that inform policing and carceral practices (Scannell, 2019). As Jefferson notes in an exposition on technologically mediated forms of policing and containment, "it is consequently important to pay attention to relations between political projects and the way criminal justice data are produced, encoded, and used. It is also important to foreground the historical contexts that establish the conditions for criminal justice data production" (2020, 10). Technologically mediated carceral practices operate not just to catalog and contain the biometric information of incarcerated people and their connections outside, but also to reaffirm the categories of criminality and risk that further justify containment, surveillance, and state violence (Scannell, 2019).

In order to trace flows of power and technology access as a form of information control within carceral facilities, this section covers the existing technologies and examines how they are framed by their purveyors and within discourses about carceral security, with a focus on information control and provision. The overview offered here also covers concerns relevant to library and information professionals. It builds from and contributes to ongoing work in surveillance studies and algorithmic ethics. Through an examination of the ultimate purposes to constrict, contain, and surveil people who are incarcerated, it also counters what have often been punitive approaches to situate technology access inside of carceral facilities as a "softer" state model that provides incarcerated people with luxury items (Knight, 2015). Following a review of tablets, kiosks, and similar forms of mediated communication, this section turns to a study of the comparatively long history of biometric surveillance in carceral facilities. It outlines how biometric information is gathered from incarcerated people and is then later used to further target their communities, potentially as content used to train and refine the artificial intelligence systems that are used in predictive policing and risk assessment (Brayne, 2017; Maguire, 2018; Scannell, 2019; Wang, 2018).[1] It reviews instances when incarcerated people have, at times, been positioned as creators of digital content, even as they are unable to reliably access that content. It concludes with a short review of how library and information professionals are making access more possible through existing technologies, and the concerns that these new modes of information provision raise.

ACCESSING INFORMATION: "PRO-SOCIAL" COLLECTIONS AND THE COSTS OF ACCESS

Tablet devices have been lauded as a solution to the security needs of carceral facilities, as being able to provide resources that reduce recidivism, and as ways to enable people who are incarcerated to engage in "pro-social" behavior (American Prison Data Systems, 2018; Banks, 2019; Toms, 2018, 71). Beginning with the implementation of tablets in Colorado prisons in 2016,[2] the utilization of tablets in carceral facilities has now grown to around one in every ten prisons in the United States (Banks, 2019). Tablets are often introduced and maintained under financial contract with a prison system. Most of these tablet companies operate on for-profit models. The tablets and kiosks are provided by vendors of ICTs for carceral facilities such as JPay, GTL, and a plethora of small start-ups. When promoted to carceral facility staff, the technological aspects of these systems are brought to the fore ("a secure network with locked-down connectivity," "seven layers of security that restrict inmates to only host-related content, prohibiting all access to the external internet") (Toms, 2018, 72). Popular industry publications have focused on the oversight prisons have on what is available through the tablets, the alert systems that inform staff if the tablet is (intentionally or unintentionally) damaged, and the ability to assess the security of the device's software (Toms, 2018). When presented to families as a means to support their incarcerated loved ones, companies underscore the ability to "pass the time" and "keep informed" (Connect Network GTL, 2020). Profit models have driven the revenue generated from tablets; for instance, with the devices provided by GTL, "some tablet content and services are free, such as select reading material, utilities (dictionary, calendar, calculator, etc.), and quick links to common facility tools. Other subscription services are available at an additional cost" (Connect Network GTL, 2020). Free materials might include very basic games and access to books in the public domain and digitized through Project Gutenberg (James, 2020).

Incarcerated people and their supporters have noted the financial disparities inherent in accessing tablets, which often charge for access to desired materials at rates that are disproportionate to those charged for the general public. These are often too costly, given the meager financial resources that are available to most people who are incarcerated, even when they are employed by the carceral facility. According to a report in *Mother Jones*, which drew upon information from the families of incarcerated people, "in some facilities, a simple game like solitaire that would be free on a phone costs up to $7.99, and movie rentals and purchases range from $2 to $25" (Riley, 2018). This has enabled some states to obtain more than $1,000,000 in revenues per year from incarcerated people's tablet use, and at times to garner up to 50 percent of all the revenue generated through in-tablet purchases, with much of these financial gains generated from phone calls to friends and family (Banks, 2019; Riley, 2018). Charges have been documented for minute-by-minute access to electronic books, including books that are in the public domain (James, 2020; Waters, 2019). These practices of charging for access to materials have led the ALA to pass a "Resolution in Opposition to Charging Prisoners to Read" (2020), which notes that per-minute access "charges mean that the average cost of reading a single 'free' book such as *1984* is close to $20, while imprisoned people's wages, if any are paid, are less than $1 per day" (American Library Association, 2020). There are also precedents for people who are incarcerated to lose their access to digital items they have purchased when the state's contracts with vendors have changed over time. This occurred in Florida when the state contracted with a new private vendor for access to digitally available music (Banks, 2019; Riley, 2018).

In addition to recreational and security narratives, ICT companies have provided tablets to state prisons and local jails at free or reduced costs and advertised their ability to facilitate access to educational opportunities that are viewed as reducing the likelihood that people will reoffend (American Prison Data Systems, 2018). Much of the educational content currently available through these technologies, however, is not equal to that of formal or in-person educational programs, and it often consists of materials that were designed to be free educational content that is available online anyway (Tanaka and Cooper, 2020). Aspiring students who are incarcerated are constrained by a lack of resources that allow them to assess their academic programs and build their academic skills. The upcoming reintroduction of Pell Grant access for people who are incarcerated has combined with political processes to enable some predatory practices that occur through access to "educational" technologies (Burke, 2021). Information control and the limitations placed on accessing information while incarcerated, including the lack of access to electronic research platforms and the internet, pose especially difficult problems for educational programs in carceral facilities and for students who are incarcerated (Tanaka and Cooper, 2020). Educators and advocates making authoritative and published education resources available to people who are incarcerated are envisioning alternative approaches to information access for incarcerated students, including loading database content to intranet servers which can be accessed through tablets or kiosks in carceral settings (Tanaka and Cooper, 2020).

There are also physical constraints placed around access to tablets, kiosks, and other technologies. Access to these technologies tends to be positioned as a privilege based on where an individual is located within the carceral facility. Access is also potentially used as a punishment because it can be revoked. Access can be limited to specific periods of time each day, depending on whether or not the facility administration decides that tablets or other technologies can be accessed only under the supervision of facility staff or during official programs.

Descriptions of the information access provided through tablets echo the prevailing emphasis on "pro-social" behaviors and access to information and entertainment media, thus potentially slipping into narratives of information control that mimic those in biblio-therapy and early approaches to librarianship in carceral facilities. Overdrive, which provides access to some of the collections held on American Prison Data Systems (APDS) tablets—and which also facilitates a large share of e-book access for public libraries and their patrons—has partnered with APDS to create an electronic resource collection that contains more current materials than are usually found in the collections offered by other companies. An interview between staff at Overdrive and a member of the APDS staff regarding the National Corrections Library reveals some of the pitfalls present when electronic materials are selected to heavily align with the restrictions placed by institutions. In the interview, the APDS staff member underlines the content focus of the collection along lines of positivity and self-growth, stating that it contains "engaging, informative, aspirational, and inspirational titles to inmates at all reading and educational levels" (Overdrive, 2015).[3] This description leaves little room for titles that may be purely recreational, or which may be viewed by the facility as not encouraging "pro-social" behaviors or as presenting a security risk.[4] The National Corrections Library is positioned as a replacement, rather than a supplement, for access to physical books. In the aforementioned interview, the staff member from APDS builds upon security fears to depict access to the curated electronic library as a safety solution, and claims that it both reduces violence in the facility and can serve to replace the physical threats and inconveniences that are viewed as inherent in accessing physical materials (Overdrive, 2015).[5] This assessment pits digital collections against physical access to materials, sidestepping the types of limitations that exist for digital materials and ignoring the restricted distribution of tablets and other technologies within carceral facilities.

Since people who are incarcerated are not often considered to have rights to privacy, tablet devices, which log and transmit data about people's information access over time, pose a particular tension for librarians who are committed to information access.[6] A curated, digital collection designed to align with carceral restrictions may already stand in opposition to portions of the ALA's statement on "Prisoners' Right to Read." For instance, such a collection offers little room for oversight into how collection development occurs or how information providers navigate the challenges from carceral staff or facilities. That said, APDS is one of the companies that is more open about its practices. The lack of opportunities for oversight extends beyond the APDS collection and into those maintained by established and conglomerating companies like GTL (formerly Global Tel*Link) and Securus (JPay/Aventiv), which provide free or paid access to the Project Gutenberg materials, some additional content, and charge fees to access other materials.

TECHNOLOGIES AND BIOMETRICS

Carceral facilities are often imagined to be low-technology environments in which the day-to-day activities of the facility depend on pencil and paper as much as they do on video monitoring, and perhaps some jail or offender management software (Martinez, 2017). In reality, sophisticated technologies are increasingly present in carceral facilities, and the Integrated Justice Information Systems (IJIS) Institute predicts that these technologies will eventually "become mandatory" (IJIS Institute, 2017, 24). Joseph, in a 2017 criminology textbook on technologies for policing and incarceration, identifies the following types of technologies that are in use in carceral facilities in the United States:

- Advanced X-ray devices
- Closed-circuit TV monitoring
- Drug and alcohol abuse testing packages
- Magnetic "friskers" and officer tracking/alerting systems
- Telemedicine
- Videoconferencing[7] (Joseph, 2017, 172)

Joseph focuses on a few areas of the "technoprison." Among these are technologies that increase surveillance, including the use of radio-frequency transmitters (RFID) in facility-issued identification materials and technologically enhanced perimeter fences; technologies for detecting activities forbidden by the prison or by law, including the possession of cell phones and the facilities potential use of cell-phone jammers or reduced scope signal interruption to limit cell phone signals; and the use of teleconferencing and videoconferencing technologies instead of in-person visitations or court appearances. It is important here to remember that there may be multiple motives for utilizing the unapproved technologies that these carceral technologies are designed to block. Johnson and Hail-Jares (2016) cite the high cost of phone calls as part of the appeal of contraband cell phones, and also note that despite the seemingly large numbers of cell phones inside American prisons, rarely few instances of violence are linked to cell phone access. Rather, the authors believe that these clandestine cell phones are used to communicate with family members and are preferred because they are much less expensive than in-prison ICTs.

The use of video- and teleconferencing technologies has special importance for librarians and information professionals who are seeking to facilitate connections between people who are incarcerated and their families and social support networks. While some public libraries have successfully created free video visitation programs to help families maintain contact with their loved ones in incarceration (Telestory, n.d.), carceral facilities and ICT companies have consistently marketed that technology as a way to reduce or completely cease in-person visitation while also increasing surveillance and facilitating data-gathering (IJIS Institute, 2017; Sims, 2017). Library and information professionals might also feel concerned by the use of telephonic and video communications to provide health information and psychiatric diagnoses at a distance (Arndt, 2018; Joseph, 2017).

The use of RFID and other tracking systems inside the carceral facility reveals the extent to which people who are incarcerated do not have rights to autonomy or privacy—their bodies and movements become data points and their actions are regulated from a distance. The use of information generated by the movements and physical bodies of people who are incarcerated has a long history and has been well-established in carceral contexts. From medical experimentation to the positioning of people's bodies and activities as data, people who are incarcerated have been especially susceptible to being used to test and perfect new technologies. Joseph (2017) opens the chapter on technology in prisons with a review of how biometric information is gathered and used in carceral facilities, including facial recognition, fingerprinting, eye scanning (iris and retinal), and hand geometry. Shoshana Magnet (2010) offers a detailed timeline of the implementation of biometric technologies in carceral contexts.

Biometric identification, specifically geometric hand scanning and fingerprint analysis, has been used in policing and incarceration for more than five decades. Eye-scanning technology was implemented in a prison in the United States in 1988, and biometric technologies entered prisons over the course of the 1990s (Magnet, 2010). Due to the increase in the scale of incarceration and the number of carceral facilities, which occurred alongside a time of technological development and reduced social resources, many of these biometric technologies were specifically designed to be tested in and marketed to carceral facilities (Magnet, 2010). Iris and retinal scanning, both of which are unpopular in American markets because of the uncomfortable nature of the scan and the possibility of biometric failure (i.e., a person might be misidentified), have nevertheless gained widespread use in prisons—where people do not have the option of refusing the scan. Facial recognition technologies had also been implemented in some prisons in the United States by the early 2000s.

Magnet's analysis is notable because it combines information about mass incarceration with technology development and training, making clear that "prisoners' bodies are valuable commodities to biometric companies, providing the industry with a captive test population for assessing the efficacy of these new identification technologies" (2010, 63). In environments where people are unable to refuse to be cataloged by biometric technology, their information (and bodies) are then utilized to train and refine the technologies into ways of seeing while also instantiating their identities into fixed categories (such as race and gender) (Magnet, 2010). As machines "learn" from people who are incarcerated, they reproduce the categories that they have been trained to identify and use in cataloging individuals. Technologies refined through their use in carceral facilities have then been implemented in other sectors, including immigration, policing, and welfare, and into global contexts following the post-9/11 declaration of a "war on terror."

It is not speculative to claim that information gathered from people in carceral facilities is being used to train and refine surveillance systems that may be implemented in other facilities and will potentially leak into larger-scale forms of community surveillance. The IJIS Institute advocates ongoing experimentation in creating systems that use information gathered in carceral contexts in order to refine technologies, including ones that use artificial intelligence, to meet the goals of the facility (IJIS Institute, 2017). The institute's 2017 report clearly states that information-gathering should occur beyond the limits of the carceral facility: "Correctional agencies will be collecting increasing amounts of *data from inside and outside the criminal justice system* to assess impacts of sentencing and corrections policies" (33, emphasis in original).

There are a few examples of how incarcerated people's biometric information is fed into systems that are then used to increase the scope and likelihood that they, and their social support networks and neighborhoods, will be further policed. In some instances, as in Florida, where the state has had a facial recognition program for twenty years, biometric forms of surveillance that are used in the sphere of the general public were originally preloaded to recognize individuals whose photos are in mug-shot databases (Valentino-Devries, 2019). This practice emerged frequently in the development of early facial recognition systems (Paglen, 2019; Rouvalis, 2020). In addition to this, people who are incarcerated have shared their experiences of being informed that they would lose privileges unless they contributed information to voice surveillance technologies (Joseph and Nathan, 2019). This process, which is used to train and refine a technology that can identify people by their voice, may currently be one of the largest biometric information-gathering projects taking place in U.S. prisons. Third-party contractors create and maintain databases of voiceprints from people who are currently and previously incarcerated, and (in at least some instances) the voiceprints of the people with whom they communicate. This system is marketed as increasing security within the facility, and often entails embedding company employees in the prison setting as security experts (Francescani, 2019; Joseph and Nathan, 2019). Some voiceprint technologies make it possible "for investigators to query for any calls where an inmate's voice is heard—whether the call was initiated by that inmate or if the inmate entered the conversation after the call was already in progress" (GTL, 2017), thereby adding family members, friends, and people who have been charged but not convicted of a crime into these large-scale data-gathering practices.

The voiceprint and other biometric systems used in prisons are remarkably opaque—there is often no obligation for state actors, carceral facilities, or third-party vendors to share information about the ways in which biometric information is collected and used to identify, track, or confirm the identity of individuals. Moreover, it is routine that individuals whose information is being used to train and refine these technologies are not informed about the intents to refine the technologies or that their information will be retained for long periods of time (Gullo and Lynch, 2019; Joseph and Nathan, 2019). Private companies are not accountable to the supposed transparency of public institutions, or to established legal processes for gaining information about state practices (such as FOIA) (Van Oort, 2020). This lack of transparency has also been used by government entities as a shield from responsibility when third-party technologies are revealed to be functionally discriminatory and harmful (Crawford and Schultz, 2019).[8] In some ways, though, these companies are radically transparent about their intentions, if not their technological capacity, given the fact that they advertise their ability to increase surveillance and to aggregate biometric and other data for investigative use. For instance, there is a pronounced lack of information about how long the ICT companies retain their surveillance data, but these companies often promote their long-term data retention services in their advertisements to carceral facilities. Some companies, like Smart Communications, a mail digitization company that intercepts physical mail and creates digital scans that simultaneously allow for the retention, aggregation, and technologically mediated analysis of any non-legal communications between incarcerated people and those who communicate with them, have boasted of their ability to retain this information for years (Sims, 2017). Sutherland points to ongoing legacies of racism and white supremacy in the creation of these "carceral archives," in which "justifications for oppression . . . are codified, reinscribed, and reinforced" (Sutherland, 2019, 6).

Biometric forms of surveillance that have been developed or refined in carceral facilities are increasingly used outside of the carceral facility. Magnet (2010) notes that white supremacist logics have driven how and when biometrics are utilized as security tools. For instance, large-scale facial recognition information-gathering systems have been used by the FBI and by Immigration and Customs Enforcement to review driver's license photos in states across the country (Edmondson, 2019; Raviv, 2020). This data collection takes place in both physical and digital spaces and involves private-public partnerships and contracts, including ones with well-established technology companies (Mijente, n.d.). Villa-Nicholas (2020) has traced the ongoing biometric surveillance of the border and its extension into both the majority of the geographic area of the United States, as well as into the virtual realms of data storage and access. Villa-Nicholas (2020) frames this virtual space as a "data body milieu" in which actors coexist but, due to technological imposition and cataloging, do not interact in forms of exchange that occur when parties are physically present with one another. Villa-Nicholas (2020) notes that, in the expanding trajectory of data collection within the digitally constructed border, the technology that detects, identifies, and leads to digital and potentially physical capture of individuals is positioned as the "hero" in national and media narratives. So, too, are the mainstream narratives of biometric surveillance as securing the prison and reducing the cost of incarceration, which overlook or sidestep the opportunities people who are incarcerated have to be seen and potentially recognized as deserving of care, or as capable of resistance to inhumane conditions (Magnet, 2010).

INFORMATION WORK

In addition to being coerced into contributing to data-gathering and algorithmic refinement, people who are incarcerated have been positioned as producers of actual digital content and as exploitable labor for ICT companies and call centers. Kaun and Stiernstedt place this work alongside the tracking and data-gathering of incarcerated people as a continuance of "prison media work," including an example of the work of incarcerated people in Finland to improve the machine learning capabilities of an AI system (2020, 1278). Instances of information-based work, including digitization, are present in the United States. Incarcerated workers are employed as braille transcribers across the United States (American Printing House for the Blind, Inc., n.d.). Logsdon (2019) has traced a few of the projects in which people who are incarcerated have been recruited by government entities, the Mormon church, and others to digitize physical materials as a form of employment or religious service. Instances of this include a multistate project using the labor of incarcerated people to index the Mormon church's Family History Project and the digitization of high-school yearbooks by incarcerated people in Oklahoma (Associated Press, 2014; Bauer, 2015). People who are incarcerated in federal (under UNICOR, formerly Federal Prison Industries) and state facilities are employed (typically for very little pay) as call center workers for both public and private industries, providing customer service by phone for DMV offices, and have been employed by well-known electronics and ICT companies such as Hitachi and Microsoft (Cao, 2018; Goodridge et al., 2018; MSNBC.com Staff and NBC News, 2012). State and federal prison systems, as well as private prisons, work with private-sector partners to generate revenue through in-prison labor and, at times, transport people who are incarcerated to job sites that are outside of the prison (Goodridge et al., 2018). Nationalistic rhetorics of using American labor (as opposed to outsourced labor) and an emphasis on a reliable employee base have undergirded the push for call centers to capitalize on the low-wage labor of people who are incarcerated. UNICOR, in particular, underlines the point that unlike in the general public, people who are incarcerated cannot routinely leave these types of work (Cao, 2018). Some state prison systems, such as those of Arizona, Oregon, and Tennessee, include call center or other technology-based work (including design services) as part of the type of labor they generate through incarceration. Televerde and ProCom are two of the private companies that are creating private-public partnerships with prisons for their call center functions. It is likely that many other companies, industries, and groups are generating income or otherwise benefiting from the technology-based labor of people who are incarcerated. Information about private partnerships with prisons is quite closely guarded, but future research might reveal connections between various ICT companies and industries and their use of incarcerated people's labor.

CONCLUSION

Turning to technologies that are present in carceral contexts widens the plain in which librarians and information professionals might position the information practices, needs, and desires of people who are incarcerated. If "prisons continue to be an integral part of the technological revolution" (Joseph, 2017, 199), LIS professionals must consider the ways in which the technologies being implemented in carceral institutions shape people's life experiences. Some effort has gone into organizing research bodies to explore the possibility of providing incarcerated people with greater access to technologies (Verbaan et al., 2018), but more work is needed in this area. The lack of access to information, which is increasingly mediated by access to technologies, is a sign of the extreme power differentials within carceral facilities.

Even less attention has been given to the types of technologies that are already present in carceral contexts and how these technologies shape the flows of information between people who are incarcerated and those in contact with them, who are often aware of, and made uncomfortable by, their unwilling participation in that surveillance (Cahn, 2020; Owens, Cobb, and Craner, 2021). Owens, Cobb, and Craner (2021) offer a useful overview of the types of surveillance that cross the walls of carceral facilities, drawing from information provided by ICT companies and the lived experiences of family members of people who are incarcerated. Their work creates an opening for further research on this topic.

People who are incarcerated do engage with information through technologically mediated access (through, for instance, more traditional technologies such as television, telephones, and radio, and more recent forms of technological access, such as tablets), but they are also forced into technological engagement as unwitting or coerced producers of information. As scholars of surveillance and race and racism have illustrated, the technologies used in carceral facilities and along the national borders continue long histories of racialized surveillance, targeting particular communities for greater levels of policing and furthering the momentum of incarceration (Benjamin, 2019; Browne, 2015; Newell, Gomez, and Guajardo, 2017; Villa-Nicholas, 2020; Vukov, 2016; Vukov and Sheller, 2013; Wang, 2018). Accounts of the use of technologies to permeate the carceral context—by accessing cell phone or by using drones to bring materials over the prison walls—illustrate the possibility that forms of surveillance can occur from the ground up as well as from the state and that systems of control are rarely as airtight as they are purported to be (Benjamin, 2019; Browne, 2015). While sensationalist news stories of these events (actual or possible) are often widely circulated and used to justify the strengthening of surveillance in carceral contexts, Johnson and Hail-Jares (2016) emphasize that the permeability of carceral facilities is often made possible by carceral staff members themselves, who are in a particular position to profit by supplying people who are incarcerated with access to prohibited technologies.

Surveillance of access to media, library materials, and other information should greatly concern librarians and information professionals, especially as the profession moves to counter the mass surveillance of the general public (American Library Association, 2016; Knox, 2019; Zimmer, 2019). When thinking through how technologies can potentially create access to digital resources, or lead to new modes of communication between incarcerated people and LIS professionals, professionals will need to move toward these types of services with a critical eye on the overall purposes of most ICTs that are available in carceral facilities. This will involve assessing how technologies might be used to push against censorship and categorical exclusion of certain types of materials. The creation of services that are not used to further restrict information access and which do not use access to information as a means of punishment or reward can guide this work.

Resisting approaches to information access which don't support incarcerated people's actual information practices (including recreational access) will serve to ensure that "the injustices and painful nature of imprisonment"—and the provision of paltry or heavily controlled access—are not concealed "behind claims of fairness, benevolence and care" (Cheliotis, 2014, 17). Moving from an understanding of the current geography of carceral technologies, information flows, and the asymmetrical role of ICTs in maintaining power through information aggregation and control will enable LIS professionals to not only better assess their engagements with existing technologies, but to envision more ethical ways of facilitating information access for people who are incarcerated.

New and innovative approaches were developed in response to the coronavirus pandemic, a time when many carceral facilities entered lockdown conditions, individual's time spent out of cells was limited to one hour a day in many cases, and in-person visitations were prohibited. Among these are the Hennepin County Library's efforts to add a function to existing in-unit kiosks that allows people who have access to the kiosk to e-mail a librarian their book requests. The librarian is then able to deliver the requested books to the facility, where they are made available for distribution. The Brooklyn Public Library and the Queens Public Library have developed a system for including "Ask a Librarian" functionality on available tablets, which allows librarians and staff to continue their former on-site reference services. This service includes a reminder about the surveillance of the communications that take place through the tablets, as well as information about how to contact those libraries through the mail. Providing this alternative allows patrons to have some level of control over the medium they use for reference requests, which has implications for their own privacy as they seek to access information.

The Brooklyn Public Library and Queens Public Library are also offering at-a-distance library programming through available technologies, including programs that librarians know will be of high interest from information gleaned during in-person services. These include programs on American Sign Language, cooking, drawing, an introduction to astrology, and upcoming programs featuring people who are successfully employed in careers that hire people with conviction histories. Providing prerecorded content through the tablets allows the libraries to extend their in-person programming while facilities are locked down, but they may also serve to supplement in-person programming after it resumes. The programs actually held in carceral facilities often meet with a number of barriers, including the length of time taken up by the clearance process for outside presenters, whether or not there are staff available to allow people to move from their cells or units into programming spaces, and other concerns on the part of the facility. Making some programming available through tablets will potentially provide a way to work around the procedural barriers to providing programs inside carceral facilities, thus ensuring that more people have access to library programs.

Librarians and staff at the Dauphin County Library System have successfully advocated for people incarcerated at the Dauphin County Prison access to the library's e-book collection. Through careful negotiations, they have been able to pilot access to a curated collection of e-books through tablets under the control of GTL. This collection is primarily developed by librarians, and incorporates suggestions from incarcerated people, the prison education coordinator, prison staff, and volunteers. At the prison's behest, the collection does not include materials that portray graphic violence or graphic sexual content. Licensing models for e-books are a concern for the ongoing development of this collection, as some licensing models create more access but become prohibitively more expensive due to demand and the size of the patron base. This example of creating access to digital resources for patrons who are incarcerated illustrates future possibilities and concerns that libraries may explore as they assess and extend their existing patron bases.

The second half of this book includes information about direct and indirect information access for incarcerated people, existing library and grassroots programs, and information about reentry as a site of library service. Due to the current conditions of technology implementation in carceral facilities, technologies are rarely mentioned in relation to the existing programs and services that are examined in the second half of the book.

NOTES

1. There is an international trend toward algorithm-based decision-making, with most of the people who contributed feedback at the 2019 Technology in Corrections Summary Report gathering and using data about incarcerated people when justified as a security concern or without limits. When asked about how risk assessment technologies could be implemented, most respondents identified them as useful in the ongoing functions of the prison (programs and reentry) (Technology in Corrections, 2019).
2. Riley, writing in 2018, found that JPay had marketed tablets as early as 2012. JPay is now owned by Securus, under the umbrella company Aventiv.
3. The National Corrections Library can be viewed at https://apds.libraryreserve.com/.
4. The materials that are censored in some facilities for posing a security risk have included language learning, LGBTQIA+ information, racial and cultural histories, and urban fiction, in addition to materials that are categorically banned from most facilities, like those related to maps or weapons.
5. Overdrive has also partnered directly with the National Institute of Corrections to create and curate an electronic collection. This collection is intended for people working in the carceral system and not for incarcerated people. It is available at https://nic.overdrive.com/.
6. In the case of the National Corrections Library, Overdrive provides the same amount of privacy for patrons who are incarcerated as for patrons in the general public (personal communication, 2020).
7. Some of these technologies became more ubiquitous, both within and outside of carceral facilities, during the COVID-19 pandemic, but they had been implemented in carceral contexts before the pandemic began. It is not far-fetched to speculate that some of these technologies were refined through their compulsory use in prisons.
8. Ananny and Crawford (2018) caution against relying on a narrative of transparency as one that necessarily reveals the implications and functions of algorithmic systems. The authors provide examples of the limitations of transparency and how transparency can be curtailed even when it is mandated in some fashion. Their work offers new ways of framing accountability in relation to algorithmic systems.

REFERENCES

American Library Association. 2016. "Resolution for Restoring Civil Liberties and Opposing Mass Surveillance." www.ala.org/rt/sites/ala.org.rt/files/content/SRRT/Resolutions/2016/Mass -Surveillance01-12-16-CD20.1.pdf.
———. 2020. "Resolution in Opposition to Charging Prisoners to Read." www.ala.org/aboutala/sites/ ala.org.aboutala/files/content/ALA%20CD%2041%20Resolution%20in%20Opposition%20to%20 Charging%20Prisoners%20to%20Read.pdf.
American Printing House for the Blind, Inc. n.d. "National Prison Braille Network." https://sites.aph.org/ pbf/.

American Prison Data Systems. 2018. https://apdscorporate.com/.

Ananny, M., and K. Crawford. 2018. "Seeing without Knowing: Limitations of the Transparency Ideal and Its Application to Algorithmic Accountability." *New Media & Society* 20, no. 3: 973–89.

Arndt, R. Z. 2018. "Prison Inmates Access Mental Health Services through Telepsychiatry." *Modern Healthcare* 48, no. 2: 18.

Associated Press. 2014. "Oklahoma Prisoners Help Digitize School Yearbooks in Mississippi." *The Oklahoman*. https://oklahoman.com/article/3919704/oklahoma-prisoners-help-digitize-school-yearbooks-in-mississippi.

Bagaric, M., D. Hunter, and C. Loberg. 2019. "Introducing Disruptive Technology to Criminal Sanctions: Punishment by Computer Monitoring to Enhance Sentencing Fairness and Efficiency." *Brooklyn Law Review* 84, no. 4: 1227–86.

Banks, A. M. 2019. "Please Don't Stop the Music: Using the Takings Clause to Protect Inmates' Digital Music. *Vanderbilt Journal of Entertainment & Technology Law* 22, no. 1: 121–53.

Bauer, S. 2015. "Your Family's Genealogical Records May Have Been Digitized by a Prisoner." *Mother Jones*. www.motherjones.com/politics/2015/08/mormon-church-prison-geneology-family-search/.

Benjamin, R. 2019. *Race after Technology: Abolitionist Tools for the New Jim Code*. Cambridge, UK: Polity.

Brayne, S. 2017. "Big Data Surveillance: The Case of Policing." *American Sociological Review* 82, no. 5: 977–1008.

Browne, S. 2015. *Dark Matters: On the Surveillance of Blackness*. Durham, NC: Duke University Press.

Burke, L. 2021. "After the Pell Ban." *Inside Higher Ed*, January 27. www.insidehighered.com/news/2021/01/27/pell-grants-restored-people-prison-eyes-turn-assuring-quality.

Cahn, A. F. 2020. "Listening beyond the Bars: New York's Artificial Intelligence Surveillance of Prisoners and Their Loved Ones." Surveillance Technology Oversight Project.

Cao, L. 2018. "Made in America: Race, Trade, and Prison Labor." *N.Y.U. Review of Law & Social Change* 43, no. 1: 1–58.

Center for Media Justice. 2019. "No More Shackles: Why We Must End the Use of Electronic Monitors for People on Parole." https://mediajustice.org/wp-content/uploads/2019/05/NoMoreShackles_Parole Report_UPDATED.pdf.

Cheliotis, L. K. 2014. "Decorative Justice: Deconstructing the Relationship between the Arts and Imprisonment." *International Journal for Crime, Justice, and Social Democracy* 3, no. 1: 16–34.

Connect Network GTL. 2020. "Inmate Devices & Content." https://web.connectnetwork.com/inmate-devices-content/.

Crawford, K., and J. Schultz. 2019. "AI Systems as State Actors." *Columbia Law Review* 119, no. 7: 1941–72.

Edmondson, C. 2019. "ICE Used Facial Recognition to Mine State Driver's License Databases." *New York Times*, July 7. www.nytimes.com/2019/07/07/us/politics/ice-drivers-licenses-facial-recognition.html.

Equal Justice Initiative. 2019. "Defendants Driven into Debt by Fees for Ankle Monitors by Private Companies." https://eji.org/news/defendants-driven-into-debt-by-fees-for-ankle-monitors/.

Francescani, C. 2019. "US Prisons and Jails Using AI to Mass-Monitor Millions of Inmate Calls." *ABC News*. https://abcnews.go.com/Technology/us-prisons-jails-ai-mass-monitor-millions-inmate/story?id=66370244.

Goodridge, J., M. Schwartzer, C. Jantz, and L. Christian. 2018. "Prison Labor in the United States: An Investor Perspective." North Star Asset Management. https://northstarasset.com/wp-content/uploads/2018/05/revMay2018_Prison-Labor-in-the-Supply-Chain.pdf.

GTL. 2017. "GTL Increases Inmate Identification and Fraud Prevention with New Voice Biometrics Feature." Press release. www.gtl.net/wp-content/uploads/2017/08/Voice-IQ-Search-PR.pdf.

Gullo, K., and J. Lynch. 2019. "When Facial Recognition Is Used to Identify Defendants, They Have a Right to Obtain Information about the Algorithms Used on Them, EFF Tells Courts." Electronic Frontier

Foundation. www.eff.org/deeplinks/2019/03/when-facial-recognition-used-identify-defendants-they-have-right-obtain.

IJIS Institute. 2017. "Corrections Tech 2020: Technological Trends in Custodial and Community Corrections." www.correctionstech.org/publications.

Immigration and Customs Enforcement. 2020. "Intensive Supervision Appearance Program IV (ISAP IV) Support Services." https://beta.sam.gov/opp/df1b63595f19eb5ea8724539ff394f3b/view.

James, E. R. 2020. "Prisoners Pay to Read: Corrections Departments Turn to Private Companies for Profits." *American Libraries*. https://americanlibrariesmagazine.org/blogs/the-scoop/prisoners-pay-to-read-prison-tablets/.

Jefferson, B. 2020. *Digitize and Punish: Racial Criminalization in the Digital Age.* Minneapolis: University of Minnesota Press.

Johnson, R., and K. Hail-Jares. 2016. "Prisons and Technology: General Lessons from the American Context." In *Handbook on Prisons,* 2nd edition, ed. Y. Jewkes, B. Crewe, and J. Bennett. London: Routledge.

Joseph, G., and D. Nathan. 2019. "Prisons across the U.S. Are Quietly Building Databases of Incarcerated People's Voice Prints." *The Intercept*, January 30. https://theintercept.com/2019/01/30/prison-voice-prints-databases-securus/.

Joseph, J. 2017. "Technoprison: Technology and Prisons." In *Criminal Justice Technology in the 21st Century,* 3rd edition, ed. L. J. Moriarty, 172–205. Springfield, IL: Charles C. Thomas.

Kaba, M. 2021. "I Live in a Place Where Everybody Watches You Everywhere You Go." In *We do This 'Till We Free Us: Abolitionist Organizing and Transforming Justice* (88–92). Chicago: Haymarket Books.

Kaun, A., and F. Stiernstedt. 2020. "Prison Media Work: From Manual Labor to the Work of Being Tracked." *Media, Culture, & Society* 42, no. 7-8: 1277–92.

Knight, V. 2015. "Some Observations on the Digital Landscape of Prisons Today." *Prison Service Journal* 220: 3–10.

Knight, V., and S. Van De Steene. 2021. "The Digital Prison: Toward an Ethics of Technology." In *Prisons and Community Corrections: Critical Issues and Emerging Controversies,* ed. P. Birch and L. Sicard. Taylor and Francis.

Knox, E. J. M. 2019. "Information Access." In *Foundations of Information Ethics,* ed. J. T. F. Burgess and E. J. M. Knox, 37–46. Chicago: ALA Neal-Schuman.

Logsdon, A. 2019. "Ethical Digital Libraries and Prison Labor?" Paper presented at Digital Library Federation Forum, Tampa, Florida.

Magnet, S. A. 2010. *When Biometrics Fail: Gender, Race, and the Technology of Identity.* Durham, NC: Duke University Press.

Maguire, M. 2018. "Policing Future Crimes." In *Bodies as Evidence: Security, Knowledge, and Power,* ed. M. Maguire, U. Rao, and N. Zurawski, 137–58. Durham, NC: Duke University Press.

Martinez, J. 2017. "Jail Tech: Phones, Tablets, and Software behind Bars." *PC Magazine,* February, 120–29.

Mijente. n.d. "#NoTechforICE." https://notechforice.com/about/.

MSNBC.Com Staff and NBC News. 2012. "Inside the Secret Industry of Inmate-Staffed Call Centers." NBC. http://usnews.nbcnews.com/_news/2012/01/12/10140493-inside-the-secret-industry-of-inmate-staffed-call-centers?lite.

Nellis, M. 2019. "'Better Than Human'? Smartphones, Artificial Intelligence, and Ultra-Punitive Electronic Monitoring." Challenging E-Carceration. www.challengingecarceration.org/wp-content/uploads/2019/01/TI-and-Smart-EM-Final-.pdf.

Newell, B. C., R. Gomez, and V. E. Guajardo. 2017. "Sensors, Cameras, and the New 'Normal' in Clandestine Migration: How Undocumented Migrants Experience Surveillance at the U.S.-Mexico Border." *Surveillance and Society* 15, no. 1: 21–41.

Osberg, M., and D. Mehrotra. 2020. "When Your Freedom Depends on an App." Gizmodo. https://gizmodo
.com/when-your-freedom-depends-on-an-app-1843109198.

Overdrive. 2015. "How Digital Librarians Are Helping Prisoners across the Country." https://company
.overdrive.com/2015/03/26/how-digital-libraries-are-helping-prisoners-across-the-country/.

Owens, K., C. Cobb, and L. F. Craner. 2021. "'You Gotta Watch What You Say': Surveillance of
Communication with Incarcerated People." ACM CHI Conference on Human Factors in Computing
Systems (CHI'21).

Paglen, T. 2019. "They Took the Faces from the Accused and the Dead . . . (SD18)." De Young Museum, San
Francisco. https://deyoung.famsf.org/trevor-paglen-they-took-faces-accused-and-dead-sd18.

Pittman, J. 2020. "Released into Shackles: The Rise of Immigrant E-Carceration." *California Law Review*
108, no. 2. www.californialawreview.org/print/released-into-shackles/.

Raviv, S. 2020. "The Secret History of Facial Recognition." *Wired*. www.wired.com/story/secret-history
-facial-recognition/.

Riley, T. 2018. "'Free' Tablets Are Costing Prison Inmates a Fortune." *Mother Jones*, October. www.mother
jones.com/politics/2018/10/tablets-prisons-inmates-jpay-securus-global-tel-link/.

Rouvalis, C. 2020. "How Machines See Us—and Why." *Carnegie Magazine*. https://carnegiemuseums.org/
carnegie-magazine/fall-2020/how-machines-see-us-and-why/.

Scannell, R. J. 2019. "This Is Not *Minority Report*: Predictive Policing and Population Racism." In *Captivating Technology: Race, Carceral Technoscience, and Liberatory Imagination in Everyday Life,* ed. R.
Benjamin, 107-29. Durham, NC: Duke University Press.

Schenwar, M., and V. Law. 2020. *Prison by Any Other Name: The Harmful Consequences of Popular Reforms.*
New York: New Press.

Sims, T. 2017. "Smart Communications Tackles Contraband with Technology." *Correctional News*,
November 6. http://correctionalnews.com/2017/10/06/smart-communications-tackles-contraband
-technology/.

Sutherland, T. 2019. "The Carceral Archive: Documentary Records, Narrative Construction, and Predictive
Risk Assessment." *Journal of Cultural Analytics* 1, no. 1. https://culturalanalytics.org/article/11047
-the-carceral-archive-documentary-records-narrative-construction-and-predictive-risk-assessment.

Tanaka, K., and D. Cooper. 2020. *"Advancing Technological Equity for Incarcerated College Students:
Examining the Opportunities and Risks."* Ithaka S+R. https://sr.ithaka.org/publications/advancing
-technological-equity-incarcerated-college-students/.

Technology in Corrections (TIC). 2019. "Technology in Corrections: Digital Transformation." Summary
Report. International Corrections and Prisons Association. https://icpa.org/wp-content/
uploads/2019/07/TIC2019_Summary_Report_v2.pdf/?download.

Telestory. n.d. "Brochure." New York Public Library. www.nypl.org/sites/default/files/video_visitation
_brochure.pdf.

Toms, S. 2018. "An Innovative Behavior Management Tool." *American Jails* 32, no. 3: 71-73.

Valentino-Devries, J. 2019. "How the Police Use Facial Recognition, and Where It Falls Short." *New York
Times*, January 12. www.nytimes.com/2020/01/12/technology/facial-recognition-police.html.

Van Oort, M. 2020. "Employing the Carceral Imaginary: An Ethnography of Worker Surveillance in the
Retail Industry." In *Captivating Technology: Race, Carceral Technoscience, and Liberatory Imagination in
Everyday Life*, ed. R. Benjamin, 209-23. Durham, NC: Duke University Press.

Verbaan, S., C. Aldington, R. McNaney, and J. Wallace. 2018. "Potentials of HCI for Prisons and
Incarcerated Individuals." ACM CHI Conference on Human Factors in Computing Systems (CHI'18).

Villa-Nicholas, M. 2020. "Data Body Milieu: The Latinx Immigrant at the Center of Technological
Development." *Feminist Media Studies* 20, no. 2: 300-304.

Vukov, T. 2016. "Target Practice: The Algorithmics and Biopolitics of Race in Emerging Smart Border
Practices and Technologies." *Transfers* 6, no. 1: 80-97.

Vukov, T., and M. Sheller. 2013. "Border Work: Surveillant Assemblages, Virtual Fences, and Tactical Counter-Media." *Social Semiotics* 23, no. 2: 225-41.

Wang, J. 2018. *Carceral Capitalism*. South Pasadena, CA: Semiotext(e).

Waters, M. 2019. "Free Tablets for the Incarcerated Come with a Price." The Outline. https://theoutline .com/post/8329/jpay-free-tablet-program-ripoff?zd=1&zi=gavkd33m.

Zimmer, P. 2019. "Privacy." In *Foundations of Information Ethics*, ed. J. T. F. Burgess and E. J. M. Knox, 47-56. Chicago: ALA Neal-Schuman.

CHAPTER 5

Models of Direct Service

O verall, publications within the field of librarianship (and subsequently in library and information science) have focused on the practical aspects of services in carceral facilities and have paid only limited attention to the theoretical facets that inform those library services and collections. The practical features of these services must be positioned within the culture of librarianship, which has historically prioritized white, middle-class, and hetero- and gender-normative modes of conduct and ways of knowing. This chapter and the next one draw upon prior research and information from jail and prison library staff to position current and possible library services to incarcerated people within the framework described in the first half of the book.

This is not to overstate the reach of the critical stance described in previous chapters. Rather, this chapter and those that follow, all of which address the more practical aspects of library services for people who are incarcerated, can be read alongside critical interrogations of how and to what ends incarceration functions in the United States, especially in regard to accessing information. Pairing histories of the state-enforced dehumanization of incarcerated people, as illustrated through piecemeal and limited access to information, with the ongoing projects of racial criminalization described in the previous chapters provides readers with a stance from which to critically assess how and in what ways they might conceive of, develop, and advocate for library and information services to people who are currently incarcerated (as well as services that work to support people as they are released from carceral facilities). Readers can hold the racializing and racially motivated histories of incarceration alongside the fact that some of the earliest publications on library services to incarcerated people described the limited availability of reading materials and the pitiful state of those materials that were present. In many carceral facilities, this situation remains unchanged—library collections still partially or completely consist of donated or heavily circulated discarded books. Librarians and information professionals can interrogate the ways that access or denial of access to personally meaningful information equates to how people who are incarcerated are socially and politically valued.

The chapter focuses on the direct provision of library services as they occur in juvenile detention centers, jails, and prisons in the United States (services to children in the process of immigration are profiled in this chapter, but formal library and information services to people in immigration detention facilities are not widespread).[1] It provides a review of library services in carceral facilities before moving on to highlight some existing programs as described by the academic, prison, public, and special librarians who provide them. Information related to public libraries is given somewhat more weight than information about library services inside of prisons because the library services maintained by prison librarians have received more attention in recent publications. (Few recent publications have explored the role of the public library in supporting prison librarians, currently incarcerated people, or people in reentry.)

Beyond supplementing the existing literature, the second half of this book extends a much earlier call. In a 1972 review of library standards, Bailey noted the redistribution of carceral facilities as a reason for public libraries to become involved in more direct services to incarcerated patrons, stating that "since there is movement away from the large isolated [carceral] institution to smaller facilities located in populated areas, it is logical to assume that the public library will be called upon to participate more actively in the service provided to correctional institutions" (1972, 264). While the time between Bailey's advocacy for a greater focus on library services to incarcerated people has revealed that carceral facilities did not always move to more populated areas, the sheer number of people currently detained, incarcerated, or under state supervision means that the experience of incarceration has permeated society in ways that demand a response on the part of librarians. Examining the ongoing efforts of prison and public librarians can reveal a variety of approaches that are available to the profession. The programs described in this chapter offer some courses of action to increase library services to people impacted by incarceration, and, in the process, to address the ongoing prioritization of whiteness that has been part and parcel of the field of librarianship in the United States.

This chapter also deviates from the emphasis on library standards for people who are incarcerated (including the IFLA and ALA standards) in order to review the actual, on-the-ground practices of library and information science professionals. The existing standards are outdated, for the most part, and research has shown that the ALA's standards for adult facilities do not match the reality of services that are actually provided inside prisons (Conrad, 2017). The existing services reveal the shaping power of carceral facilities, their inconsistencies, and the possibilities for enduring and meaningful library services. There are also ongoing concerns over both the funding and the scale and administration of the libraries which provide those services; and this chapter calls for increased funding and presents the activities of a few well-funded and or otherwise established programs. Together, this and the next chapter advocate for the development of models that are critically situated, that recognize incarceration in both rural and urban contexts, and that are responsive to how incarceration shapes the lives of people who are incarcerated, their families, and their social support networks.

PRISON LIBRARIES

Rule 64 of the United Nations' Standard Minimum Rules for the Treatment of Prisoners (the Nelson Mandela Rules) states that "every prison shall have a library for the use of prisoners, adequately stocked with both recreational and instructional books, and prisoners shall be encouraged to make full use of it" (United Nations, 2015, 19). Despite the fact that standards for library services in carceral facilities have been developed by professional associations at the international and national levels, including the IFLA's "Guidelines for Library Services to Prisoners," developed by Lehmann and Locke in 2005, the ALA's "Library Standards for Adult Correctional Institutions" (last updated by the ASCLA in 1992), and "Library Standards for Juvenile Correctional Facilities" (last updated by the ASCLA's ad hoc Subcommittee on Library Standards for Juvenile Correctional Institutions in 1999), the actual library services in carceral institutions rarely match the requirements outlined in those standards.[2] Conrad, in *Prison Librarianship: Policy and Practice*, offers "an attempt to look at the professional field of librarianship [in prisons] without bias and try to determine reasons for the ambiguities between policies and practice" (2017, 15). Using surveys and in-depth interviews with prison librarians, Conrad identifies the intervening factors that limit or curtail library services within prisons in the United States. Conrad holds information about actual practices to the ALA's 1992 standards for adult prisons, and makes clear that an emphasis on materials in the collection, space provision for the library, and other similar requirements does not adequately address the ways in which carceral facilities curtail access to information through oversight or due to the intentional disregard of library services.

Drawing from a tradition that emphasizes the role of librarians in the rehabilitation of incarcerated people, Conrad outlines the requirements of the ALA's standards and the literature on library services to incarcerated people in order to philosophically situate the library within the carceral context. This approach is modified by a discussion of security, which is often noted as the primary concern of carceral facilities, and is used to justify the censorship of materials. Conrad states that "materials that are occasionally but not consistently banned include materials such as hate literature, literature on gangs, homosexuality, road maps, true crime novels, information on Satanic worship, literature on survival, medical topics, and anything about organized crime" (2017, 51). The prison librarians in Sweeney's research echo these restrictions (2010).

This list reveals some troubling possibilities. "Hate literature" has been broadly defined in many cases to encompass literature related to Black, Indigenous, and Latinx history and culture as well as materials that explicitly espouse white supremacist views; and white supremacist-related materials have, in some instances, not been banned in carceral facilities even when materials related to Black political thought are viewed by the facility as a security threat (Austin et al., 2020). Reviewing Conrad's list also reveals a troubling trend in publications about library services to incarcerated people: LGBTQIA+ people (and especially LGBTQIA+ people who are Black, Indigenous, and people of color and those who were living in poverty) are rarely explicitly mentioned in library literature as groups targeted through policing and incarceration. The library literature on jail and prison services seems to only (and even then, quite rarely) acknowledge LGBTQIA+ people in conversations about censorship. This occurs despite research, personal accounts, and the ongoing efforts by community-based groups to explicitly provide materials and to communicate with LGBTQIA+ people who are incarcerated—groups such as Black & Pink, LGBTQ Books to Prisoners, and the Transgender Gender-Variant and Intersex Justice Project (TGIJP) (Austin et al., 2020; Black & Pink, 2019; TGIJP, n.d.).

Censorship is a hallmark of library services in prisons in the United States (Krolak, 2019). Despite censorship and the justifications for security, Conrad argues that the literature on library services in adult prisons has generally leaned toward advocacy for people's rights to read and to access information and technology. One of the ways that prison librarians have done this is by turning to needs assessments and patron-driven collection development. Several factors intervene in this possibility. Among these are the commonly encountered resistance of carceral facilities or governments to apportion a section of their budget to library materials and library staff in carceral facilities, thus leaving libraries funded through overly expensive commissary-budget funds (inmate welfare funds), which are distributed to various programs in the prison. In some instances, these types of budgetary issues have been addressed through agreements between public library systems and carceral facilities (Clark and MacCreaigh, 2006, describe this model in their public library and carceral facility partnership), allowing librarians to build collections that reflect the needs and interests of patrons within some of the strictures set by the carceral facility. In addition to formal censorship by facilities and informal censorship through limited funding, librarians have also actively engaged in self-censorship, due either to their own biases or because they were navigating or resisting directives from carceral staff (Arford, 2016; Sweeney, 2010).

Conrad's research consisted of surveys conducted with prison librarians, which were followed by interviews with a subset of respondents. Her research reveals that prison librarians continue to navigate processes of censorship, space limitations for materials, limited budgets, and their own biases and preferences as they select materials (and self-censor certain materials) when creating and maintaining their library collections. The librarians responding to Conrad's survey were, at times, quite explicit about their power to purchase or to deny access to specific materials. While some creatively worked around the language of censored materials in official Department of Corrections policies in order to provide the broadest array of materials possible within imposed strictures, others relied on their own personal preferences (and their own conceptions of "good" reading for persons deemed criminal by the state) in their collection development efforts. For instance, one librarian interviewed stated that "any items that I feel are not suitable for the inmate population" were not included in the library collection (Conrad, 2017, 133).

Conrad found important patterns in the limitations placed on prison librarians. Librarians recounted how issues of funding, training, being split between roles (at times acting as law, recreational reference, and even academic librarians), overseeing libraries with limited staffing and often few trained librarians and with collections subject to severe budget restrictions or only supplemented through donations, restrictions placed by the physical space of the library and whether or not people were able to access it, and more set the parameters of library service. Conrad also notes that there are only limited educational and professional resources that focus on the professional development of librarians in prisons. This lack may be caused by the devaluation of library services for people who are incarcerated within the field of library and information science. Because of the dearth of resources, librarians must rely on interpersonal communication with other prison librarians as they build and sustain their services, or else they must develop those services on the fly. Even when publications on library services in carceral facilities are genuinely relevant to the work of librarians in prisons, these publications are probably constrained by what it is possible to say in a carceral context. The ideological reach of incarceration and the ability of carceral facilities to curtail any type of program, including recreational library access, may partly explain why so many publications about library services to incarcerated people tend in their discussions to mirror the logics of the general literature on the function of incarceration—librarians may be positioned to speak as the facility speaks, utilizing its available logics (rehabilitation or punishment) to justify their own efforts.

Whether or not this is true, Conrad's work outlines areas of extreme disconnect between how libraries in carceral facilities are actually administered across the United States and the "Standards for Adult Correctional Facilities." According to Conrad, "the discrepancies between the ASCLA standards and the actual practices are troubling, especially to the future ability of prison libraries to continue to sustain a certain level of service" (2017, 126). In practice, librarians in prison libraries often have to fulfill multiple roles—providing hard-won access to legal resources as well as access to recreational materials while also facilitating access to library spaces (when available); providing book cart services and in-unit collections for people in administrative segregation and medical units; and finding innovative ways to address the myriad needs that arise when running a library likely managed by a single librarian or library staff person. These actions are undertaken even as most prisons continue to underfund recreational materials (Conrad, 2017).

Because opportunities to provide well-rounded library services are minimal and the number of people who will probably rely on those services for regular access to recreational reading and information is very high, library and information professionals outside of carceral facilities should consider how they can support the work of prison librarians. One way to do this is to address the extreme professional isolation that prison librarians expressed in their communications with Conrad (2017), and to create collaborations that bridge the access gap between prison libraries and public (and other) libraries (Millsap, 2018).[3] In order to better determine how and when prison-public library collaborations occurred, I initiated an informal discussion with librarians on the prison-l and asgcla-incarcerated-detained discussion lists in May of 2020.[4] During this informal inquiry, prison and public librarians on these e-mail lists were asked two questions not commonly included in the literature about library services to people who are incarcerated:

1. Do you currently receive support from public or other libraries in the community (including but not limited to book donations, interlibrary loan, professional development, programming in the prison, reentry related programming, etc.)? If yes, please describe.
2. Are there ways that public libraries or other libraries in the community could support your work in the prison library? If yes, please describe.

The responding librarians worked in many different contexts (including juvenile detentions, jails, prisons, and state library systems). Their replies provide insight into collaborative services, their collection development practices, and the condition of libraries and library services generally in carceral facilities. The following overview includes information gathered by e-mail and through phone conversations. Respondents gave permission for their information to be included.

In one instance, a library system in a county jail in the Southwest that relies exclusively on donated books and materials to build its collections used and expanded the public library's seasonal reading programs to create a way for individuals to request books they wanted to read. This is a way of addressing the stark limitations of a completely donation-based collection, as well as the limited staff who are available to provide library services. In this pared-down approach, incarcerated people read books available in the units where they are detained or which they can access through library cart service, and they log their reading as they complete each book. After reading a predesignated number of books that are on hand, the readers are able to request a title of their own choosing. If available, this title is then delivered from the jail library's collection. The reading program is available year-round, and reading logs are distributed in English and in Spanish. The program is regularly promoted through posters in the units of the jails and through PDF files uploaded to the in-facility tablets.

In some instances, library services in juvenile detention centers are provided by the education program in the juvenile detention, but they are also often (when they exist) supported by public libraries or by librarians who have taken it upon themselves to create new services and apply for outside funding (such as obtaining materials through the ALA's Great Stories Club). Public librarian Paula Wiley suggested that materials access and programming for youth are important not only because of the beneficial impact of library service in general, but also because these efforts communicate to youth who are detained or incarcerated "that the national library community has not forgotten them." Wiley's collaborative program was built in partnership with other programs in a juvenile detention center, and the collaborators included a caseworker, the principal of the school at the facility, and teachers. They were able to bring authors and to promote library access through this network. This was especially important since, outside of staff time, the program had no established institutional library funding (Wiley, 2017).

A public librarian at a library system in Arapahoe County, Colorado, described the impact of including a set budget for formal library services in carceral facilities. In the Arapahoe library system, the Sheriff's Department is responsible for the budget for materials (including recreational and legal materials) as a line item in the system's official budget. This funding provides a foundation for ongoing and innovative services in the county's jail. Librarians are employed by the public library system to provide in-jail services and also design and promote passive programming. Public librarians and staff working in the carceral facilities receive funding for their own professional development. They also receive and circulate materials that are withdrawn from the public library collection, and they use the library's resources to create promotional posters and other materials.

A librarian who was previously employed in a prison on the west coast described a heavy reliance on donations for collection development in the prison library. The collection was refreshed annually by contributions from a Friends of the Library group at a local public library. The Friends group would alert the librarian of upcoming opportunities to collect free materials, and the librarian gave special attention to collecting nonfiction materials that could support the prison's Education Department, in addition to materials for recreational reading. (While not part of their own collection development practices, the librarian also mentioned an academic library that donated sets of journals to an education program in another prison.) The librarian went beyond soliciting donations from public libraries and was able to acquire legal texts from local law firms that were updating their in-house collections. Drawing from their experience in the library, which included denials of requested interlibrary loan materials, this librarian envisioned collaborative relationships between law librarians and prison librarians, who often have only limited experience with legal research during their LIS education. Given the need for more "space, staff, technology," and training for prison librarians, the librarian was clear that prison librarians would benefit from collaborations with other types of libraries. They imagined professional exchanges that built upon the collaborating parties' shared recognition of the limitations on resources in the prison and the limited funding and staff for prison libraries. One simple step this librarian proposed is for public librarians to provide local reentry information to prison librarians, so that this information can be made available to people inside of the prison.

The Washington State Library has provided reentry information within prisons in that state and has established robust library services and staffed libraries through a funded program that is detailed later in this chapter. The Washington State Library recently began a large-scale collaborative project with public libraries in many areas of the state. In this collaboration, a prison librarian works with people who are preparing for their release to ensure that they have public library cards. Part of this process involves addressing the anticipated barriers to library access (such as library fines or being released without a permanent address). While the process for issuing cards within the prisons varies between public libraries, the prison library staff are all given guidance on issuing cards and informing public libraries of the cards that have been issued (Kinney, Sherbo, and Herrlinger, 2018).

This informal review has presented some possibilities for collaboration between various types of libraries (and other information providers) and prison librarians. The partnerships described here are dependent on the local context. Collaborations and library services are shaped by the resources available within a facility, whether or not there are library staff, the number of people incarcerated in a facility, the ways in which materials access occurs inside the facility, and whether or not other programming staff exist or have enough resources to collaborate within the facility. Many of these limitations can be connected to themes in the first half of this text, including the criminalization of Black, Indigenous, and people of color, the rehabilitative or punitive philosophies of carceral facilities, the rhetorics that are used to justify incarceration, and the forms of policing, surveillance, and legal policies that have led to mass incarceration.

PUBLIC LIBRARIES

Writing in 2004, de la Peña McCook noted that "while there is a solid statement of policy on public library service to people in jail, there is little information about the number of libraries that choose to do so" (27). De la Peña McCook reviewed a few notable programs operating at that time, including programs that continue to operate today in Alameda County (CA), Arapahoe County (CO), and Hennepin County (MN). Since 2004, some popular and scholarly articles on public library services to people who are incarcerated have chronicled the work of public librarians and library systems. Lilienthal's 2013 article revisits the Hennepin County Library's services and also introduces services at the New York Public Library, through the San Diego County Library, and through the Colorado State Library. The public library services that Lilienthal reviews involve programming both inside of carceral facilities and at public libraries. These include book cart services, literacy and job-searching programs, programs related to employment, entrepreneurship, and financial literacy, and outreach to sites where people recently released from prison are required to live or to attend programs or meetings (Lilienthal, 2013). The Denver Public Library's Free to Learn program, mentioned by Lilienthal, focused on three main areas of literacy —career development, technology, and knowledge of library services (Morris, 2013). Morris's article includes information about training for librarians, as well as example texts for reentry facilitation packets. (Chapter 7 discusses programs specifically focused on release and returning to the community after incarceration.) Bilz, in a 2020 review of the library literature on services to incarcerated people and people detained in immigration detention centers, identifies seven prominent types of programming and services. These are library outreach to people who are detained or incarcerated, family-centered programming, literacy and education, events (author readings, book clubs, etc.), the creation of reentry resources, access to library collections, and by-mail reference services (Bilz, 2020).

Conrad (2017) includes a review of publications and websites related to partnerships and other forms of collaboration between public and prison libraries. In this review, Conrad identifies library programs that facilitate opportunities for people who are incarcerated to record themselves reading to their children, to invite in families of people who are incarcerated, to host book clubs and talks inside of carceral facilities, to provide indirect library services through donated materials, and to provide reentry-related skills and information for formerly incarcerated people after they are released. Conrad notes that many of the programs and services currently offered by public libraries are probably not in the public record, and encourages public library systems to engage in outreach to patrons who are incarcerated (2017).

The most thorough recent review of public library services to people who are incarcerated was conducted by Klick in 2011. Klick contacted staff at all public library systems in California to determine whether or not they offered services or materials to those in juvenile detention centers, jails, or prisons. In the review Klick also highlights three model programs, those administered through the Alameda County, Arapahoe County, and Multnomah County libraries, which involve partnerships between public libraries and carceral facilities. This approach allows Klick to show that while public libraries can and do engage in providing these services, many libraries in California had not effectively implemented services for or outreach to people who are currently or formerly incarcerated. Klick utilized a tiered system to designate levels of services, listing 27 library systems that directly provided library services (including materials and programming), 27 systems that provided some level of primarily indirect service, and 128 systems that provided neither direct nor indirect service. More information about existing services and collaborations is sorely needed within the field.

In lieu of a large-scale data-gathering project, this chapter includes profiles written by librarians and information professionals working in jails and prisons, public librarians who directly and indirectly support library services to people who are incarcerated, and librarians working to increase information access inside of immigrant detention centers. The following profiles highlight the differences between various types of programs and how programs are shaped both by their home institution and by the context of an individual jail, prison, or other carceral facility.

The programs detailed here were chosen for their unique or exemplary work, and may not fully reflect the very real difficulties and restrictions summarized earlier in this chapter. Some of these profiles, including the one of REFORMA's Children in Crisis Project, convey the continuing needs and limitations that librarians face. Together, the profiles underscore the importance of access to funding and institutional and administrative support from the library.[5]

REFORMA'S CHILDREN IN CRISIS PROJECT

ORALIA GARZA DE CORTÉS AND PATRICK SULLIVAN

In 2014, in response to the influx of unaccompanied minors seeking asylum at the U.S. border, REFORMA, the National Association to Promote Library and Information Services to Latinos and the Spanish Speaking within the American Library Association (ALA), established the Children in Crisis (CIC) Project. The Children in Crisis Project is a task force of librarians within REFORMA committed to procuring and distributing children's and young adults' books in Spanish or bilingual Spanish/English. At that time there were thousands of children from Central America crossing the southern border, and their reception ranged from supportive efforts to strident protests. REFORMA was committed to ensuring that these children, who have encountered so many hurdles in their struggle to escape violence in their home countries, receive books for the journey to their final destination. Many of these children came from environments where libraries were nonexistent, and one of our goals was to ensure that they were made aware of the support that libraries and librarians in the United States could provide when they were finally reunited with family members here.

Since those early days, the Children in Crisis Project has been providing books to the children wherever they are: detention centers, bus stations, shelters on both sides of the border, and basically anywhere they are being housed or detained. In addition to our book donations to some very dedicated groups and individuals who provide the children with food, shelter, instruction, and so much more, we were also able to connect some of the shelters to their local libraries so that the children could visit the library and become aware of what awaited them in the local communities when reunited with their families. The educators at the shelters were able to work with REFORMA CIC volunteers to coordinate their classes at the shelters with the library materials available and to share all the technology and resources available.

While CIC worked with shelters across the country, we were also developing new alliances with groups like Team Brownsville that work cross-border to make sure that even though the asylum-seeking process has slowed, the children still have a library and a school in Matamoros on the Mexican side of the border. These efforts provide an opportunity for our CIC project to piggyback on these established, grassroots volunteer organizations. We have also been blessed to have the support of organizations such as the International Board on Books for Young People, First Book, Believe in Reading, the Young Adult Library Services Association, and many other authors, publishers, and distributors in our efforts to connect the children with books.

In each book that we donate there is a bookplate that contains the following quotation: "Un libro es un compañero que te da luz y cobijo," or "A book is a companion that gives you light and shelter." There is also a spot for each child to claim the book as theirs by signing their name. Please stop by our Facebook page: https://www.facebook .com/REFORMAChildreninCrisis/ or our web page: http://refugeechildren.wixsite.com/ refugee-children/, and please consider donating to ensure that asylum-seeking youth are greeted by books and librarians who can work with them.

Thanks for your support, REFORMA Children in Crisis Taskforce
[The authors can be contacted at oraliagarzacortes@gmail.com (Oralia Garza de Cortés) and sullivan@mail.sdsu.edu (Patrick Sullivan).]

SAN FRANCISCO PUBLIC LIBRARY'S JUVENILE JUSTICE CENTER LIBRARY

RACHEL KINNON

The San Francisco Public Library (SFPL) began providing library service at the city's Juvenile Justice Center (JJC, then called the Youth Guidance Center) in the 1990s. The program's early iterations involved a librarian bringing a book truck to the youths' living spaces at the facility. When a new facility was built in 2007, its plans included a designated school area, managed by the San Francisco Unified School District (SFUSD); that wing of the facility included a dedicated library space to be run by the SFPL. The SFPL provides staff, materials, and a programs budget for that library.

Since 2007, the SFPL has partnered closely with the SFUSD to ensure that youth in the Juvenile Justice Center visit the library consistently. The English/Language Arts teacher there incorporates a library visit by the youth into her weekly schedule. Youth browse for and select books to bring back to their rooms, with the librarian providing in-depth reader's advisory to each youth, as needed. The visits to the library also include activities such as a scavenger hunt using the Dewey Decimal System; supervised internet use as the youth plan their return to the community; informal book discussions; and unstructured time to peruse magazines and books, much like in a public library. Per the facility's rules, each youth can have up to five books in their room at a time. The youth return library books via a large, locked book return bin inside each living unit, which is emptied weekly by SFPL staff.

The library's collection has been built based in part on the librarian's selections, and in part on youth and staff requests. This helps ensure that the collection reflects the interests and information needs of its patrons, who are primarily Black and Latino young men. The collection includes comics and manga; current magazines; nonfiction and fiction books, including a wide selection of urban biographies and urban fiction for youth; and high-interest oversize, photo-heavy books. The books are selected at a range of reading levels, from early elementary through adult, in order to accommodate the patrons' range of literacy skills and interest in reading. Patrons can place holds on titles that are currently checked out, or request new titles to be purchased for the collection. The books are marked as library property with stamps and with barcoded stickers. The collection is catalogued in Koha, a password-protected, open-source database, which is used only by the library's staff. (The system can also be searched, and holds placed, by teachers or by youth inside the classrooms using its OPAC.)

For years the SFPL partnered with a local nonprofit group, Sunset Youth Services, to provide youth who are young parents or older siblings the chance to record themselves reading a picture book for a child in their life. Sunset Youth Services created an audiobook, complete with background music and page-turn cues, which could be gifted to the young child along with a copy of the book. These recordings help to support the bond between the youth and the child, as the child can hear their loved one's voice reading to them, while also supporting early literacy for the child. Youth who do not wish to make an audiobook can still select some board books and picture books from a collection maintained in the library, so that they can gift a book to the children in their life.

The librarian regularly schedules author visits to the JJC. Youth have been excited to meet YA authors such as Jason Reynolds and Coe Booth, motivational speaker Eric Thomas, and a number of local and nationally known advocates for criminal justice reform and youth leadership. The speakers' visits are coordinated by the librarian with the support of the SFUSD and the facility's administration, and when possible, the SFPL provides an honorarium. The guest speakers are frequently scheduled in coordination with librarians at other Bay Area juvenile halls, so that youth in several facilities can benefit. Many of the youth at the JJC are aspiring writers and artists, and they often express their gratitude for these inspiring visits. The librarian has also facilitated numerous book groups, but finds that the most engaged discussions take place spontaneously in the library when youth recommend to each other books they've recently read, share their opinions, and have heated arguments about who is reading better books and why.

The library inside the Juvenile Justice Center is a sunny, colorful room, and many patrons have described their weekly visit to the library as their favorite part of the week. It provides a sharp contrast to the rest of the institution, both in its appearance and in its focus on providing individualized attention to each youth. Youth take advantage of the librarian's offer to purchase books that are requested, and they look forward to receiving the brand-new copy that arrives, usually within a few weeks. Countless youth request public library cards while they are in custody, so that they can use their local branch upon their release. The library functions as a relaxed space that provides a short break from the institutionalized experience, and allows the youth to request materials of special, unique interest to them. One long-term juvenile hall staffer commented that the library has "made reading cool" for youth in custody; this, combined with the youths' excitement over their next batch of good books to read, illustrates the immense value of the juvenile hall's library.

NEW YORK PUBLIC LIBRARY'S CORRECTIONAL SERVICES

SARAH BALL

The New York Public Library (NYPL) formed a Correctional Services department in 1980 when an initiative and accompanying funding from New York State mandated public libraries to conduct outreach to the jails and prisons in each of their districts. While many upstate public library systems already worked with prisons that had libraries and librarians on staff, the New York City jail system that includes the Rikers Island complex, had only law libraries—there were no general library services standardized at that time. The NYPL's first correctional services librarian, Steve Likosky, started three foundational services that still constitute the department's core services today: circulating book service at the city's jails; Reference by Mail services to people in prison; and *Connections*, a regularly updated, reentry resource directory, printed and mailed free to incarcerated and formerly incarcerated people. The Correctional Services department had no more than one staff member for many years, although staff working in the NYPL's branches often joined for book service in the jails. The department has expanded during the last decade, with the aim of supporting increased regular programming, and alongside the growing national conversation about mass incarceration and the needs and interests of those inside.

There are several accounts of library collections that existed in New York City's jails at various points in history, sometimes serving certain groups or designated areas, but at no time was there a comprehensive, systematized library service that reached every potential user. While that remains true today, the combined efforts of New York City's three public library systems (the New York Public Library, Brooklyn Public Library, and Queens Public Library) allow library services to reach a significant portion of the people incarcerated in the city's jails. Book service is delivered in various formats, and is adapted to the varied and inconsistent physical environments and institutional cultures inside each of the city's nine jail facilities. Most areas are served using mobile book carts, with some carts rolling inside each housing unit, and others parked for service in a vestibule or bridge area. There are dedicated library spaces, which are designed and used solely for the public library. A pop-up library model in a gymnasium has also been used, where the collection is set up and put away for each day of service. Each collection of materials—made up of books, magazines, graphic novels, and manga—is meticulously chosen by Correctional Services staff based on patron interests and requests. The NYPL staff values patron input as the only driver for collection development, and avoids collection development that imposes cultural, moral, or educational conventions. The only materials that can be found in a public library but are censored from the jail collection are those that describe unsafe activities in an *explicitly instructional* way, such as how to make a weapon. The materials checkout and return policies follow general guidelines across the various facilities, but the staff have flexibility to adapt the rules to the unique circumstances of each site and audience. Book services are an excellent way to gauge the needs, interests, and strengths of our patron base, to build healthy professional relationships with them, and to develop programming that can further support them.

Part of supporting people in jail and prison is helping them prepare for release and returning home. New York City has an incredible network of resources and services designed to support people in transition, but navigating that landscape can be overwhelming. *Connections* is a reentry resource guidebook that was first published in 1982 as a staple-bound pamphlet. In 2021 the *Connections* book is now nearly 400 pages long and lists over 600 organizations and agencies. It contains narrative text on a wide variety of laws and policies that impact criminalized and incarcerated people, including a full chapter of guidance about employment for those with a criminal conviction. The book includes resources relating to housing, education, financial support, physical and mental health, and legal services, plus information gathered to serve specific groups such as LGBTQIA+ people, people with disabilities, older people, and more. The more recent editions also feature writing and artwork created by formerly and currently incarcerated people. The book is updated annually, with a rigorous fact-checking and editing process, including improvements to usability and accessibility. The book is printed and distributed to people in prisons across the state and to formerly incarcerated people in the community, often via service providers who request multiple copies, and it is available at all NYPL branch locations and digitally on the NYPL website.

A fundamental condition of prison is isolation, and a lack of access to information is, by design, a primary means of punishment. Since before the Correctional Services department existed, people incarcerated in New York State and across the country have sent questions and research requests via mail to the NYPL. This reference service became the responsibility of the correctional services librarian, and in recent years the project has responded to ever-increasing demand with a streamlined process utilizing a larger team of respondents. Patrons who use the service ask every type of research question imaginable. They are often seeking practical information to prepare for release, or other information relating to their incarceration. But almost just as frequently, the queries are fun, obscure, and one-of-a-kind. Responding both to patrons' needs and to their curiosity makes the project a unique and rewarding experience for staff. The Reference by Mail service is managed by a supervising librarian who opens, reads, and assigns each letter to a team of volunteers and students working to respond to the high volume of requests, about fifty letters per week. A partnership with the Pratt Institute's School of Information allows graduate students, who each answer three letters from prison, to hone their real-world reference skills, a process that is contextualized by the glaring impacts of information access inequity.

Beginning in 2010, the Correctional Services department began implementing various programming to be delivered regularly at several facilities across the city. A family literacy program, Daddy/Mommy & Me, teaches incarcerated parents and caregivers about early literacy practices and maintaining family reading habits from a distance. An audio recording of each parent reading a storybook for their children is made, and the program culminates with a special family day event, where each child receives the recording, along with a new copy of the book, and extra library goodies. Another family program is the Video Visitation program, available at all New York City public library systems, where families can go to a neighborhood branch to have an hour-long visit via video conferencing with a loved one incarcerated in a city jail facility. The program is ideal for families who cannot make the arduous commute to Rikers Island, or those who want to supplement their regular in-person visits with video visits. The program is available in the neighborhoods most affected by incarceration, and in those with convenient public transportation access. Regular book discussion groups occur with people in federal custody in the city, and a wide range of literature and nonfiction is explored. The discussions are casual, and there are semi-regular exchanges with patrons in neighborhood branches reading the same title, using a letter template entitled "Dear Fellow Reader." The department's most formal literacy program is English for Speakers of Other Languages (ESOL), with classes that take place for students on Rikers Island. The class format and curricula are adapted to the jail environment and to the distinct needs of the students, who range widely in many aspects, including their English proficiency level, their literacy in their native language, and their cognitive ability. The goal of the classes is to increase the students' confidence in the ability to speak and understand English, and nearly all of the students self-report a noticeable positive change in that ability after six weeks of attendance.

WASHINGTON STATE LIBRARY'S INSTITUTIONAL LIBRARY SERVICES

LAURA SHERBO

The Washington State Library's Institutional Library Services are unique in their administration through the state library system and their instantiation as a part of Washington state law. The services were added to the state librarian's duties in the 1960s. The most recent version of the law, RCW 27.04.045 part 13, states that the duties of the state librarian include "providing for library and information service to residents and staff of state-supported residential institutions." Under this provision, *the libraries in state prisons are branches of the Washington State Library.*

The Washington State Library funds all materials and all staff with state and federal money (through Library Services and Technology Act funds). All prison library staff are employees of the Washington State Library, which is a division of the Office of the Secretary of State. In addition, there is a contractual arrangement with state's Department of Corrections about how the library services are provided and managed. The contract between the Washington State Library and the Department of Corrections is reviewed and renewed biannually. The Department of Corrections manages the law libraries, and the Washington State Library manages the "public libraries" administered by the Washington State Library.

All staff in the prison libraries are professional (MLIS) librarians. All prison libraries are staffed with one librarian, so the expectations are that they perform a wide variety of tasks in order to manage the branch library. Our current job announcement reads:

> Institutional Library Services is a program of the Washington State Library that provides library services to the inmates and patients in Washington's prisons and State Hospitals. These positions provide library and information services to inmates and patients by performing complex technical library duties and problem-solving related to collection development, reference/information delivery, and automated circulation systems.

> Branch staff maintains day-to-day library services and operations, performs collection management duties, participates in branch library programs and assists other

branches, and performs bibliographic and information searches and answers reference questions.

The number of people served by any library varies by prison, due to the size of
population (prison populations in Washington state prisons range from 500 to 2,100 people)
and the size of the library (its fire code capacity). People in administrative segregation,
medical, or other restricted housing units receive some service, in the form of individuals
submitting written requests for information. Library staff receive the requests and send
internet printouts or photocopies of library materials back to the individual who made
the request. In the past, books were sent to people in these units—they would request a
particular author, title, or subject, and the library staff would supply it—but the Department
of Corrections ended this practice. Donated paperbacks are supplied by library staff to
these units as available.

Library programming (community reads, author and poet visits, Humanities
Washington speakers, trivia night, and more) is encouraged and supported. Supporting
reentry is a very big part of what the librarians do, and this includes a customized reentry
resources request form, reentry seminars, and issuing public library cards.

NORTH DAKOTA'S PRISON LIBRARIES

BECCA SORGERT

The North Dakota prison library system is structured under the North Dakota Department
of Corrections' Education Department. The Education Department oversees funding for
materials and staffing. While the juvenile facility has had a full-time paid school librarian on
staff for many years, the state's three adult male facilities only received a full-time and part-
time library staff around 2014. Prior to this, the collection was maintained by a consulting
librarian who assisted in ordering and cataloging, and the library was maintained by
incarcerated people. This consulting librarian advocated for more staff.

The librarians are expected to manage all library operations such as ordering,
cataloging, preparing books, readers' advisory, program implementation, management of
incarcerated staff, and more. Patrons in administrative segregation receive books twice a
week through a home delivery method. These patrons can browse a printed catalog, where
each book is labeled "paperback" or "hardcover," in order to have a higher successful
fill rate, depending on their security level. Medical units can also request books, though
this is seen at a significantly lower rate. Legal materials are overseen by correctional staff
outside of the Education Department. Legal reference materials and computers with legal
information were located in the library and were accessible during library hours.

The library has a robust interlibrary loan program facilitated through the North Dakota
State Library. A maximum of 200 total loans are allowed, and it is typical for loans to float
around the 150 range.

The library system has encountered challenges, such as needing to be creative with
the budget in place in order to meet the needs of a wide variety of readers and reading
levels. Spanish-language materials are in high demand, but approving content is a
challenge that can be hard to overcome due to the lack of bilingual staff. The interlibrary
loan program in place is a way to supplement the budget—and has been embraced by a
large portion of users.

A challenge at one facility was that patrons were only able to access the library during recreation time, which was scheduled by unit and was scheduled between morning and evening, which made it difficult to engage with all the patrons. Though all patrons could communicate in writing to library staff, patrons preferred in-person communication. Engaging patrons in reading contests and celebrations were instant triumphs.

EDUCATION JUSTICE PROJECT

BECCA SORGERT AND THE EDUCATION JUSTICE PROJECT TEAM

The Education Justice Project (EJP) offers educational programming at the Danville Correctional Center through the University of Illinois at Urbana-Champaign. The EJP has a two-room library and computer center that is operated separately from the Department of Corrections library. The EJP oversees funding for the library and supplements the collection with library books from the University of Illinois academic library system, which are delivered by EJP volunteers. There is a library committee that consists of an EJP volunteer and incarcerated students. In addition to materials cataloging and maintaining the space, student librarians also contribute to the library by fostering information literacy, building a thoughtful collection of print and digital resources, and organizing library events that stimulate critical thinking and discussion outside the classroom. Both recreational and educational materials are in the library's collection. Legal materials are seen as out of the scope of EJP and are provided by the Department of Corrections. The students created a library catalog through Python and enter books and subject headings into it.

In 2019, the staff at the Danville Correctional Center removed more than 200 books from the EJP library, many of which focused on race, including the autobiography of Frederick Douglass and *The Souls of Black Folk* by W. E. B. Du Bois. After many unsuccessful attempts to work with the prison directly, EJP went to the press and the books were ultimately returned.

Taken together, these profiles highlight issues that are critically explored throughout this book. They take into account the information needs and interests of patrons, placing them within the context of mass incarceration. They relate information requests, access, and censorship to the impact of incarceration and detention practices on Black, Indigenous, and people of color and draw from this knowledge to create collections that reflect the needs and interests of people who are incarcerated. They are situated in grassroots and professional networks, which often act as points of association between community resources and information organizations outside of detention centers, jails, juvenile detention centers, and prisons. These services recognize the people impacted by incarceration and detention as knowledgeable about their own information needs and practices, as situated in the context of detention, immigration, or incarceration, and as people who carry with them a history, a present, and a future.

Even as profiles of notable services, the library services described above are not isolated or completely independent. Some are supported by individuals and professional associations, which help them to perform their tasks or to resist large-scale censorship. One service is networked with other types of libraries in order to provide consistent services during and after incarceration. The other services describe the value of shared resources, specifically interlibrary loan materials, in creating a collection that is responsive to patron requests. These collaborations and connections are necessary not only because of the scale of incarceration, but also because they resist isolation and raise public awareness about information and incarceration.

The coordinated efforts of the New York Public Library, Brooklyn Public Library, and Queens Public Library demonstrate how collaborations can be built to better meet the information needs and desires of incarcerated people. Together, these three libraries provide library services and information access for people incarcerated across New York. Each of these libraries has a set parameter for service, ensuring that more people who are incarcerated have more frequent access to services. The NYPL's services are profiled above. The Brooklyn Public Library provides similar book cart services to people in the New York Department of Corrections. The Queens Public Library has long been recognized for its exceptional services for people who are incarcerated, including its work on reentry, which is described in chapter 7 of this book. All three of New York City's library systems host video visitations, connecting people in the neighborhoods around the libraries with their family members and friends who are incarcerated.

The Brooklyn Public Library (2021) hosts programs through its public libraries not only to raise awareness of incarceration, but to also promote critical thinking about justice, criminalization, and legal rights. The library system hosts an ongoing book club and discussion that centers on "sparking conversations about social power, dismantling oppressive systems, and fostering collective action." It partners with organizations that provide services to currently and formerly incarcerated people to provide introductory sessions on ways to support incarcerated people, including guidance on how to write to them, which encourages people who are not directly impacted by incarceration to become pen pals with people who are. The library system hosts workshops on rights to privacy, resisting surveillance, and the possibility of enacting legislation so that certain activities (like drug use or sex work) might not be considered criminal in the future, thereby reducing the reach of incarceration into communities. Brooklyn Public Library's programming series is exceptional in and of itself, but also within the field—it recognizes Black, Indigenous, and women of color and LGBTQIA+ people are often targeted for incarceration. Brooklyn Public Library's programs draw from knowledge of this impact, working to build not only awareness of how carceral systems function and who is most likely to be surveilled, but also to build relationships and material bonds between people on the outside and people who are incarcerated.

Granting bodies have provided some means to address the lack of funding provided for library and information services to people who are incarcerated. Recently funded projects through the Institute of Museum and Library Services concern college libraries as resources for people in reentry and possibilities for library collaborations to extend existing resources and services (Chicago, IL, based at Chicago State University), digital literacy and information access (Cherokee Regional Library, GA; University of North Carolina at Chapel-Hill), increasing reentry-related services and information access (Free Library of Philadelphia, PA; New Jersey), reentry outcome assessment (Colorado), and visual and media arts programming for youth in juvenile detention centers (King County, WA, based at the University of Washington; Los Angeles, CA; Miami, FL). The Andrew W. Mellon Foundation has provided funding to support higher education access for people who are incarcerated, as well as funding for arts-based programming inside of prisons. Funded projects include an online digital archive of newspapers created in prisons (through Reveal Digital), a project to create or increase book collections within prisons (Freedom Reads, based at Yale and headed by Reginald Dwayne Betts), and a forthcoming archive of mass incarceration in Los Angeles (based at UCLA and headed by Kelly Lytle Hernández).

The profiles provided by the librarians at times contrast with the accounts in Conrad (2017) and with other research on library services in prisons reviewed earlier in this book. The librarians, for instance, repeatedly call for library services inside of prisons to reflect public library models (this is the approach that Coyle critiqued so strongly in 1987), but issues of inadequate funding, formal and informal censorship, and institutional philosophies have shaped the materials provided inside of carceral facilities across the country (Arford, 2016; Conrad, 2017). Granting bodies have recognized and reacted to the need for increased financial support to improve information access inside of carceral facilities. Other funding models may emerge to build library and information services to people who are incarcerated, potentially through cross-institutional library collaborations that involve sharing access to collections or librarian and staff time, or through the redistribution of materials in prison budgets to create a line item for library collections and services.

As is illustrated in the example of collection building at the county jail in the Southwest, where staff relied on discards and donations to build a collection and people incarcerated had limited access to the materials they would prefer to read, funding is a continuing issue for library collections. Funding, or lack thereof, determines how collection development occurs. This chapter closes by reflecting on collection development as a central aspect of direct services.

COLLECTION DEVELOPMENT

Collections should, as much as possible, reflect the informational and recreational needs and interests of the people incarcerated in a given facility. In practice, collection development is complicated by facility rules, informal standards for access, facility staff assessments of classification and specialized restrictions, correctional staff's perceptions of access and reading, and the budgetary support that exists for collection development.

Outside of access to the law and to religious material, people who are incarcerated don't have a guaranteed, constitutionally protected right to access information. In *Turner v. Safley* (1987), the Supreme Court ruled that the constitutional rights of incarcerated people are limited by the security concerns of carceral facilities, concerns which are defined by facility administrators or overseeing administrative bodies. The *Turner* standard ostensibly required that there be legitimate concerns given for restricting access to specific materials. In practice, the option to legitimize the censorship of information and materials as a threat to security has been used to ban *The Autobiography of Malcolm X*, Barack Obama's autobiography, images of cats, books by John Updike, James Joyce's novel *Ulysses*, printed material from the internet, and even entire types of materials such as newspapers and magazines (Shapiro, 2016). Censorship is an enduring feature of prison libraries - Glennor Shirley's (2007) survey documented similar trends. These bans and forms of censorship tend to occur at the level of individual facilities, and so the practices at individual institutions will shape what materials it is possible to have in a collection. Carceral facilities vary in what types of materials are allowed, with some limiting access only to softcover books and others allowing hardcover and nonbook materials in the collection. Some facilities may allow magazines while others do not (this will also be a budgetary consideration, since a subscription to a magazine can quickly become expensive).

Higgins prioritizes the reading interests and desires of people in carceral facilities in the Public Library Association's guide to jail and prison service, *Get Inside: Responsible Jail and Prison Library Service* (2017). Drawing on his experience as a jail librarian, Higgins states that prior to starting a new service, "[a] good first step is to ask a jail official to send out a survey to people incarcerated there to collect info on what genres, authors, specific titles, reference material, and other items interest them" (2017, 37). The languages that people read can also be assessed through an initial survey, and the survey can be distributed in multiple languages as needed. The survey will probably set expectations for collection development, so it should only present materials and services that can actually (or realistically) be provided. If a genre or type of book is censored by the facility, or the library system can't guarantee access to a type of book or books in a specific language, then a listing of those materials in a survey might fracture trust between potential patrons and the future librarian and library staff. Any exclusions from the survey can be supplemented, however, by an option for future patrons to write in their own interests. Doing this can provide much-needed guidance for collection development and may address oversights in the survey's design. Requesting information about patrons' information interests not only creates a foundation for a meaningful library collection; it also informs people who are incarcerated of forthcoming library services and communicates to them that their interests, needs, and desires will be incorporated into (and will likely continue to shape) the library collection. The patron survey's results may indicate the existence of other programs in the facility, including educational programs, programs for people who are veterans, and more. A version of the survey can be developed for and distributed to these program staff too, if desired.

The survey's results may also help communicate the need for a materials budget to library or facility administrators. Many libraries in juvenile detention centers, jails, and prisons reflect small branch collections and include a range of nonfiction, fiction, and comics. The racialized nature of incarceration in the United States has shaped the demographics of people who are incarcerated, and collections should reflect people's identities, histories, and cultures.

Higgins's guide describes the lengths to which librarians and volunteers have gone in order to develop meaningful collections for their patrons in carceral facilities, including networking with publishers and bookstores in order to obtain donated copies of books, purchasing books secondhand, raiding their personal book collections for materials, and otherwise using their personal time in order to ensure that the patron-centered collection development suggested through a survey process will result in a materials collection that reflects patrons' actual interests and needs (2017). While revealing the dedication that librarians and volunteers have and the importance people who are incarcerated place on receiving a requested book or materials on a requested topic, this type of collection development is far from ideal. Support and funding from library administration can guarantee that a library service is able to recognize (and satisfy) the information needs and desires of incarcerated patrons. As was previously illustrated in the profiles, strong cross-library collaborations can help to meet the more niche information needs and desires of some patrons and supplement areas not yet developed in the library collection.

Collection development budgets, censorship, and other professional concerns are discussed in chapter 8 of this book. Here, though, it is important to highlight the tensions between intellectual freedom and library services that are socially and politically aware of how experiences of oppression shape the information landscape (Knox, 2020). This is true within library services generally (Knox, 2020), but is often amplified by the ways in which carceral facilities formally or informally segregate people by racial group or perceived, claimed, or imposed gang affiliation and by the historically racialized and racist tensions that systems of incarceration create and amplify. Carceral facilities have historically been more likely to censor or restrict information related to Black, Indigenous, and Latinx identities and their histories and knowledges than they have been to restrict information that reinforces white supremacist or white nationalist beliefs. This means it may often be the professional duty of a librarian developing collections to be aware of which materials advocate white nationalist ideologies or other forms of oppressive violence (including transphobia and homophobia). As in other areas of professional practice, librarians who are building collections or providing other services for people who are incarcerated "may want to take the consequences of certain types of speech into account in their professional lives" (Knox, 2020, 8) and in their collection development practices. It is probably the case that the NYPL's Correctional Services guidelines that exclude any material that "describes unsafe activity in an *explicitly instructional* way" will limit the weight given to this consideration.

CONCLUSION

Drawing from the library literature, information provided by librarians, and in-depth profiles written by librarians providing information to people in carceral facilities present a wider view of the range of direct services inside of carceral facilities. The services to people who are incarcerated are shaped by budgets, carceral facility restrictions, formal and informal agreements and practices, and collaborations across types of libraries. The partnerships described in this chapter open the possibility of as-of-yet unrecorded collaborations between types of libraries and among librarians and library staff. While the programs highlighted in this chapter are successful models partly due to cross-institutional support and access to reliable funding, it is probable that, as Conrad's (2017) research revealed, many library services to people who are incarcerated are personally meaningful to them even in the midst of extreme limitations.

The barriers to providing direct services in some facilities (such as federal policies in immigrant detention centers) can combine with the limited attention to and funding for library and information services for people who are incarcerated and create massive barriers to providing direct services. While library systems, librarians, and information professionals may not be able to do much more than put pressure on policies that restrict information access, LIS as a field can interrogate why information access for incarcerated people has been such a low priority, both internally and in the general dominant discourse about incarceration, its effects, and its scale. Library systems might consider how their existing services can be used to provide information, materials access, e-resources, and programming to people in carceral facilities; how to connect patrons inside with those outside through coordinated services (such as the programs profiled earlier in this chapter); and how to best protect people's access to autonomy, privacy, and their information freedom in that process. Changes in the overall field of LIS, including defining the people in carceral facilities as library patrons, might impact how library budgets are allocated toward library services for the people most negatively impacted by incarceration. These can be coupled with advocating for the redistribution of carceral facility budgets from allocations for the monitoring of people's information access to practices that will better support the libraries and information access within those facilities.

The next chapter offers additional paths to increasing incarcerated peoples' information access. It covers indirect services, such as collection redistribution and by-mail reference. In this moment, the limited and highly regulated information access through technologies inside of carceral institutions and the limited priority given to funding library services and information access necessitates the creation of programs that do not require large financial investments from library systems. Library and information professionals do not have to be isolated in this effort. The next chapter presents opportunities for libraries to use their existing resources and collection maintenance processes to collaborate with community groups that are already working to increase materials access for people who are incarcerated.

NOTES

1. This is not for lack of effort. The ALA issued the "Resolution for Library Service for Children in Detention at Migrant Detention Centers" in 2019. The American Civil Liberties Union (2021) maintains that the difficulties present in accessing and providing information at detention centers are a consequence of the absence of any "regulations or enforceable standards regarding detention conditions."
2. The American Correctional Association (ACA) includes information about libraries in its Standards for Adult Correctional Institutions. The 2018 version of these standards includes new criteria for assessing aspects of library services, including interviews with staff and incarcerated people, but this version of the Standards is only available digitally and so is not widely distributed to prison librarians. The 2003 version of the standards, still in use by some prison librarians, provided little detailed information about the requirements for library service or how the standards were enforced (2003).
3. Washington State Library's Institutional Library Services department has maintained a directory of prison libraries and librarians since the early 2010s. That directory is available at https://washstatelib.libguides.com/directoryofstateprisonlibraries.
4. Both of these lists were previously under the ALA; the prison-l discussion list is now administered through Colorado, the ASCGLA list is no longer in use.
5. All of these profiles were written before the COVID-19 pandemic and reflect services prior to the lockdown conditions in many facilities.

REFERENCES

American Civil Liberties Union (ACLU). 2021. "Immigration Detention Conditions." www.aclu.org/issues/immigrants-rights/immigrants-rights-and-detention/immigration-detention-conditions.

American Correctional Association. 2003. *Standards for Adult Correctional Institutions, Fourth Edition.* Alexandria, VA: American Correctional Association: 75-76, 158-159.

———. 2018. *Performance-Based Expected Practices for Adult Correctional Institutions, Fifth Edition.* Alexandria, VA: American Correctional Association: 100-101, 114-117, 238-240.

American Library Association. 2019. "Resolution for Library Service for Children in Detention at Migrant Detention Centers." www.ala.org/aboutala/sites/ala.org.aboutala/files/content/governance/council/council_documents/2019_ac_docs/ALA 20CD 2052 Resolution on Library Service for Children in Detention at Migrant Detention Centers_0.pdf.

Arford, T. 2016. "Prisons as Sites of Power/Resistance." In *The SAGE Handbook of Resistance*, ed. D. Courpasson and S. Vallas, 224-43. London: Sage Publications.

Association of Specialized and Cooperative Library Agencies. 1992. "Library Standards for Adult Correctional Institutions."

Association of Specialized and Cooperative Library Agencies, Ad Hoc Subcommittee on Library Standards for Juvenile Correctional Institutions. 1999. "Library Standards for Juvenile Correctional Facilities."

Austin, J., J. Lincoln, K. C. Briggs, M. Charenko, and M. Dillon. 2020. "Race, Racism, and the Contested Ground of Information Access for Incarcerated People." *Open Information Science*, 4, no. 1: 169–85.

Bailey, A. 1972. "Standards for Library Service in Institutions: A. In the Correctional Setting." *Library Trends* 21: 261–66.

Bilz, K. 2020. "Public Library Services for the Incarcerated and Detained." *Kentucky Libraries* 84, no. 2: 16–23.

Black & Pink. 2019. www.blackandpink.org/.

Brooklyn Public Library. 2021. "Justice Initiatives Book Club: *Parable of the Sower* by Octavia Butler." www.bklynlibrary.org/calendar/justice-initiatives-book-virtual-20210322.

Clark, S., and E. MacCreaigh. 2006. *Library Services to the Incarcerated: Applying the Public Library Model in Correctional Facilities*. Santa Barbara, CA: Libraries Unlimited.

Conrad, S. 2017. *Prison Librarianship: Policy and Practice*. Jefferson, NC: McFarland.

Curtis, F. R. 1918. *The Libraries of the American State and National Institutions for Defectives, Dependents, and Delinquents*. Minneapolis: Bulletin of the University of Minnesota.

de la Peña McCook, K. 2004. "Public Libraries and People in Jails." *Reference & User Services Quarterly* 44, no. 1: 26–30.

Higgins, N. 2017. *Get Inside: Responsible Jail and Prison Library Service*. Chicago: Public Library Association.

Kinney, B., L. Sherbo, and T. Herrlinger. 2018. "Prison Walls, Library Doorways: Improving Library Access for Releasing Inmates." *ALKI* 34, no. 1: 13–14, 17.

Klick, L. R. S. 2011. "Uncommon Services: Public Library Services to Incarcerated Patrons." *InterActions: UCLA Journal of Education and Information Studies* 7, no. 1.

Knox, E. 2020. "Intellectual Freedom and Social Justice: Tensions between Core Values in American Librarianship." *Open Information Science* 4, no. 1: 1–10.

Krolak, L. 2019. *Books beyond Bars: The Transformative Potential of Prison Libraries*. Hamburg: UNESCO Institute for Lifelong Learning.

Lehmann, V., and I. Locke. 2005. *Guidelines for Library Services to Prisoners*. 3rd edition. IFLA Professional Report No. 92. The Hague: International Federation of Library Associations and Institutions.

Lilienthal, S. M. 2013. "Prison and Public Libraries." *Library Journal*, 138, no. 2: 26–32.

Millsap, K. 2018. "Building Partnerships with Correctional Libraries." *Texas Library Journal* 94, no. 3: 79–80.

Morris, J. 2013. "Free to Learn: Helping Ex-Offenders with Reentry." *Public Library Quarterly* 32: 119–23.

Revised Code of Washington, 27.04.045 § 13. https://app.leg.wa.gov/RCW/default.aspx?cite=27.04.045.

Shapiro, D. M. 2016. "Lenient in Theory, Dumb in Fact: Prison, Speech, and Scrutiny." *George Washington Law Review* 84, no. 4: 972–1028.

Shirley, G. 2007. "Censorship and Prison Libraries." *Behind the Walls*. www.ala.org/ala/olos/outreach resource/btw0207.htm.

Sweeney, M. 2010. *Reading Is My Window: Books and the Art of Reading in Women's Prisons*. Chapel Hill: University of North Carolina Press.

Transgender Gender-Variant and Intersex Justice Project (TGIJP). n.d. www.tgijp.org/.

United Nations. 2015. "Standard Minimum Rules for the Treatment of Prisoners." www.unodc.org/documents/justice-and-prison-reform/Nelson_Mandela_Rules-E-ebook.pdf.

Washington State Library. 2021. Directory of State Prison Libraries. https://washstatelib.libguides.com/directoryofstateprisonlibraries.

Wiley, P. 2017. "Juvie 101: Six Things I Learned Doing Outreach at a Juvenile Detention Center." Programming Librarian. https://programminglibrarian.org/articles/juvie-101-six-things-i-learned-doing-outreach-juvenile-detention-center.

CHAPTER 6

Models of Indirect Service

I ndirect library and information services for people who are incarcerated present an opportunity for library and information professionals to meet the needs and interests of
incarcerated people even if they are unable to interact face-to-face with library patrons.
Some justifications for indirect services might include a library system's limited staffing
for outreach, distance from carceral facilities or proximity to facilities with existing librarians, and yet-to-be finalized discussions with carceral facility administrators regarding the
provision of direct services. Indirect services can break ground for library systems to create
established programming for incarcerated people, to create a connection between people
who are incarcerated and the local library system, and to support the work of existing prison librarians who are fulfilling multiple roles and must often operate their libraries with
limited funding. Indirect library services also provide a means to continue library services
when physical services are disrupted. Having an established way of conducting indirect
library services means that some access to information may still be available to patrons in
jails and prisons even when those facilities are under orders not to admit anyone other than
staff or when units are closed to programming.

This chapter focuses on two types of indirect information services. These are reference services by mail and donations to library collections or programs within the carceral
facility or to nonlibrary groups that provide people who are incarcerated with reading
materials for free (these are often referred to as Books to Prisoners programs). After
reviewing information from library systems, the chapter closes with information about
other indirect ways that librarians and information professionals can support programs
and increase the resources for people who are incarcerated even when they cannot physically enter the carceral facility.

REFERENCE BY MAIL

As discussed in chapter 4, people who are incarcerated encounter a number of barriers to
information access. Among these barriers are prohibitions on access to the internet and limited access to library and information professionals who have the time and other resources
to locate authoritative sources, assist with information-seeking, or support research. Reference by mail services are one way to address information needs that are unmet due to
the carceral facility's control of information access. Through a reference by mail service,
libraries can indirectly provide reference services to people who would otherwise have little

or no opportunity to obtain the information they want and need. Unlike e-mail-based and phone-based services, which can be prohibitively expensive to access while incarcerated, by-mail service enables patrons who have little or no funds to still access the information they need or want.

Formal reference by mail service was started by the New York Public Library (NYPL) more than fifty years ago (Jacobson, 2018). The NYPL's Correctional Services program has run a reference by mail service that provides information to people who are incarcerated across the entire country (until 2018, when the services were shared with the newly formed Jail and Reentry Services program at the San Francisco Public Library, and staff at these libraries collaborated to identify other libraries providing this type of formalized service). The NYPL's program serves as a strong model for providing reference by mail. Through NYPL's service, patrons can request information from the library twice per month. They can receive up to ten pages of information as a response to each request letter, with information printed on the front and back of each page. All mail that passes into and out of a prison is potentially examined by mailroom staff, and many carceral facilities have particular regulations regarding what types of information or media are allowed or will not be allowed. NYPL librarians have extensive experience with this process and have refined their rules and regulations to reflect what types of information are most often not allowed inside of prisons in the United States. The rules that the NYPL follows are given in the text box.

EXAMPLE OF RULES AND REGULATIONS FOR A REFERENCE BY MAIL SERVICE

NEW YORK PUBLIC LIBRARY

The New York Public Library's Correctional Services staff is committed to answering your reference questions. In order to offer you the best service possible, we ask that you follow the below rules & regulations:

1. Because of the volume of letters we receive, we cannot answer more than two letters per person, per month. If you do send more than two letters per month, your requests will go unanswered. We deal with a backlog of letters and as a result, you will experience a delay in your reply. Please do not send the same request more than once. We appreciate your understanding.
2. We can only send you 18 pages of information at a time. As a result, we may not be able to send all of the information you request.
3. We do not get into contact with a third party for you, nor can we send any mail or correspondence on your behalf. Any requests for this will go unanswered.
4. We are unable to offer legal advice of any kind. For information on how to file discrimination or wrongdoing complaints in your correctional facility, please contact the grievance office of your facility. Please be aware that we will not respond to questions asking us for legal opinions or advice of any kind.
5. We do not send any adult materials, including images or text. This also includes the names of companies that produce adult materials.

6. We do not send information promoting violence or the use of weapons, including lists of weapons/ammunition or any information pertaining to acquiring weapons.
7. We are unable to send you individual books/magazines/newspapers/etc. Please reach out to Books through Bars c/o Bluestockings Bookstore, 172 Allen Street, New York, NY 10002.
8. We do not provide personal correspondence (pen pal services) for any individual, nor can we contact a pen pal service on your behalf.
9. We do not send an individual's contact information. This includes phone numbers, addresses, or e-mail addresses for any individual. We do not engage with social media or newspaper articles either about you or anyone else. We also do not research your criminal history, nor anyone else's on your behalf.
10. We do not send maps or directions.
11. Library services are free, and so you do not need to provide postage. Also, please do not send original documents you wish returned. Nothing you send to the library will be mailed back to you.

12. If any part of your letter requests prohibited information, the entire letter will not be answered. Prohibited information is determined at the discretion of NYPL staff.

NYPL also offers a reference service by phone, for easy-to-answer questions, at 917-ASK-NYPL (917-275-6975). Patrons may have to wait in a queue (usually under two minutes). Depending on their facility, patrons may have to put AskNYPL on their approved call list.

Please be advised that a team of volunteers answer letters. To ensure your privacy, all identifying information, including your name and facility, is redacted and only seen by NYPL staff. NYPL shreds your letters after they are answered, and no identifying information is kept.

While every effort is made to provide accurate information, NYPL specifically disclaims all express and implied warranties with respect to the information and materials provided to patrons. NYPL and representatives shall have no liability for any damages, including, without limitation, direct, indirect, consequential, compensatory, special, punitive, or incidental damages arising out of or relating to the use of our services.

Due to the difficulties that people who are incarcerated encounter when seeking information, there is no end to the amount of letters that a reference by mail service might receive. The limits set on the number of letters a patron can submit each month are a way to create a service that is not deluged with information requests, while also affording more equitable access for all patrons who request information and research. Various libraries that provide these types of services—including the Brooklyn Public Library (NY), Carson City Library (NV), Harris County Library (TX), the St. Louis County Library (MO), the Queens Public Library, and the no longer extant medical information service in Texas (Couvillon and Justice, 2016)—have scoped their rules and workflows to ensure that they are able to adequately meet patrons' information requests in a timely manner. Volunteer groups, such as the Prison Library Support Network (PLSN), have also stepped in to answer requests from and provide information to incarcerated people (2020). It is possible that fewer restrictions will be placed on the frequency with which patrons can write and receive a response, or on the number of questions answered in each response, as more library services share the responsibility for providing needed information to incarcerated patrons.

Typically, the letters are addressed to and received by a specific department in the library. Upon receipt, the letters are opened, assigned some form of tracking information, and basic information about the letter is recorded in a tracking document (taking care to not record any information that would not be recorded for public library patrons). A tracking system allows the librarians who supervise the reference by mail service to follow up if there are any issues with completing responses, and to monitor the time spent between the receipt of a letter and the mailing of a response.

Depending on the workflow model developed by the library system and the supervising librarian, there are several ways that letters might be distributed. If letters are answered by all the librarians in the system, the overseeing librarian can physically distribute the designated number of letters to each librarian or library branch. This type of workflow often requires that providing reference by mail services form part of the position description for all librarians in a system. This model has the benefit of creating a system-wide awareness of the information needs and desires of people who are incarcerated. A possible shortfall can occur when individual librarians' biases against providing the service, which may be rooted in criminalizing narratives or in philosophies that see the carceral facility as necessarily punitive, are reflected in the quality of work provided by those respondents.

Another workflow model is to create opportunities for librarians to "opt in" to participate in the reference by mail service. Librarians in the library system can be provided with background information on the service and the reasons for providing it, sample materials, and with direct training or instructions from the librarians who supervise the service. This model may mean there are fewer librarians who are actively responding to letters (which increases the delays between receipt and response), but the result may be that the high quality of the librarians' work reflects their willingness to provide this type of service. The distributed model also allows for the possibility of recruiting respondents from outside of the library system. Some reference by mail services, for instance, provide opportunities for volunteer LIS professionals to answer reference requests, some involve collaborations between public and specialized librarians (medical and academic librarians, for instance), and some services work directly with library and information science programs to provide coursework and internships for students who are interested in learning more about library services for people who are incarcerated (Austin and Villa-Nicholas, 2019; Drabinski and Rabina, 2015; Jacobson, 2018; Rabina and Drabinski, 2015).

In this model, the librarian who oversees the reference by mail service will probably need to create a somewhat more complex mode of tracking in order to trace when requests were sent to respondents and when they are returned. The service will also need to anonymize the letters received. In a model which relies entirely on respondents within the library system (and forgoes the use of outside respondents), the respondent librarians are already expected to respect patron privacy and to not share patron information as part of their professional duties. People who are incarcerated are followed by their conviction histories. In most states, it is possible to see the conviction history of anyone who is currently incarcerated by searching their full name or jail or prison identification number in the locator for the facility. For jails, this information includes actions they have been accused, but not always convicted, of committing. Given the structuring of the carceral system in the United States, reviewing conviction histories and charges must always be done with the awareness that this information is limited. While people, both incarcerated and not incarcerated, do engage in real harm to other people, in no circumstances will the conviction history of a patron reveal the fullness of their life, nor will it reveal much about their need for information. By protecting patrons' privacy by anonymizing their letters, the librarian that oversees the reference by mail program can work to reduce the possible bias that might accompany knowledge of convictions or accusations of certain actions. Of course, the letters distributed within a library system can also be anonymized in order to better protect patron privacy.

Anonymization is simple, though it does require an additional step. In order to anonymize letters, the librarian who opens the reference requests mailed from people who are incarcerated can place a sticky note over the name of the patron, their facility identification number, and the name of the facility, when these are listed. The librarian can then digitize the letter by using a scanner, creating an anonymized digital version of the letter. This method, created by librarians at the New York Public Library, makes possible the easy distribution of letters to volunteers, other librarians, or LIS students. An anonymized, scanned letter can be sent as an e-mail to the respondent, who can then reply to that e-mail with a digital file as a response. The librarian overseeing the reference by mail program can then review the content and fit of the response and can then use the original physical correspondence to address and mail the response. This method serves to protect patron privacy, facilitate letter distribution, and streamline the reference by mail process.

Librarians overseeing this type of service will probably want to be mindful of the steps to take to protect patron privacy in digital spaces, including e-mail communications and any tracking documents maintained. If the library has a privacy specialist, involving that staffer in these conversations can lead to innovative ways to minimize access to the digital records and digital traces of patron requests. People who are incarcerated are subject to myriad surveillance technologies; mitigating further surveillance, as much as possible, should be part of a reference by mail service.

Emily Jacobson, a Correctional Services librarian at the New York Public Library, notes a few particularities of administering a reference by mail service (2018). Since requests for information vary in complexity and specificity, respondents must be able to gain enough background information on a given topic in order to ascertain whether or not a given resource fits the information request, the level of prior knowledge a patron has about a topic, and whether or not a resource authoritatively meets the patron's request. The inability to conduct a reference interview means that respondents must use deductive reasoning to match materials with patrons' expressed level of prior knowledge, any other information provided, or patrons' literacy levels as interpreted through the wording of their requests. However, respondents should keep in mind that what could be read as indicators of lower literacy levels may actually reflect that a patron's primary literate language is a language other than English; that it is sometimes difficult for patrons to access paper inside and so their letters may be brief in order to use part of a piece of paper for other purposes; and that their requests for information may have been transcribed hurriedly. Keeping this in mind will assist respondents as they try to find the resources that best fit patrons' requests, but sometimes compiling the information for a response does involve making a best guess about which information to include. When it is not possible to evaluate a patron's familiarity with a topic or current research, respondents might list other areas related to the topic or suggest resources that can be requested in the future. These practices convey an understanding of the impact that incarceration has on information access, and also facilitate patrons' own information-seeking. Finally, the length of time between sending a reference request and receiving a response involves delays, so it should be standard practice for respondents to restate all of the information requests received in a letter (even those that are not answered in the response) in case the patron has forgotten the information they requested or would like to pursue an area that was not included in the response (Jacobson, 2018).

The information must be formatted in ways that make sense in a physical letter. Much of the information that is requested is available online—and sometimes is only available online—and so it needs to be formatted to a print mailing. This involves editing the information from a digital (and often highly visually coded) medium to the printed page, removing internal indications of hyperlinks, and assessing when copying and pasting the contents of an article or taking a screenshot of the information would best convey the information requested. Reformatting the information is also a necessary step in order to avoid causing confusion for patrons who have limited familiarity with present-day web design or who, due to the length of their incarceration, may have never personally accessed the internet.

The tone of the response is another factor to consider. Any response will most likely include an introductory letter that restates the information originally requested, describes the information enclosed, and explains why the sources included were deemed to be authoritative or the best fit for the information requested. In many of the library systems that provide by-mail references services to people who are incarcerated, the tone of these letters skews heavily professional. In part, this is to ensure that patrons understand the role of the service as differentiated from a pen pal service. It also serves to represent the library as a professional and trustworthy institution. The strongest reason, though, for implementing a standard form of response that uses a professional tone is so that patrons will not have a perception of being treated any differently from anyone else. This is a way to communicate that all information requests (that fall within the rules of a given service) are seen by respondents as equally valid and worthy of research and attention.

Many libraries receive letters from people who are currently incarcerated. Often, these letters are answered in a piecemeal fashion (depending on which librarian receives the letters and whether or not they respond), or the letters don't receive a response because librarians feel unsure about the regulations about sending information to people who are incarcerated. Creating a formalized service with an experienced manager who coordinates the letters received, reviews the outgoing responses for their adherence to established rules and regulations, and is professionally qualified to supervise volunteers and librarians, recruit librarians as respondents, and provide insight into the best modes of approach for specific questions, helps to ensure that patrons' requests are answered professionally and that no enclosed materials potentially violate the mailroom regulations of a specific facility.

There are probably models for providing reference by mail services that are largely unexplored because they have yet to be implemented. One possible model is to create a statewide association of librarians who work together to provide reference service to individuals in all the carceral institutions in a given state. This model could be centralized through a specific library or orchestrated by the state library or the state library association that coordinates the incoming and outgoing mail and the distribution of letters to respondents. This would be useful because the funding models for libraries don't often fit the geospatial location of prisons—prisons tend to be located in rural areas, and often near smaller libraries that may not have the funding or staff time available to meet the information requests of people who are either temporarily their local patrons or are from areas other than the one a given library serves. A distributed model of service enables different libraries to work together to answer letters, share the cost of postage and printing materials, and share resources from across the state as patrons ask about reentry-related resources in specific areas.

A distributed model of service could also be used to create and provide language-specific information services for people who are detained and incarcerated. More information access in the non-English primary literate languages of people who are incarcerated is desperately needed. This is especially true when considering the number of people who are currently being detained in immigration detention facilities and the recorded lack of information available therein.

Reference by mail and other by-mail services present opportunities for creating at-a-distance programming inside of facilities. For instance, the New York Public Library has also used its by-mail service to offer programming content that is high-interest and culturally relevant to people who are incarcerated. The Schomburg Center for Research in Black Culture has been instrumental in this process. The Schomburg Center created a Black history packet, which included information and activities, that was then made available to patrons incarcerated on Rikers Island. This mode of delivery can be used to supplement existing in-person programming, or as focused programming when facilities are locked down or are otherwise prohibiting in-person access.

BOOK DONATIONS

Prison libraries are often funded through the inmate welfare fund at a given institution, which is created through purchases made at commissary (Conrad, 2017). These funds are typically in short supply and are insufficient to enable the library to meet patrons' requests for materials and information. There are many reports of understocked libraries and of books that have been read until they disintegrate. The condition of the library materials in carceral facilities often represent the repercussions of mass incarceration, as well as the systems that permeate racial criminalization, which fundamentally involve devaluation and oppression.

Even library collections that have been developed to truly meet the interests and information needs of people who are incarcerated involve balancing collection development tasks against the existing budget (if there is one), patrons' interests and desires, and the limitations placed by the carceral facility on library materials. Some prison libraries are subject to purchase cycles that may only allow them to purchase new materials a few times a year, leaving the collection somewhat stagnant between funding periods. The need to regulate the collection to ensure the widest possible access—to guarantee that books are returned on time, that they are not shared between patrons but instead always pass through the library before being recirculated, and that library loans are not extended for books that are heavily in demand—can position prison librarians to function as extensions of the carceral facility, imposing punitive measures on people who are trying to access popular library materials that are often in short supply.

Public, academic, law, and special libraries can all collaborate with prison librarians to supplement the library collections and general access to books that are available in facilities. Donated materials should always align with the fictional genres and nonfiction areas that are of interest to the patrons in a given facility. Although supplementing library collections with donated materials cannot address the discrepancies between funding for library materials and the funding spent on general operations of the facility or any of the other myriad factors that shape incarceration in the United States that are discussed in this book, they can help to alleviate the pressure librarians in carceral facilities might feel as they navigate patron's desires for access and limited available materials. External librarians and library systems can collaborate with prison librarians to locate materials that those librarians know are heavily requested and fit with ongoing programming in the facility. These outside librarians can also help connect the readers inside of facilities with readers outside through their joint participation in various programs, such as One City, One Book programs. Some public libraries do already provide prison librarians access to their discarded materials, or intentionally set aside discarded books that are in high demand in carceral facilities (such as novels by best-selling mystery authors, books on Black and Latinx history, and urban fiction). Another model might be to work with a local juvenile detention, jail, or prison librarian, educator, or other group that provides programming or services to people who are incarcerated to purchase some materials that can be circulated in the prison. Doing this not only increases information access for people who are incarcerated, it also provides a means by which libraries can informally conduct outreach to the people inside of carceral facilities. Displays in the prison library's space could, for instance, inform viewers that some of the materials available there were purchased by the local library and could include general information about public and other library services or obtaining a library card upon release. Educators and others who provide programming in the carceral facility can work in tandem with outside librarians to create joint programming that takes place both inside of the facility and in the library, creating modes of communication around donated materials that facilitate connection to the larger public. These programs can build public awareness of the realities of incarceration while also increasing the amount of library materials available for people who are incarcerated.

Another option is to coordinate with groups that already provide books to incarcerated people. These groups are often referred to as "books to prisoners" programs. They have a long history of resisting censorship in carceral facilities, increasing access to reading materials, providing materials specifically related to race, gender, and sexuality and experiences of incarceration, and coordinating volunteers and fund-raising to facilitate access to donated materials. Some of these groups focus specifically on providing books to women or to LGBTQIA+ people. Michelle Dillon, a longtime Books to Prisoners member, contributed a description of these types of programs for this book.

BOOKS TO PRISONERS PROGRAMS

MICHELLE DILLON

Prison book programs, also sometimes known as *books to prisoners programs*, are grassroots organizations which provide free books, magazines, zines, and other reading materials upon request to people who are incarcerated in jails, prisons, and detention centers. These groups are organized and maintained by volunteers who have an interest in ensuring that incarcerated individuals retain access to vital tools for education, recreation, and self-empowerment, as well as opening communication lines to people who are outside of carceral facilities. The volunteers who work with these groups perform duties such as reading request letters for books from incarcerated individuals, selecting appropriate books based on the content of these letters, and preparing packages of books to be shipped to the person who made the request. Many prison book programs also coordinate pen pal programs, book clubs, writing workshops, and educational classes inside of carceral facilities to complement the reading materials which they provide.

Although efforts to provide reading materials to incarcerated individuals are probably as old as incarceration itself, the history of modern prison book programs began in 1972 with the founding of the Prison Book Program in Quincy, Massachusetts. Some of the earliest programs began with the explicit purpose of providing support to political prisoners and politically progressive incarcerated individuals (Books to Prisoners, 2019; Prison Book Program, n.d.). However, the scope of operations for most groups has expanded since those early years. The array of prison book programs now includes groups that serve readers nationwide, groups that serve specific demographics (such as LGBT Books to Prisoners, which serves LGBTQIA+ individuals, and Liberation Library, which serves incarcerated youth), and groups that serve individuals incarcerated in one state or region (Prison Book Program, n.d.). Prison book programs may operate in connection with a local bookstore, with assistance from colleges and universities, or as autonomous programs. A prison book program may be a 501(c)(3) nonprofit, may be fiscally sponsored by a 501(c)(3) nonprofit, or may prefer to remain independent.

Despite these differences, two common themes unite these groups. The first theme is that each group will strive to provide a variety of reading materials, and its volunteers will tailor packages as best they can to the desires of the requesting person without superimposing their own political or religious beliefs. The second theme is that each group has been organized to provide a mechanism for the direct delivery of free reading materials to people whose only option for book ownership otherwise would be for friends and family members to purchase expensive new books from a bookstore or publisher. Prison book programs exist to solve a troubling issue for incarcerated individuals and their support networks: if you want to provide a book or magazine to somebody who is incarcerated, you cannot simply select a book from your bookshelf and mail it to the facility. Prisons and jails classify used books which have been sent directly by individuals as contraband, and those books will be barred from reaching the person inside. Unfortunately, jail and prison administrators use claims of contraband not only to bar reasonable access to books sent from well-intentioned friends and families, but sometimes even books from prison book programs and publishers as well. These claims intersect with entrenched issues of incarceration as a system of control over bodies and minds, and underscore the need for prison book programs and advocates to work continually to ensure the fewest possible restrictions on content and vendors, more access in more facilities, and new routes for access (Schorb, 2014).

Prison book programs exist to provide a consistent delivery service for books in a system with few existing options, but the barriers to carceral book access extend beyond restrictions on vendors and content. The unfortunate reality is that most jail and prison facilities are underequipped to provide reading materials to incarcerated individuals. Prison libraries are typically underfunded and de-prioritized; the library's open hours may be short, and high-quality reading materials may be scarce. Some Washington state prisons were found to have been accessible to people in those facilities less than half of their scheduled times in 2018 due to staffing shortages, lockdowns, and other service disruptions (Books to Prisoners, @B2PSeattle, 2020).[1] In 2018, a journalist in Illinois discovered that the Illinois Department of Corrections had spent just $276 on books for its prison libraries during the previous year (Gaines, 2018). An analysis of prison libraries in Georgia in 2019 revealed that those facilities were being stocked with as few as two books per person (Thieme, 2019).

The nature of incarceration in the United States has ensured that those who are incarcerated, as well as their loved ones, typically lack the means to offset these widespread insufficiencies with personal book purchases. The exploitative wages which are paid for prison labor (some immigrant detainees are not even paid for their labor, and are only compensated with candy bars [Urbina, 2014]) prevent most incarcerated people from purchasing books. Furthermore, given the ways that policing and incarceration target communities with high rates of poverty, as well as the many additional good and services for which loved ones must pay to support those who are incarcerated, regular purchases of books and magazines are impossible for most families (deVuono-Powell et al., 2015).

Prison book programs have been organized to offset these systemic challenges, but they themselves face ongoing obstacles. Censorship by prison officials continues to be one of the biggest obstacles for information access. Censorship limits what content incarcerated people can read, from whom incarcerated people can receive information, and in what formats incarcerated people can receive information. Broadly speaking, carceral facilities may impose content-based or content-neutral bans on various types of books, and the official regulations for content-based bans are "construed so broadly that they essentially serve as convenient justifications for arbitrary bans" (PEN America, 2019). The materials mailed by prison book programs that have been censored in jails and prisons include dog breed encyclopedias and maps of the moon (which were restricted because they presented an alleged escape attempt) (*Prison Legal News v. Secretary*, 2018). More insidiously, there appears to be a significant tendency to restrict books about Black history and political theory (Onyenacho, 2020).

Given the opacity of carceral systems, these unjust bans can be difficult to identify and rescind, especially when the decisions are made by prison officials without proper accountability. In 2019, Washington State's Department of Corrections (DOC) attempted to ban prison book programs by claiming that mailed books were being used to smuggle in contraband. The DOC released a statement that seventeen such incidents had occurred during the last twelve months. However, a journalist discovered that the DOC's statement had been based on a bad database query, wherein officials had simply queried the keywords "book" and "contraband" together. The alleged incidents which had been used to try to restrict access included a case in which "an inmate was *book*ed with contraband" and "contraband was located by Officer *Book*er"; not a single incident could be linked to mailed books (O'Sullivan, 2019). With the allegations dismantled, the Washington DOC quickly rescinded its book ban—but notably, only because the public eye was now on the issue.

New technologies may also provoke new restrictions on communication and information. Following the introduction of prison tablets—devices similar in form to an iPad or a Kindle, but with fees attached for virtually every service—facilities across the country have attempted to stop in-person visitations, postal mail, and book deliveries (Raher, 2020). In one of the most egregious examples to date, in 2019 the West Virginia Division of Corrections and Rehabilitation signed a contract with a prison tablet provider in which incarcerated people would be charged $.05 per minute to read books (Appalachian Prison Book Project, 2019).

Volunteers with prison book programs have been at the forefront of the fight to overturn senseless and harmful restrictions on access to reading materials and other information, from Pittsburgh's Book 'Em program writing an op-ed in the *Washington Post* to overturn an attempt to ban mailed books in 2018 (Lincoln, 2018), to Books to Prisoners (Seattle) coordinating a campaign to restore access in Washington prisons in 2019 (Constant, 2019), to the ongoing work of the Appalachian Prison Book Project to eliminate the pay-per-minute fees on e-books (James, 2020). In the words of one prison librarian who spoke about the frustrations of ongoing barriers to information access for incarcerated people, "Books aren't the problem, and censorship isn't the solution" (Orlofsky, 2019). In general, prison book programs have made it their mission to uphold that tenet.

If these ideas and issues interest you, you might consider becoming involved with the prison book program movement:

- Find out if a program exists in your area and volunteer for it or donate to it. Most programs maintain lists of books they need, including used books and specialized books that might not be on most people's bookshelves, such as dictionaries and GED preparation books. However, note that for most groups, money and volunteer time are the most prized resources that you might be able to donate. A list of current programs is available online at the website for the Prison Books Program in Quincy, Massachusetts. [An extensive list of groups that provide this service is available online at https://prisonbookprogram.org/resources/other-books-to-prisoners-programs/.]
- Stay updated on the current needs and new barriers faced by prison book programs, and boost this advocacy on social media and in your networks. When censorship has happened in the past, one of the best mechanisms to fight it has been public engagement and outcry. Your phone call or e-mail to a legislator, governor, or prison official will help tremendously.
- If you've looked at the scope of current prison book programs and decided that you are interested in starting a new program to fill an unmet need, the Prison Book Collective has compiled an excellent guide which you can find online (Prison Books Collective, n.d.). Do not, however, undertake to form a new program without serious consideration, as experience shows that word about your program (and the excitement over the promise of free books) is likely to exceed your capacity quite quickly, and significant groundwork for financial stability, volunteer coverage, and storage capacity will be necessary to ensure stability. It's hard work, but it's rewarding!

OTHER INDIRECT SERVICES

The libraries outside of jails, prisons, and detention centers can and do offer indirect services other than those listed above. Indirect services might include regularly sharing information about library programs and resources with prison librarians and programming staff, as well as the staff at parole and probation offices and sites for community reentry, so that it can be displayed in the programming areas of facilities or in reentry-service offices. Another indirect service might consist of providing distance reference and collection development support for existing programs inside of carceral facilities. Prison educational programs and education-by-correspondence programs may be particularly interested in supporting their students' work through regular access to reliable resources and scholarly materials. With the ban on Pell Grant eligibility for incarcerated people lifting in 2023, these programs will likely experience new growth and will benefit from additional support. Academic librarians may be especially well-positioned to work in coordination with higher education programs in carceral facilities and to expand academic resources to those patrons who are not involved in formal academic programs (Asher, 2006; Sorgert, 2014). External libraries with language specialists can also support programs in carceral institutions by offering translation services or resource support in languages other than English.

Interlibrary loan is a formalized service that can be extended to prison libraries (Asher, 2006). As Michelle Dillon notes, many prison libraries are seriously under-resourced. This means that prison librarians, when they exist at all, may have to develop their collections to serve the broadest interests possible and are unlikely to include more obscure, niche, or academic materials (Conrad, 2017). External libraries' interlibrary loan services and ILL partnerships with prison libraries can increase access, legitimate interests, open new possibilities for learning and can, as they did for lawyer and poet Reginald Dwayne Betts, provide an entry point for people who are incarcerated to develop new ways of being and creating in the world (Jacobs, 2020).

External libraries can also provide indirect services to people who are incarcerated by creating in-library resources that use live video technologies to facilitate conversations between library patrons and incarcerated people or to supplement existing visitation programs (Higgins, 2017; Jacobson, 2018). Higgins (2017) describes collaborative, multi-system programs that support video visitations and other forms of access by creating visitation areas in public library branches that connect to a video booth in Rikers Island. In the Telestory program, family members on each end of the video feed have the same book and are able to engage in co-literacy practices and establish connections through the process of reading together. Higgins outlines the steps to take to create a similar program, including assessing whether or not, and which, telecommunications are already used in the facility, working with library IT departments to create the necessary connections, creating step-by-step work plans with a partner in the facility (probably facility administration), and promoting the program to partners and political figures. Because many of the existing video interface services available in carceral facilities are prohibitively expensive to access, and many of the companies that advertise these services to carceral facilities tend to emphasize that they can replace (rather than supplement) in-person visitation, librarians involved in creating similar services should critically review their approach.

Public librarians are considering other digitally based options for increasing access. Among these is the possibility to provide access to the library's e-resources through tablets, when they exist in the carceral facility. Access to e-resources can communicate to people who are incarcerated that they are considered to be part of the public served by the library. Dauphin County Library System has piloted access to a curated collection of materials through tablets (see the chapter on technology for more information). Their pilot paves the way for this type of indirect service to be developed through other library systems. Librarians and information professionals considering this option should emphasize the established tenets of librarianship related to information access, counter attempts to utilize access as a punishment or a reward, maintain an awareness of the data-gathering practices of many tablet companies, and prioritize patron privacy as they develop this service. These services can supplement, but should never replace, in-person library and information services. Library and information services should always be used to increase, and never to decrease, access to information and the world outside of the carceral facility.

CONCLUSION

Libraries, librarians, and information professionals who are unable to provide direct library and information services in carceral facilities still have many opportunities to support information access for people who are incarcerated. Understanding the political and economic structures that shape information access, the existing collections in prison libraries, and any other resources that are available to incarcerated people in a given facility or type of facility can inform the implementation of indirect services. Identifying and supporting the work of partners who already provide programming in carceral facilities can increase incarcerated peoples' information access through that programming. Individual librarians can share information about what is and is not available in carceral facilities and propose possible partnerships to the library administration as they advocate for increased services.

Librarians and library systems can also go beyond existing programs and collections to created indirect services that are available to all individuals who are incarcerated in a given facility. Reference by mail services are a relatively affordable mode for individuals in carceral institutions to seek information that fits their own personal needs and interests. Because many prisons provide indigent packs (typically a few stamped envelopes, some pieces of paper, and possibly a writing utensil) for people who have extremely limited financial resources (sometimes defined as less than $5 a month), a by-mail reference service is often one of the most affordable modes of information access for incarcerated people who don't have any other recourse. This is especially true since incarcerated people across the country are often paid less than 50 cents an hour for their labor and are charged high markup prices for the materials in the commissary, and for communicating via phone calls or monitored electronic communication.

While libraries have created effective and innovative services to connect people who are incarcerated with both needed information and communal literacy practices (such as the Telestory program), it is not necessary to devise new programming or infrastructures in order to provide indirect services. Collection redistribution and support for the work of groups already providing book and materials access to incarcerated people are available and simple routes to increase access to people who are incarcerated. Keeping informed about the state of libraries and materials access in carceral institutions, and learning about how censorship on the part of prison administrators or across carceral systems shapes the information that crosses the barrier of the carceral wall present opportunities to advocate for and work alongside incarcerated people in order to maintain and increase their information access. Heeding the calls for support from groups and librarians who are already doing the work of expanding access to information and materials not only bolsters existing programs—it can also lead to new and generative ways of utilizing existing resources and services.

The next chapter moves from the context of incarceration to that of reentry. It draws from research on individuals' experiences of the reentry process, and the barriers they encountered, to identify existing and possible library programs that can be tailored to facilitate the process of reentry.

NOTE

1. Books to Prisoners [@B2PSeattle]. (2020). "This is a real problem in prison libraries across the country. In Washington, some of the prison libraries were open less than 1/3 of the expected time in 2018 due to staffing shortages, lockdowns, and other disruptions" (tweet). https://twitter.com/B2PSeattle/status/1216556222398156800.

REFERENCES

Appalachian Prison Book Project. 2019. "How Much Does It Cost to Read a Free Book on a Free Tablet?" https://appalachianprisonbookproject.org/2019/11/20/how-much-does-it-cost-to-read-a-free-book -on-a-free-tablet/.

Asher, C. 2006. "Interlibrary Loan Outreach to a Prison: Access Inside." *Journal of Interlibrary Loan, Document Delivery & Electronic Reserve* 16, no. 3: 27–33.

Austin, J., and M. Villa-Nicholas. 2019. "Information Provision and the Carceral State: Race and Reference beyond the Idea of the 'Underserved.'" *The Reference Librarian* 60, no. 4: 233–61.

Books to Prisoners. 2019. *Dear Books to Prisoners: Letters from the Incarcerated.* Tallinn, Estonia: Left Bank Books.

Books to Prisoners [@B2PSeattle]. 2020. https://twitter.com/B2PSeattle/status/1216556222398156800.

Conrad, S. 2017. *Prison Librarianship: Policy and Practice.* Jefferson, NC: McFarland.

Constant, P. 2019. "Access to Information Is Not an Easy Thing to Come by in Prisons." *The Seattle Review of Books*, April 24. https://seattlereviewofbooks.com/notes/2019/04/24/access-to-information-is-not-an -easy-thing-to-come-by-in-prisons/.

Couvillon, E., and A. Justice. 2016. "Letters from the Big House: Providing Consumer Health Reference for Texas Prisons." *Journal of Hospital Librarianship* 16, no. 4: 281–86.

deVuono-Powell, S., C. Schweidler, A. Walters, and A. Zohrabi, A. 2015. "Who Pays? The True Cost of Incarceration on Families." Ella Baker Center, Forward Together, Research Action Design. http:// whopaysreport.org/who-pays-full-report/.

Drabinski, E., and D. Rabina. 2015. "Reference Services to Incarcerated People: Part I, Themes Emerging from Answering Reference Questions from Prisons and Jails." *Reference and User Services Quarterly* 55, no. 1: 42–48.

Gaines, L. 2018. "Illinois Prison System Spent Less Than $300 on Books Last Year." Illinois Public Media News. https://will.illinois.edu/news/story/illinois-prison-system-spent-less-than-300-on-books-last -year.

Higgins, N. 2017. *Get Inside: Responsible Jail and Prison Library Service.* Quick Reads for Busy Librarians. Chicago: Public Library Association.

Jacobs, J. 2020. "With Books and New Focus, Mellon Foundation to Foster Social Equity." *New York Times*, June 30. www.nytimes.com/2020/06/30/arts/mellon-foundation-elizabeth-alexander.html.

Jacobson, E. 2018. "Reference by Mail to Incarcerated People." In *Reference Librarianship & Justice: History, Praxis, & Practice,* ed. K. Adler, I. Beilin, and E. Tewell, 151–59. Sacramento, CA: Library Juice.

James, E. R. 2020. "Prisoners Pay to Read." *American Libraries*. https://americanlibrariesmagazine.org/ blogs/the-scoop/prisoners-pay-to-read-prison-tablets/.

Lincoln, J. 2018. "Incarcerated Pennsylvanians Now Have to Pay $150 to Read. We Should All Be Outraged." *Washington Post*, October 11. www.washingtonpost.com/opinions/incarcerated-pennsylvanians-now -have-to-pay-150-to-read-we-should-all-be-outraged/2018/10/11/51f548b8-cbd9-11e8-a85c-0bbe30 c19e8f_story.html.

Onyenacho, T. 2020. "Prisons Are Banning Black History Books, and the Law Has Made It Possible." *Daily Kos.* www.dailykos.com/stories/1922523.

Orlofsky, V. L. 2019. "Windows, Not Walls: Defending Incarcerated People's Right to Read." Office for Intellectual Freedom of the American Library Association. www.oif.ala.org/oif/?p=18499.

O'Sullivan, J. 2019. "Corrections Officials' Claims of Contraband in Used Books Mailed to Washington Inmates Don't Add Up." *The Seattle Times.* www.seattletimes.com/seattle-news/politics/corrections -officials-claims-of-contraband-in-used-books-mailed-to-washington-inmates-doesnt-add-up/.

PEN America, J. 2019. "Literature Locked Up: How Prison Book Restriction Policies Constitute the Nation's Largest Book Ban." https://pen.org/wp-content/uploads/2019/09/literature-locked-up -report-9.24.19.pdf.

Prison Book Program. n.d. "Our Story." https://prisonbookprogram.org/about/our-story/.

———. n.d. "Other Books to Prisoners Programs." https://prisonbookprogram.org/resources/other-books
-to-prisoners-programs/.

Prison Books Collective. n.d. "How to Start a Prison Books Collective." https://prisonbooks.info/resources/
how-to-start-a-prison-books-collective/.

Prison Legal News v. Secretary, Florida Department of Corrections. 2018. Brief for Amici Curiae Prison Books
Clubs in Support of Petitioner, No. 18-355.

Prison Library Support Network. 2020. https://plsn-nyc.tumblr.com/.

Rabina, D., and E. Drabinski. 2015. "Reference Services to Incarcerated People: Part II, Sources and
Learning Outcomes." *Reference and User Services Quarterly* 55, no. 2: 123–31.

Raher, S. 2020. "The Company Store and the Literally Captive Market: Consumer Law in Prisons and Jails."
Hastings Race and Poverty Law Journal 17, no. 1: 3–86.

Schorb, J. 2014. *Reading Prisoners: Literature, Literacy, and the Transformation of American Punishment.* New
Brunswick, NJ: Rutgers University Press.

Sorgert, R. 2014. "Forgotten and Elusive Partners: Academic Libraries and Higher Education in Prison." *St.
Louis University Public Law Review* 33, no. 2: 429–41.

Thieme, N. 2019. "Georgia Prison Libraries Short on Books and Titles, AJC Analysis Finds." *Atlanta-Journal
Constitution.* www.ajc.com/news/crime--law/georgia-prison-libraries-short-books-and-titles-ajc
-analysis-finds/aKi5FxMIcLpYY92JoQBjPL/.

Urbina, I. 2014. "Detained Immigrants a Pool of Cheap Labor." *The Seattle Times.* www.seattletimes.com/
nation-world/detained-immigrants-a-pool-of-cheap-labor/.

CHAPTER 7

Reentry Support and Programming

R *eentry* is a popular term for the release of people from juvenile detentions, jails, and prisons and their relocation to areas and communities outside of the carceral facility (though, as chapter 3 makes clear, typically not outside of carceral surveillance).[1] Libraries tend to facilitate the process of reentry by drawing upon their existing programs, providing in-facility preparatory courses and materials, and raising public awareness about the effects and aftereffects of incarceration. This chapter draws upon the literature on the process of reentry to examine existing and possible ways that library and information professionals can assist people who are formerly incarcerated.

Reentry is a somewhat deceptive term because it implies a return to the community or society in which a person previously lived. As communities are impacted, over time, by gentrification, policing and incarceration, changes in resources, changes in technology, and other temporospatial changes, the people who are entering the community after years in jails or prisons may not return to the same place they left, even if they return to the same geographic area where they once lived (Middlemass, 2017; Wacquant, 2010). Middlemass draws upon interviews with people in the process of reentry who discuss their needs and the difficulties they face in managing both the state's expectations of parole and their own requirements for daily survival. Middlemass points to the fact that reentry for people with a traceable conviction history (specifically felonies, though this can be extended to people who had their accusations or convictions published in newspapers or posted online) is a back-end process of continued punishment and penalization. Wacquant points to the cyclical nature of oversight, the social and political disinvestment in communities where people who are more likely to be surveilled, policed, and incarcerated, and the movement of people back and forth between those communities and carceral facilities as an *"ongoing circulation between the two poles of a continuum of forced confinement"* (2010, 611). Moreover, the requirements of oversight bodies—principally with regard to probation, supervised release, and parole—imposed on those released from incarceration are often impossible to meet, or are often fractured or selectively enforced. The concept of reentry also fails to hold when considering people who are detained in immigration detention centers, who are often civilly detained when seeking entry to the United States. These critiques can be used as tools to guide library programming and information services related to people's movement from the environment of the carceral facility to the publics served (or as of yet unserved) by the library.

Due to its popularity in the literature of various disciplines, this chapter will continue to use the term *reentry*. The first section of this chapter offers a review of people's experiences of reentry, and reveals the realities of navigating state supervision. The next section discusses recent programming implemented by libraries that is related to reentry. The chapter closes by proposing ways in which libraries can better recognize the impact of incarceration by creating new programs, information sources, and approaches that simultaneously acknowledge the rigors of reentry while also seeking to push against the systems that move people from communities back into carceral facilities and flourish when reentry processes are unsuccessful.

REENTRY AS A LIVED EXPERIENCE

"It's like they want me to fail"
—participant in Middlemass's study of the reentry process for people with felony convictions. (2017, 121)

Reentry is not an easy undertaking. Even being detained for a short time can have a landslide effect on how people are treated when they are released from jail as they may lose their employment, housing, or other resources and potentially experience strained relationships with their families and social support networks (Cross, 2016; Freudenberg et al., 2005; Mears and Cochran, 2015; Raphael, 2011; Story, 2016). Experiences of reentry can vary in ways that are affected (or determined) by an individual's gender, race, age, and sexuality (Cross, 2016; Freudenberg et al., 2005, Greene, 2019; Maschi, Rees, and Klein, 2016), but similar themes with regard to resources and access arise across many personal accounts and a large body of research.

Middlemass's study of men and women with felony convictions reveals that political and social structures enable the systemic oppression of people who are followed by this type of conviction even after their release. Drawing from multiple interviews and ongoing engagements with people who accessed services at a nonprofit focused on reentry, Middlemass traces the compounding forces that create a post-incarceration system of control through the regulation of peoples' access to resources. First and foremost among the struggles that the people in Middlemass's study describe is access to employment (which is hindered by systemic and individual discrimination against people with felony convictions, by criminal background checks, and by moral character requirements for occupational certification and licensing). This is followed in importance by their difficulties in securing housing, food, and other basic resources (which are curtailed through federal and state public-housing legislation, regulations on access to health care, and state-by-state variations in lifetime bans on accessing food assistance programs). These themes arise time and time again in the literature on reentry (Freudenberg et al., 2005; Mears and Cochran, 2015; Raphael, 2011).

Even what are generally considered to be minor legal violations can have lasting effects on individuals' ability to access basic services (Californians for Safety and Justice, 2018; Middlemass, 2017). The consequences of this can be life-changing. For instance, the surveillance and policing of people who are undocumented can lead to their detainment or deportation (Californians for Safety and Justice, 2018). People with conviction histories may be unable to obtain drivers' licenses or access basic support care when needed

(Californians for Safety and Justice, 2018). Legal and social sanctions affect communities and families, and re-entrench the ongoing nature of racialized state violence (Californians for Safety and Justice, 2018). Reuben Jonathan Miller vividly describes the tensions that people in reentry, and their support networks, face:

> The history of punishment and black incarceration, of racism and the production of race, the whole history of crime and criminality haunt the people we've accused of crimes. It whispers in the ears of prospective employers and landlords, urging them to reject applications. And it whispers into the ears of grandmothers and girlfriends as they make life-or-death decisions on behalf of their loved ones, forcing them to withhold a couch to sleep on or risk eviction to help them because the state has labeled the people they care about criminals. (Miller, 2021, 6)

The lack of access to basic resources is compounded as people return from carceral systems under probation, parole, or supervised release or are released from immigrant detention centers under state supervision. Often, the requirements of the overseeing agencies conflict with the lived realities of people in the process of reentry. For example, people in reentry may be required to obtain legal employment, but often they only receive employment offers for low-skilled and low-paying jobs, which don't provide enough income to afford basic necessities (Freudenberg et al., 2005, Mears and Cochran, 2015; Middlemass, 2017; Raphael, 2011). In response to policies that penalize people with a felony or other conviction histories, "ban the box" campaigns have pushed for states and private employers to remove questions about criminal convictions from their applications (All of Us or None, n.d.; Middlemass, 2017; Stacy and Cohen, 2017). Removing the request for a conviction history from employment applications has made some difference in hiring practices, but in at least some instances this has been replaced by employers' assumptions about racialized criminality, assumptions that are reinforced by cycles of surveillance and policing (Stacy and Cohen, 2017). The removal of a question about criminal history on application materials does not prevent employers from personally asking applicants about their conviction histories or from administering criminal background checks (Stacy and Cohen, 2017). In order to address these barriers, grassroots campaigns and agencies have pushed for the removal of strict limitations on obtaining occupational certification, and have called for the legal removal of records of criminal convictions or the expunging of criminal records (Californians for Safety and Justice, 2018; Love, Gaines, and Osborne, 2017).

The barriers that people in reentry encounter play out along lines of intersectional oppression. Black, Indigenous, and women of color who have experienced interpersonal violence when not incarcerated often face the compounding effects of the trauma of incarceration, and may face further violence after they are released (Cross, 2016). Women may be less likely to receive the assistance they need to extricate themselves from dangerous situations, due to the qualifications required to receive assistance from organizations designed to support people experiencing interpersonal violence, and owing to the social stigma against people with conviction histories. In some cases, interpersonal violence compels women to break the conditions of their probation or parole in order to escape situations that are violent, and this can potentially lead to their re-incarceration and thus further exacerbate their trauma (Cross, 2016; Survived and Punished, n.d.).

LGBTQIA+ people face heightened levels of difficulty obtaining housing, including transitional housing (Maschi, Rees, and Klein, 2016). Often, housing is not LGBQIA+ or transgender-competent, thus further penalizing people who must live, due either to state supervision requirements or to a lack of financial resources, at in-house transitional programs upon their release. The severity of this varies by age, disability status, and health status (Maschi, Rees, and Klein, 2016) and is especially pronounced for Black transgender women (Greene, 2019). For LGBTQIA+ people, access to housing after incarceration can be limited due to homophobia in their own families and even in community organizations that are supposed to offer support to people upon their release (Maschi, Rees, and Klein, 2016). Additionally, access to in-prison programming (when and if it is available), including educational programming, is often foreclosed to LGBTQIA+ people while they are incarcerated under the carceral narrative of protection (Maschi, Rees, and Klein, 2016). During reentry, the social marginalization of some LGBTQIA+ people who have experienced incarceration can present another set of difficulties related to their ability to build community and access resources (Maschi, Rees, and Klein, 2016). The larger society's reliance on mainstream definitions of gender means that transgender people, and especially Black transgender women, who have often experienced traumatic violence while incarcerated, are forced to rely on social services that negate their identities and potentially put them in a position to experience ongoing confrontations related to their gender identities or to continuously navigate their gender as an aspect of reentry (Greene, 2019). When Black and Indigenous transgender women and transgender women of color respond to conditions that include ongoing confrontations and stressors by asserting themselves or by acting in self-defense, their actions are then read through racism and transphobia and used to remove them from programming and access to housing, leading to a life increasingly lived in public and subject to police surveillance and to possible breaches of state supervision requirements (Greene, 2019).

When their own families are available, able, and willing to support people in the process of reentry, family members may themselves face the penalizing aspects of their relative's parole or probation. Family members and roommates must be willing to submit to surveillance and possible searches of their property by parole and other agencies (Middlemass, 2017; Miller, 2021). This and other factors act as stressors that can impact the health and well-being of family members as they support people in reentry (Grieb et al., 2014). Family members exhibit great care in their ongoing support of incarcerated people and people recently released, but they may also feel obligated to act as support systems for recently incarcerated people due to the lack of other available support and the knowledge that surveillance and policing negatively impact the lives of people in reentry and increase the likelihood that they will be re-incarcerated (Grieb et al., 2014). The stress and health effects that supportive families experience may also be exacerbated by behavioral changes that have taken place in their relatives while incarcerated (Grieb et al., 2014).

Looking to research and community-level information about the lived realities of reentry provides library and information professionals with the background knowledge they need to create meaningful reentry-related programs. Library and information professionals can apply their awareness of some of the issues raised in this section to aspects of the services, including literacy services, within their own libraries. Individuals' experiences reveal oversights that might arise when planning library programs. For instance, a librarian or information professional conducting a job-seeking workshop might not be, but should be, aware of the ways in which types of convictions can limit possible professional pursuits, and that some people under state supervision are forbidden from associating with specific people or with all people with conviction histories. Some libraries have already made headway in this area, and are focusing on reentry as they create programs and resources to connect people in carceral facilities to their family and community on the outside and build infrastructural support for people in the process of reentry.

LIBRARIES AND REENTRY PROGRAMMING

Many of the programs that libraries already provide—such as technological support and employment workshops—can address the difficulties and barriers that people face during the process of reentry. Throughout the 2000s, libraries in the United States built upon the professional tenets of librarianship to create or expand programs that support people as they move through reentry and as they migrate to the United States. A 2007 *Public Libraries* article detailed the range of reentry-focused programs and information packets offered by public libraries:

- Creation and distribution of reentry guides and reentry packets
- Employment, financial preparation, and job development programs
- Legal services
- Traditional literacy-building programs (Dowling, 2007)

Several of the librarians in Dowling's article discussed the need to create connections to people while they were incarcerated as a way of welcoming them to the public library upon their release. In some instances, public librarians partnered with prison librarians to provide library-based programming inside of carceral facilities in order to connect people who were being released with the public library. These librarians provided reading-based programs to support connections between parents and their children (using facility-approved video or audio technology), attended job fairs in prisons to promote their library's materials and services, distributed paper materials or videos about the library that were made available or shown during the release process in jails or prisons, and offered reentry-based preparation classes inside of carceral facilities. The public librarians who provided library services inside of jails and prisons often drew upon their existing knowledge of the prison release process to identify potential partnerships between the public library and carceral facility staff, nonprofits and community groups concerned with reentry, and employers who might hire people with conviction histories (often referred to as "second chance" employers). The librarians also provided library collections and outreach to transitional housing and shelters (Dowling, 2007).

Most articles about the library's role in reentry are published in trade magazines and profile the efforts of various library systems. Highlighted libraries and programs include:

- The Brooklyn Public Library facilitates reentry-oriented courses in jails and coordinates free video visits with incarcerated people at public library locations (Witteveen, 2017).
- The Colorado State Library provides library services for people incarcerated in Colorado, including financial literacy programs created in coordination with Wells Fargo (Lilienthal, 2013).
- The Denver Public Library created the Free to Learn program in connection with transitional housing programs to develop job-seeking skills, including how to respond to questions about conviction histories. The program gave classes specifically related to reentry, provided resource guides, and worked to ensure that classes attended in the public library counted toward parole

and probation requirements for people in reentry (Cottrell, 2017; Lilienthal, 2013; Morris, 2013).

- The Free Library of Philadelphia provides an in-jail library collection and facilitates a program for incarcerated parents to read to their children during visitations (Witteveen, 2017).
- The Hennepin County (MN) Library has a Freedom Ticket program focused specifically on reentry support and raising public awareness of the realities of incarceration (Cottrell, 2017; Witteveen, 2017).
- The Multnomah County (OR) Library provides in-facility book groups and oversees courses related to the National Career Readiness Certificate program (Witteveen, 2017).
- The New York Public Library system coordinates with the Brooklyn Public Library and Queens Public Library to provide in-person library services at Rikers Island, oversees reference by mail services for people who are incarcerated, publishes a reentry guide, conducts library outreach to shelters, and has created and implemented numerous early-literacy programs connecting people who are incarcerated and their children through recordings and book distribution (Cottrell, 2017; Higgins, 2013; Lilienthal, 2013).
- Salt Lake County Library Services provides a life skills course inside of the carceral facility and coordinates library card sign-ups or fine reductions as part of its reentry-based services (Witteveen, 2017).
- The San Diego County Library provided monthlong trainings on employment and job-seeking and coordinated connections to library resources through outreach to Parole and Community Team (PACT) meetings (meetings that people who are paroled from California prisons must attend) (Lilienthal, 2013).

IN-DEPTH PROFILE: INTERVIEW WITH DANIEL MARCOU, HENNEPIN COUNTY OUTREACH LIBRARIAN

Hennepin County's reentry services are upheld as a model for designing services that connect people inside of correctional facilities to public libraries, and many of their ongoing services have been developed by Daniel Marcou, an outreach librarian for the Hennepin County Library (Minneapolis, MN). He has provided library service and programs for incarcerated adults and their families since 2006. Previously, he was employed in a variety of public, special, and academic library settings, including positions as a consumer health librarian and a public library director. In 2009 he was recognized as a Mover & Shaker by *Library Journal* for promoting public libraries as a reentry resource for people leaving corrections facilities. (More information about his work can be found at www.librarian.info.)

Q: How did the program begin?

A: The Hennepin County Library began bringing books to the Hennepin County Adult Corrections Facility in 1971. We began regular visits with direct library service in 1976. That history of almost fifty years of partnership between the library and the facility is significant and allowed us to develop a strong relationship of trust and understanding. I'm able to offer the library programs and service that I do now because of a strong foundation built over time and the positive work done by the librarians who had the job before me.

If you're just starting an outreach program for a corrections facility, patience and adaptability are key. Take the time to build trust with the facility.

Q: How has the service evolved over time?

A: The service began as an outreach opportunity to provide recreational reading materials at the facility. We still do that; however, we have developed additional programs and resources that specifically focus on reentry needs, as well as families affected by incarceration.

Q: Have changes in the service taken place due to the library administration, or to the changing needs of people who were formerly incarcerated, and so on?

A: We have been very fortunate that both the facility and the library administration have supported library outreach to corrections since the service began. The Friends of Hennepin County Library also have shown their strong support through their ongoing funding of our programs. We would not be able to do the work we do without the trust and understanding of these three very different organizations. This support has been ongoing for a very long time, but recently, there's been an even stronger commitment and focus on reducing disparities in the community and the role that the library can play in addressing them.

Q: How does your perspective on reentry inform the work you do?

A: The biggest challenge in my work, and incarceration as a whole, is the revolving door of recidivism. When I started this job, my background had been in a variety of public libraries where you get to know the people who regularly visit your library and catch up with them if they've been away for a while. After the first six months on the job at the facility, I had my first direct experience with seeing the effects of recidivism. I had gotten to know some residents and enjoyed talking with them, so it was an eye-opening moment of awareness to be happy to see someone but then realize that they were back in jail. After that experience, I realized that we needed to do more than just provide recreational reading material, because our community libraries were doing so many good things that could help people leaving corrections facilities make positive changes in their lives. I decided I wanted to make the residents more aware of that.

After that experience, I developed the Freedom Ticket program to promote the library as a reentry resource. Public libraries made a huge difference in my life as I grew up because I didn't like school. As a kid, my real school was the neighborhood branch of the library. So I wanted to take some of that experience and develop reentry-related programs and resources to make people leaving corrections facilities more aware of what libraries could offer them, and to encourage them to use the library to make positive changes in their lives. We provide information about library and community resources in the Going Home guide, and there are programs at the facility like employment workshops, book discussions, and author visits that tie into a reentry theme.

Q: Reentry support often involves the existing resources and programs in the library. How did you get other library staff on board and informed?

A: The Hennepin County Library's staff and administration have been very supportive of our outreach to corrections facilities. My coworker Heather Fisch and I have felt that one of our roles, in addition to providing library service at the facility, is to create opportunities for awareness and advocacy of criminal justice issues in the community, including within our library system. We have offered public film screenings and author visits, we've coordinated community library staff to facilitate our Read to Me program at the facility, provided staff trainings through a play based on facility residents' stories, hosted panel discussions on homelessness, and provided an author visit by Maya Schenwar, the author of *Locked Down, Locked Out*. If community library staff have a better understanding of the complex issues that lead to incarceration and the challenges after release, they will be better informed and more empathetic in providing library service to people who have left corrections facilities, and their families.

We rely on community library staff to send us books and magazines that we use at the facility, but more importantly, we depend on them to provide reentry help to people after they leave the facility. In some ways, we see our work inside the facility as a bridge to connect residents to their neighborhood library. If they have a positive experience at the facility library, then they are more likely to visit their community library with their families or to get help with a job search or some other reentry need.

Q: Have you noticed changes in the relationship between the library and the communities targeted for policing and incarceration (Black, Indigenous, and people of color, LGBTQIA+ people, and people living in poverty) as you've continued your reentry support over time?

A: The Hennepin County Library staff have been very innovative across our library system to develop restorative justice practices with youth, community engagement with people experiencing homelessness, and LGBTQIA+ programs and resources. This focus has strengthened the library's relationship with the community and demonstrated that libraries are places where all are welcome.

In library outreach to corrections facilities, it can be challenging to know details about community library usage after release. The intent to use the library is very clear—based on program evaluations, we generally see an increase of 30 percent or more in library use from before incarceration to the intention of using the library after release. Assistance with employment needs is one of the primary reasons people tell us how they plan to use the library. We've seen a similar percentage increase in the people who have participated in our Read to Me family literacy program and who say that they intend to visit the library with their children upon their release. It's important to be clear that our statistics reflect intent because actual numbers are very difficult to gather, and I've found that with even the best of intentions, life after release can very quickly become complicated by factors that people might not be able to control. If you're working three part-time jobs, for example, you might want to take your kids to the library for books, but just not have the time.

In the past three years, we've tried very hard to provide programs for the public at our community libraries that promote advocacy and awareness of criminal justice issues.

We've had authors like Susan Burton, Shaka Senghor, and Howard Zehr talk about their books and have held screenings of films like *Mothers of Bedford*, *Tribal Justice*, and *Milwaukee 53206* with the filmmakers. We try to offer these programs at both the corrections facilities and our Minneapolis Central Library. Based on evaluations, we see that these types of programs have increased awareness and advocacy related to criminal justice issues, and we also note that people view the public library as a safe space to learn and talk about bigger societal issues.

The New Jersey State Library has created a scalable program for reentry support in libraries. The program, named Fresh Start @ Your Library, is focused on employment and reentry (New Jersey State Library, 2020a) and is funded by the Institute of Museum and Library Services in coordination with the New Jersey Department of Labor and Workforce Development and the New Jersey State Parole Board. This grant-funded, multi-library, statewide project positions libraries as "Reconnection Centers" which can "conduct individualized assessments and provide referrals to employment opportunities, library resources and classes, and occupational skills training" (New Jersey State Library, 2020b; Fresh Start @ Your Library, 2020). The grant also funds the cost of GED exams for fifty participants, includes financing for GED preparatory materials, and allows libraries to focus their programming on employment opportunities for people in reentry (New Jersey State Library, 2020b).

The Queens Public Library hosts both established and innovative programming for people preparing for reentry and people who are recently released from carceral facilities. These programs often span the walls of a jail or prison to create connections between the programming inside and the library's resources that will be available to people after they are released. The library's "see you on the outside" reentry program, which provides professional support to incarcerated people and people in reentry, explicitly links these resources. It distributes a thirty-page reentry-specific guide, which covers library basics and introduces resources that may be useful to people in reentry. These resources include programs related to employment and health, as well as digital literacy and recent immigration, two areas profiled in more depth later in this chapter. The guide presents specifically local resources that can be utilized alongside the NYPL *Connections* reentry resource. As a member of the Queens County Reentry Taskforce, the Queens Public Library advocates for people in reentry and works to increase the resources available to people who are recently released. The library's reentry services are responsive to the circumstances of reentry, as is evident in its innovative work to support people released during the coronavirus pandemic. The library has tried to counter the limited access to resources and subsequent social isolation experienced by people after their release by partnering with a local legal group—the Queens Defenders—to supply recently released people with smartphones, data plans, and technology training which can facilitate their access to the library's resources and the larger world.

Recent ALA white papers have underscored existing programs that support the work of reentry and work to assist people who have recently migrated to the United States. Ringrose's report, "Libraries & Reentry: The Importance of Public Spaces, Technologies, and Community to Formerly Incarcerated Patrons," foregrounds librarians as advocates for people in the process of reentry. It frames the need for reentry services in a review of the reach of mass incarceration and its economic toll at the personal and social level (Ringrose, 2020). The report identifies barriers to library access, including the requirement of a physical address to obtain a library card and library fines. The report promotes examples of programs that work to support people in reentry and their families, including early literacy development programming, employing embedded social workers, providing job development programs and mentoring, and voter registration drives for formerly incarcerated people. It concludes with a set of action items for librarians, formerly incarcerated patrons, and policy makers.

The ALA document "Library Programs and New Americans: A White Paper" (2019) is not specifically designed for people who have been detained in immigrant detention facilities, but its agenda to create a set of best practices for library work in the field means that it is pertinent to this chapter (American Library Association, 2019). The white paper opens with a review of the services libraries provide which are relevant to the needs and interests of "new Americans," which the paper defines as "people who might consider themselves new arrivals in the U.S. and anyone who is a non-native English language speaker," including "immigrants, refugees, and displaced persons" (2019, 2, 4). These services include assistance with the legal process of immigration, financial literacy, and language learning. The paper emphasizes that libraries also build better services to the areas they serve when they support local immigrants through programing and collection development.

Drawing upon a knowledge of existing programs, the white paper includes a literature review, a survey of several existing library programs, and recommendations for best practices. In addition to the programs already mentioned, the paper emphasizes the importance people who have migrated to the U.S. place on developing digital literacy skills and the need for programs that are accessible to all patrons, including patrons whose primary language is a language other than English. The paper lists myriad ways that new American patrons use the library. It moves from conversations with library professionals about their desire for increased training to providing a list of actionable steps for creating programs that can endure and collaborating with local community groups.

In addition to considering system-wide approaches for services to people in reentry and people who have migrated to the United States, libraries in communities large and small have worked to create and distribute reentry-related information. Some libraries, like the Seattle Public Library, have created landing pages on their websites that are specifically focused on resources for formerly incarcerated people or for the family members of people who have been incarcerated (Seattle Public Library, 2020a, 2020b). The Washington State Library's Institutional Library Services (ILS) program has partnered with public libraries across the state to provide people who are released from prison with public library cards before their release (see chapter 5 for more information about this collaboration). The state library's Institutional Library Services Department has also created an online reentry guide that was developed in response to requests and questions from currently and formerly incarcerated people, and draws upon existing in-print resources that are used in physical libraries in carceral facilities. The ILS program hopes to make a digital version of the guide available on technologies that are being piloted in Washington State prisons. (The guide is available at https://wiki.sos.wa.gov/ILSRe-entry/.)

In-facility education programs have been especially hard hit by legislation that reduced funding and access for incarcerated people. Although many studies link educational attainment to other resources that support people in the process of reentry, the people interviewed in Middlemass's 2017 study noted that education is often an unattainable goal as they focus instead on employment and accessing basic resources. The individuals in Middlemass's study stated that many jails and prisons offer certificates for attending classes and programming, which are useful in parole hearings but carry little or no weight upon release (2017). Access to academic programs while incarcerated, including high school and college programs, may increase the chances that individuals are able to obtain employment and push against the stereotypes of people with criminal convictions that they encounter after they are released.

The lack of internet access and other difficulties that individuals face in doing academic coursework while incarcerated have shaped the types of courses that colleges offer to people who are incarcerated (Sanford and Foster, 2006; Tanaka and Cooper, 2020). Academic libraries can support academic programs inside of carceral facilities by creating methods to do distance research (such as the reference by mail program described in depth in chapter 6). Because very few prisons have an academic library collection, academic librarians can share their material resources to develop small academic collections inside of carceral facilities, or they can work with prison librarians and educators who regularly access the prison to provide interlibrary loan systems to support their work (Sanford and Foster, 2006). When possible, academic librarians can support education programs inside of facilities by curating materials for preloaded, internal servers that can be accessed through tablets or other technologies for education courses (Tanaka and Cooper, 2020).

With the upcoming reintroduction of student financial support for higher education (through the Second Chance Pell grant), access to higher education has become a greater possibility for people who are incarcerated or in reentry. Even prior to this, colleges across the country have orchestrated academic support and mentoring for people impacted by incarceration. These programs, often based in individual community or 4-year colleges, can benefit from the research skills and expertise librarians and information professionals bring to navigating institutions, assessing the qualifications required for professional certification, and identifying relevant resources. In some instances, academic librarians or library and information science programs may be able to partner with community groups focused on reentry to identify and align existing resources with the expressed needs and desires of people in the process of reentry. (One example of this type of resource is the Root & Rebound "My Education, My Freedom" toolkit, 2018.)

ENVISIONING OTHER AVENUES OF ENGAGEMENT

Existing library programs related to reentry tend to focus on employment readiness programming and on locating resources. These are needed areas of support, but people in reentry have pointed to factors that foreclose possibilities. Library and information professionals can draw from the lived knowledge of people in reentry to create more robust, meaningful, and informed library programs. In some instances, this may mean that librarians and information professionals create shared resources that extend the programming that libraries already provide. In others, it may involve creating innovative programming, partnerships with groups focused on the well-being of people in reentry, and programs to support people in reentry while raising community awareness of the difficulties they face. The Information Justice Institute (IJI), based at Chicago State University and funded through the Institute of Museum and Library Services, provides a model for this approach (2021). As libraries and information professionals design programs and support services that incorporate the knowledge that some library patrons have in reentry, they should focus on ways that the library can share its resources, including financial resources, by providing financial support for speakers from community groups and formerly incarcerated people.

Some areas that librarians might explore for programming include community engagement, digital literacy, legal resources and clinics, presentations on navigating reentry resources, and programming related to raising community awareness about information access for incarcerated people.

Community engagement-related programming is one way to communicate to people in the process of reentry that the library is aware of how convictions and incarceration shape their experiences. Community engagement runs the gamut from information about voting rights for people with specific types of conviction histories, to programming related to local campaigns and political structures that shape incarceration. Speakers can be invited from groups that are specifically focused on the areas of concern examined earlier in this chapter. For example, inviting people from groups involved with the "ban the box" campaign or from groups that coordinate reentry resources to speak in the library or at transitional housing or programs where people who are in reentry and mandated to attend can raise public awareness of these groups' activities and foster important community conversations about experiences of reentry. Programming in the library can communicate librarians' awareness of the challenges involved in reentry, while programming outside of the library offers a chance for librarians to better network with other groups and institutions in the community, and communicates a recognition of some of the restrictions that people in reentry might face.

People in the process of reentry have recently been released from facilities that restricted their access to materials and information and severely limited their access to technology, and typically afforded them no internet access whatsoever. There is some clandestine access to technologies inside of carceral facilities, but the information about "the rate of digital technology penetration in prisons, and if and how incarcerated individuals are using them" is extremely limited (Magassa, 2020, 11). Reisdorf and Rikard (2018) have focused on digital technologies that can facilitate reentry, framing this as "digital rehabilitation." Digital literacy is crucial because technology has become the primary mediator for many aspects of life, such as connecting to family and friends, education, employment and job-seeking, obtaining state identification, and shopping (Magassa, 2020). Magassa's work to establish a definition for everyday digital literacy foregrounds his study of the actual digital literacy levels and practices of people in reentry. Using a questionnaire designed to assess the everyday digital literacy practices of formerly incarcerated people, Magassa found that the people in the study were aware of technologies, but faced difficulties in most areas of everyday digital literacy practices.

Digital literacy programming for formerly incarcerated people needs to be designed with consideration of the realities of reentry in mind. Ogbonnaya-Ogburu, Toyama, and Dillahunt conducted a case study of digital literacy programming (2019). In this study, interviews with formerly incarcerated people about their digital practices informed a curriculum for an ongoing digital literacy program. In practice, though, the researchers found that restrictions related to transportation and parole requirements, individuals' varying familiarity with technologies, and the technologies they had access to often conflicted with the planned program. Additionally, the authors found that participants were cautious about using social media because of parole requirements, which limited their familiarity with the social networking sites that are used for job-seeking, such as LinkedIn. The authors conclude their article by recommending that these concerns are centered in the creation of digital literacy programming for people in reentry (2019).

Partnerships between libraries and groups that provide legal resources are a needed aspect of reentry-related programming. Legal clinics might focus on expunging records, navigating published accounts of accusations or convictions, obtaining information about public figures or institutions accused of wrongdoing, and identifying possible instances of discrimination in employment or housing. Legal clinics can also focus on some of the underlying factors that can leave people more vulnerable to future incarceration. For instance, legal clinics could focus on navigating bureaucratic processes such as obtaining local- or state-issued identification without easy access to some of the paperwork required to obtain it. Legal clinics might also concern community level counter-surveillance or legal protections around practices such as filming or otherwise documenting the behavior of state supervision officers or departments. They might address topics that leave people more vulnerable to scrutiny by government officials; for example, a legal clinic on changing name and gender markers for transgender and gender-nonconforming people (Austin, 2019). All of these clinics can be provided in collaboration with lawyers or grassroots legal projects and in coordination with law libraries, which might provide resource guides or introductory materials that can help the attendees utilize their collections.

Programs related to navigating reentry can extend beyond employment support and job-seeking to include information from formerly incarcerated people about their own processes of reentry. Offering paid speaking engagements to formerly incarcerated people can help to raise public awareness about the realities of incarceration and reentry, and may build public support for ongoing programming and services through the library. Formerly incarcerated people can also act as ambassadors to others in reentry by introducing them to networks, nonprofits, and other local resources that offer support to people who are navigating reentry. Some topics might include relationships with families and working with public defenders and other legal representatives. This type of programming can be expanded to focus on the family and social support networks of individuals in the process of reentry, connecting the members of these networks to library resources and materials that might help to reduce the stress they experience as they assist their loved ones and friends during the reentry process.

A final area of reentry programming that needs to be more fully explored by libraries is the public's growing awareness and critical discussions on incarceration and the alternatives to punitive practices. Restorative and transformative justice programs and approaches are being implemented in some libraries as they try to find alternative ways to address the harm, disruption, disagreements, and injuries that can occur among library staff, between staff and patrons, and between patrons (Jackson, 2021). Restorative and transformative approaches vary, with the word *restorative* often used to imply that conditions are brought back to the point they were prior to the harm occurring, and the word *transformative* encompassing a recognition that every starting place for addressing harm is situated in historical and ongoing oppression.

These practices are rooted in Black and Indigenous feminisms. They are alternatives to addressing harms through policing, based in lived recognition that policing and incarceration either did not solve the harms or that people who experience systemic oppression can be put at risk by the presence of police (Dixon and Piepzna-Samarasinha, 2020). Librarians and information professionals can draw from these approaches to create programming and host authors and grassroots organizations to share information about their approaches to harm, conflict, and injuries and how these might be addressed without calling upon law enforcement. In addition to this, using alternative forms of accountability and group decision-making can change the culture of a library system, shift the power differentials between staff and patrons, provide opportunities for greater understanding of the situated nature of people's actions and motivations, reduce similarities between the practices of carceral institutions and libraries, and create a more welcoming library environment (Austin, 2020). A wealth of information about the philosophical foundations and practices of restorative and transformative justice is available at Transform-Harm.org, a resource created by Mariame Kaba.

Much of this book has focused on critical perspectives on mass incarceration, the history of incarceration and the racialized nature of policing, the use of technology to surveil Black, Indigenous, and people of color, and the ways that limiting access to information is used to further state oppression. Holding conversations with and programs for people who are in the process of reentry, those who have experienced incarceration, and also for people who don't directly experience the negative impacts of incarceration can provide librarians and staff opportunities to build awareness about the function of incarceration in the United States and its antecedents. Librarians can address these topics specifically through the lens of librarianship and information access—by holding skill-building and awareness workshops about library services to people in jails and prisons, technology and internet access for people who are incarcerated, censorship in jails and prisons, how to access information about immigration detention centers or juvenile detainment, facilitating letter-writing events for people interested in being pen pals with people who are incarcerated, or working with Books to Prisoners groups to increase community awareness about existing programs. This type of programming may bring librarians, staff, and patrons together to envision new ways of thinking about safety, survival, and consequences that incorporate the realities of systemic oppression with instances of interpersonal harm.

As libraries expand and deepen their existing programming to bring in more knowledge about reentry and the barriers to reentry—by, for instance, including information about felony convictions and certification access in job development workshops, or by incorporating background knowledge on how incarceration might shape recently released persons' lack of familiarity with modern technologies—library and information professionals will need to be able to critically evaluate how their work exists in relation to carceral processes. By critically engaging with incarceration and reentry as lived experiences, library and information professionals can tailor the information they provide to better fit the on-the-ground needs and interests of people in reentry. This might bring libraries to reassess their policies which require documentation to obtain a library card. If a library requires the verification of a stable address, librarians may want to advocate for a system-wide approach to creating library cards for people who are unable to provide the required documentation. If the library requires a state-issued identification card, librarians might advocate for identification that is issued by jails or prisons to be included in the list of acceptable identifications.

Community reentry guides and other resource guides can also be informed by a knowledge of the ways that difficulties in reentry create specific needs. Reentry guides can include information that responds to the experiences of people in reentry and their families. This means that in addition to providing information about how to access basic services, reentry guides should include information about resources related to interpersonal and domestic violence, LGBTQIA+ resources, information about the gender-inclusiveness of transitional housing and other programs, information about services for the children of incarcerated parents, and other topics. Libraries may choose to create or distribute a community resource guide along with a separate guide or flier that specifically lists library-generated programs that are focused on or are relevant to reentry. New York Public Library's *Connections* (2021) guide serves as a model for locating comprehensive resources related to reentry. Making information related to incarceration and reentry available in the library is one of the ways that libraries can tacitly communicate their awareness of the impact of incarceration on the communities they serve.

Library and information professionals also need to be knowledgeable about the larger context in which they create and implement their programs. Some programs might simultaneously facilitate connections between people who are incarcerated and the public while also normalizing processes of incarceration or adhering to flows of power that serve the carceral facility more than the individual. Take, for example, the introduction of video visitation programs between libraries and people who are incarcerated. While these programs facilitate connection and communication between people who are incarcerated and family or community members who may not otherwise be able to visit them in the physical location of the jail or prison, video visitation is often advertised by corporations as a way that carceral facilities can actively diminish visitor access to their facilities. Implementing these, and similar programs, requires librarians and information professionals to think through the nuances of providing access through technology without curtailing access through other venues. By framing video visitations as an additional way of maintaining contact, rather than as a replacement of in-person visitations, librarians can advocate for people who are incarcerated and assist family members as they maintain connections that might sustain their relationships during incarceration, establishing a strong foundation of support during the process of reentry.

CONCLUSION

This chapter has covered reentry-related programming from a critically informed perspective, building upon the understanding of structural issues in probation, supervised release, and parole established in chapter 3 to incorporate the lived experiences of people in reentry. It offers examples of existing and possible reentry-related programming that can take place across a variety of libraries and other information access points. Positioning programming within a large context of surveillance, policing, and incarceration reveals that there are many opportunities for libraries to expand their existing programs to better support people in reentry, their families, and their social support networks.

Reentry services might be focused on existing services, involve envisioning new services, or may call for library or institution-wide reconfiguration to better address the information needs and desires of people who have been detained in immigrant detention centers, incarcerated, or subjected to other forms of state surveillance. Shifting programming to incorporate information about reentry and providing reentry resources as physical fliers in the library and as part of a library's virtual presence are ways that librarians and information professionals can tacitly acknowledge the scale of incarceration and its impact on their patron bases. Envisioning new services that are specifically designed to support people in the process of immigration and reentry is a way the library can begin to address services that have traditionally been devalued in the history of the profession. Doing this creates opportunities for growth, change, and dynamic programming.

Alongside the previous two chapters, this chapter has offered insights into how libraries can better serve people who are or have been incarcerated and those impacted by incarceration. The next chapter steps back from possible courses of action for services to offer some practical approaches and considerations when beginning to establish such services within carceral institutions.

NOTE

1. In most popular discourse, people are "released" from immigrant detention centers (they may also be "released" from carceral facilities into ICE custody).

REFERENCES

All of Us or None. n.d. "About." Ban the Box. http://bantheboxcampaign.org/about/.

American Library Association. 2019. "Library Programs and New Americans: A White Paper." American Library Association, New Knowledge Organization.

Austin, J. 2019. "Name and Gender Marker Legal Clinics at the Public Library: A Better Practices Guide." https://jeanieaustincom.files.wordpress.com/2019/08/name-gender-marker-legal-clinics-at-the-public-library-.pdf.

Austin, J. 2020. "Restorative Justice as a Tool to Address the Role of Policing and Incarceration in the Lives of Youth in the United States." *Journal of Librarianship & Information Science* 52, no. 1: 106-20.

Californians for Safety and Justice. 2018. "Repairing the Road to Redemption in California." https://safeandjust.org/interactivereport/repairing-the-road-to-redemption-in-california/.

Cottrell, M. 2017. "Keeping Inmates on the Outside: Libraries Offer Services and Support to Ease Prisoner Reentry." *American Libraries* 48, no. 1-2: 48-55.

Cross, C. 2016. "Reentering Survivors: Invisible at the Intersection of the Criminal Legal System and the Domestic Violence Movement." *Berkeley Journal of Gender, Law & Justice* 31, no. 1: 60-120.

Dixon, E., and L. L. Piepzna-Samarasinha. 2020. "Introduction." In *Beyond Survival: Strategies and Stories from the Transformative Justice Movement*, ed. Dixon and Piepzna-Samarasinha. Chico, CA: AK Press.

Dowling, B. 2007. "Public Libraries and the Ex-Offender." *Public Libraries* 46, no. 6: 44-48.

Fresh Start @ your Library, 2020. Fresh Start Resource Center. www.freshstartlibrary.com.

Freudenberg, N., J. Daniels, M. Crum, T. Perkins, and B. E. Richie. 2005. "Coming Home from Jail: The Social and Health Consequences of Community Reentry for Women, Male Adolescents, and Their Families and Communities." *American Journal of Public Health* 95, no. 10: 1725-36.

Greene, J. T. 2019. "Categorical Exclusions: How Racialized Gender Regulation Reproduces Reentry Hardship." *Social Problems* 66: 548-63.

Grieb, S. M. D., A. Crawford, J. Fields, H. Smith, R. Harris, and P. Matson. 2014. "'The Stress Will Kill You': Prisoner Reentry as Experienced by Family Members and the Urgent Need for Support Services." *Journal of Healthcare for the Poor and Underserved* 25, no. 3: 1183-1200.

Higgins, N. 2013. "Family Literacy on the Inside." *Public Libraries* 52, no. 1: 30-35.

Information Justice Institute (IJI). 2021. www.csu.edu/macs/infostudies/centers.htm.

Jackson, S. 2021. "Restorative Libraries: Restorative Justice Practices and How to Implement Them." *Library Journal* 46, no. 4: 26-29.

Lilienthal, S. M. 2013. "Prison and Public Libraries: Programming for Prisoners - Current and Former - Helps Fight Recidivism." *Library Journal* 138, no. 2: 26-32.

Love, M., J. Gaines, and J. Osborne. 2017. "Forgiving & Forgetting in American Justice: A 50-State Guide to Expungement and Restoration of Rights." Collateral Consequences Resource Center.

Magassa, L. 2020. "I am not computer savvy." A look into the everyday digital literacy levels of formerly incarcerated people using a novel holistic digital literacy framework. [Doctoral dissertation]. University of Washington Scholarworks. https://digital.lib.washington.edu/researchworks/bitstream/handle/1773/46493/MAGASSA_washington_0250E_21999.pdf?sequence=1&isAllowed=y.

Maschi, T., J. Rees, and E. Klein. 2016. "'Coming Out' of Prison: An Exploratory Study of LGBT Elders in the Criminal Justice System." *Journal of Homosexuality* 63, no. 9: 1277-95.

Mears, D. P., and J. C. Cochran. 2015. "The Reentry Experience and Reentry Challenges." In *Prisoner Reentry in the Era of Mass Incarceration*. Thousand Oaks, CA: Sage.

Middlemass, K. 2017. *Convicted and Condemned: The Politics and Policies of Prisoner Reentry*. New York: New York University Press.

Miller, R. J. 2021. *Halfway Home: Race, Punishment, and the Afterlife of Mass Incarceration*. New York: Little, Brown.

Morris, J. 2013. "Free to Learn: Helping Ex-Offenders with Reentry." *Public Library Quarterly* 32, no. 2: 119–23.

New Jersey State Library. 2020a. "Reconnecting Returning Citizens." www.njstatelib.org/services_for _libraries/innovative-initiatives/fresh-start-your-library/.

———. 2020b. Media kit. www.njstatelib.org/services_for_libraries/innovative-initiatives/fresh-start-your -library/media-kit/.

New York Public Library. 2021. *Connections*. www.nypl.org/sites/default/files/connections_2021.pdf.

Ogbonnaya-Ogburu, I. F., K. Toyama, and T. R. Dillahunt. 2019. "Towards an Effective Digital Literacy Intervention to Assist Returning Citizens with Job Search." Conference on Human Factors in Computing Systems.

Raphael, S. 2011. "Incarceration and Prisoner Reentry in the United States." *Annals of the American Academy of Political and Social Science* 635: 192–215.

Reisdorf, B. C., and R. V. Rikard. 2018. "Digital Rehabilitation: A Model of Reentry into the Digital Age." *American Behavioral Scientist* 62, no. 9: 1273–90.

Ringrose, K. 2020. "Libraries & Reentry: The Importance of Public Spaces, Technologies, and Community to Formerly Incarcerated Patrons." American Library Association Policy Perspectives, 7.

Root & Rebound. 2018. "My Education, My Freedom: A Toolkit for Formerly Incarcerated and System-Impacted Students Pursuing Education in California." www.rootandrebound.org/resources/my -education-my-freedom/.

Sanford, R., and J. E. Foster. 2006. "Reading, Writing, and Prison Education Reform? The Tricky and Political Process of Establishing College Programs for Prisoners: Perspectives from Program Developers." *Equal Opportunities International* 25, no. 7: 599–610.

Seattle Public Library. 2020a. "Resources for Kids and Families Impacted by Incarceration." www.spl.org/ books-and-media/books-and-ebooks/staff-picks-for-kids/resources-for-kids-and-families-impacted -by-incarceration.

———. 2020b. "Resources for the Formerly Incarcerated." www.spl.org/programs-and-services/civics-and -social-services/resources-for-the-formerly-incarcerated.

Stacy, C., and M. Cohen. 2017. "Ban the Box and Racial Discrimination." The Urban Institute. www.urban .org/research/publication/ban-box-and-racial-discrimination.

Story, B. (Director). 2016. *The Prison in Twelve Landscapes* (motion picture). Ratface Films.

Survived and Punished. n.d. "Criminalizing Domestic Violence." https://survivedandpunished.org/ criminalizing-survival-curricula/.

Tanaka, K., and D. Cooper. 2020. "Advancing Technological Equity for Incarcerated College Students: Examining the Opportunities and Risks." Ithaka S+R. https://sr.ithaka.org/publications/advancing -technological-equity-incarcerated-college-students/.

Transform Harm. 2020. https://transformharm.org.

Wacquant, L. 2010. "Prisoner Reentry as Myth and Ceremony." *Dialectical Anthropology* 34: 605–20.

Witteveen, A. 2017. "Prisons & Publics: Public Libraries Are Providing Service to the Incarcerated and Their Families in an Effort to Ease Reentry." *Library Journal* 142, no. 3: 33–36.

CHAPTER 8

Building Institutional Support and Getting Started

There are tensions between creating critically informed library services for people who are incarcerated and the goals of carceral institutions. Creating new programs and services requires an understanding of how carceral systems operate, the requirements and difficulties present in forming partnerships with carceral systems, and the need to prioritize the information access of people who are incarcerated. Generating new programs may also necessitate obtaining buy-in from one's own library system in order to obtain funding for collections or programs, to create reliable indirect services, or to initiate meaningful in-library programming related to incarceration and reentry. The process of establishing partnerships between carceral facilities, the people providing resources in carceral facilities (educators and prison librarians), and academic, public or other libraries is central to increasing the information access of people who are incarcerated.

Many librarians already provide some type of programming or service for people impacted by incarceration as part of their everyday tasks. For instance, many libraries receive letters from people who are incarcerated, yet few have established formal systems for responding to information requests that originate in jails, detention centers, and prisons. Given the reach of carceral systems, not only through state supervision and technology-based monitoring, but also through the social support networks and relationships that maintain in spite of or are fractured by carceral practices, the publics, students, and other patrons who already rely on libraries as providers of reliable information and recreational materials are impacted by incarceration. This is true even when libraries or other information institutions do not offer direct or indirect services to people who are currently inside of immigrant detention centers, jails, juvenile detention centers, or prisons. Recognizing this, librarians and information professionals can identify areas for more formal service provision.

Establishing new, formal programs and services will most likely involve creating strategies and responsibilities for providing information and other resources that are designed to support library staff as services are extended, policies are shifted to better serve people impacted by incarceration, and new programs and services are developed. Established procedures can assist people who are unfamiliar with navigating the carceral constraints placed on information provision to people who are incarcerated. Having a distributed understanding among library staff and administration that library and information services to people most impacted by incarceration is central to the library's function helps to ensure that any services or programs established in the moment continue independently of one or a few passionate staff.

Establishing new in-person library services and programs in carceral facilities will not be possible without permission from (and security clearance by) the administration and staff at the facility. Institutional support within one's own library or library system can be a meaningful indicator to the administrators and staff at carceral facilities that the library will provide reliable services and will abide by the policies and regulations related to conduct in the facility. These are common concerns of carceral facilities, and addressing them early on may determine whether or not the facility's administrators will consider adding a non-required service to their facility as a worthwhile endeavor. Many programs, often volunteer-led, are designed to be implemented in carceral facilities, proposed to carceral staff or existing programs, and (due to many factors, including the difficulty of navigating a facility that has many barriers to access and can easily deny access to the facility) do not follow through on their proposed programs. The library administration's support for, and investment in, creating new services and programs in a facility can convey to both the facility and the programming staff that there is a reliable infrastructure for continuing those services.

Understanding the narratives of incarceration in the United States—that it is often either or simultaneously justified through punishment or rehabilitation—can be useful in early planning discussions. Prior to attempting to create new services in a carceral facility, however, librarians and information professionals should think about a few areas that are likely to play a significant role in how they understand their own intentions and priorities. These include issues of funding, privacy and censorship, and the formality of partnership between the library (as an institution) and the carceral facility. Considering these areas prior to opening conversations about services or programs in the facility is a useful first step because they are areas where librarians and information professionals may be able to maintain some agency in the decision-making process. Once a formal service has been established, the carceral facility administrators and staff will ultimately determine how, when, and whether services or programs are offered.

PROFESSIONAL CONCERNS

Librarians' professional ethics of privacy, intellectual freedom, and resisting censorship are often compromised in the carceral setting (Clark and MacCreaigh, 2006). At times, the restrictions placed by carceral institutions on information access or the demands for information-sharing that carceral staff make may constitute "the price you pay to get in the door" (Higgins, 2017, 39). Librarians in prisons have circumvented or resisted restrictions, especially those that involve censoring materials or limiting access, in many creative ways (Arford, 2016). There are professional tools that can guide librarians as they consider making compromises in order to establish or provide library services in carceral institutions.

For instance, Higgins (2017) recommends creating a written collection development policy that incorporates information from the ALA's "Prisoners' Right to Read" statement. This statement is a living document which has been updated since Higgins's guide was published in 2017. A section of the "Prisoners' Right to Read" statement pertinent to thinking about librarian's professional areas of concern states:

These principles should guide all library services provided to people who are incarcerated or detained, regardless of citizenship status or conviction status:

- Collection management should be governed by written policy, mutually agreed upon by librarians and correctional agency administrators, in accordance with the *Library Bill of Rights* and its interpretations.
- Correctional libraries should have written procedures for addressing challenges to library materials, including a policy-based description of the disqualifying features.
- Correctional librarians and managers should select materials that reflect the demographic composition, information needs, interests, and diverse cultural values of the confined communities they serve.
- Correctional librarians should be allowed to acquire materials that meet written selection criteria and provide for the multifaceted needs of their populations without prior correctional agency review. They should be allowed to select from a wide range of sources in order to ensure a broad and diverse collection. Correctional librarians should not be limited to acquiring or purchasing from a list of approved materials or vendors.
- Correctional librarians should make all reasonable efforts to provide sufficient materials to meet the information and recreational needs of incarcerated people who speak languages other than English.
- Correctional librarians should be given adequate support for making library resources discoverable.
- Age is not a sufficient reason for censorship. Incarcerated children and youth should have access to a wide range of fiction and nonfiction.
- Equitable access to information should be provided for people with disabilities.
- Media or materials with nontraditional bindings should not be prohibited unless they present an actual compelling and imminent risk to safety and security.
- Material with sexual content should not be banned unless it violates state and federal law.
- Correctional libraries should provide access to computers and internet content, permitted by the correctional facility's library policies.
- People who are incarcerated or detained should have the ability to obtain books and materials from outside the prison for their personal use. (American Library Association, 2019)

These points indicate some of the areas that will have to be navigated, negotiated, or potentially disregarded in order to provide library services and programs and increase information access to incarcerated people. Librarians and information professionals can anticipate some of the issues that might arise in relation to privacy and censorship by tailoring their circulation and collection development practices to prioritize access and privacy.

CIRCULATION RECORDS

While in some instances library records (including those of people who are incarcerated) may be protected under state law (Fife and Fong, 2015), Conrad notes that there are legal precedents for carceral facilities or the courts to gain information about what materials a patron who is incarcerated has accessed (2012, 2017). In the case of Hayes, records of the materials the patron accessed while incarcerated were utilized in a trial for murders Hayes was accused of committing after being released from prison (Glaberson, 2010). The court-led inquiry into the reading habits and information access of incarcerated people echoes back to the monitoring of their information access described in earlier chapters. It also provides some points for reflection as librarians and information professionals design their services, specifically with regard to the creation and maintenance of circulation records.

Circulation records have some important functions—they allow librarians and information professionals to track books and other materials and can be used to ensure the return of high-demand materials if return is delayed. Depending on the way the library service is conducted, these records may be created electronically or be handwritten. Prisons and juvenile detention centers are more likely to have a designated space that can be used for library service, and these may contain computers for library staff use. Outside of instances where there is a dedicated staff computer, the facility will probably prevent people who are not carceral staff from bringing in technologies, so it is likely that all circulation records will be initially transcribed by hand. The library's collection size and budget may dictate the need to keep detailed circulation records, since a smaller budget and a smaller collection increase a librarian's need to keep track of the materials.

The state's interest in tracking information access, and the precedents for interpreting interest in certain types of information as predicting certain behaviors, may be used to justify collection oversight as a feature of security. Although there are precedents for this at the juridical level, it is more likely that the staff who manage the library service in its daily operations are those who are most aware of individuals' reading practices and preferences. They may engage in informal censorship by requesting that specific patrons not be given access to certain titles or types of books. Additionally, their presence may chill patrons' ability to request materials, especially if the staff have made prior negative statements about a person's information-seeking or recreational reading habits.

Despite this level of in-the-moment oversight, alternative models of circulation systems may be developed to protect patron privacy over time. These might include maintaining circulation records in a manner similar to those in a public library (i.e., deleting checkout records when an item is returned or reported missing), storing paper records off-site, maintaining digital records in password-protected folders or working with IT departments to restrict access to the records on shared drives, and creating novel circulation policies. Librarians and information professionals should reflect on what purpose a circulation record serves in the provision of library service, how much information needs to be kept in the record, and for what duration.

In some instances, it may make more sense to create a system based on the number of circulated materials, rather than on records of individual titles checked out. Many carceral facilities place a limit on the amount of library materials that people who are incarcerated can check out or have in their cell at a given time. If library access or materials access is only available to a group of people on a limited basis or with limited frequency, then expecting individuals to not recirculate their books when they have finished them—and restricting their future access when they do recirculate materials—may decrease patrons' access to materials. This can also create the circumstances for further surveillance and punishment that forces librarians and information professionals to take a punitive approach to patrons' information-sharing practices. Librarians should consider whether it is truly necessary to create records that include book titles—rather than the number of books checked out to each individual. Using numbers in circulation records and marking materials in a way that indicates they are library property (such as stamping them with library information) allows patrons to trade library materials with one another when there are gaps in their access to new materials. Creating an alternative record-keeping system in this manner can better protect patrons' privacy and increase their access to materials. This system is not infallible, though, since individual facility staff may ask librarians to provide information about a patron's reading habits or enact informal consequences when they are denied access to that information (Fife and Fong, 2015).

In most states, information about people's convictions or the accusations against them is publicly available. This information can be accessed through online locators on the website of the overseeing body for the facility. This is not the case for people in civil detention in immigrant detention centers—the ICE Online Detainee Locator shows whether or not people are in custody. It is also not the case for people under the age of eighteen, who have specific legal protections as minors. Considering this, librarians and information professionals working with people who are incarcerated will need to decide whether or not the records for patrons are kept alongside the records of other patrons who utilize a library's collection, and, if so, whether or not to include information that designates that the person is incarcerated. In order to reduce bias against patrons and potential patrons (which can be heightened by conceptions of individuals that include histories or accusations of activity deemed criminal that present a lopsided and decontextualized perspective of the patron), it may be best to maintain patron records that contain individually identifying information in a system that is only accessible to the staff who work directly with those patrons.

COLLECTION DEVELOPMENT POLICIES AND CHALLENGES

Collection development plans can be used as internal documents to guide collection-building and can potentially be shared with and approved by the carceral facility's staff in the early planning stages for direct services. These plans should be tailored to fit the interests, needs, and desires of the people who are incarcerated. Collection development processes were described in chapter 5, but they are reintroduced here to discuss how justifications can be made for the inclusion of materials that are often censored by or not selected for carceral facility libraries (PEN America, 2019). For example, depending on the facility and the library, librarians might need to rephrase the clause in the ALA's "Prisoners' Right to Read" statement which says that "correctional librarians should select materials that reflect the "demographic composition, information needs, interests, and diverse cultural values of the confined communities they serve" to read "that reflect *information related to the local and other relevant history, culture, and languages* of the confined communities they serve" (American Library Association, 2019). This rephrasing would open the door (more widely) to a type of patron-centered collection development that includes materials on Afrocentric histories and Black social and political movements, Latinx and Indigenous organizing and history, contemporary fiction (including urban fiction), and LGBTQIA+ materials (including sexual health materials). It may even mean that collections might include information about contemporary and historical figures who have been incarcerated.

Conducting surveys or otherwise obtaining information about patrons' interests prior to beginning direct service, and developing the library's collections in accordance with the survey results, communicates to patrons who are incarcerated that librarians consider their suggestions for areas of collection development as useful for building a collection that meets patrons' various knowledges and interests. Balancing the information needs and desires of patrons against the strictures and regulations of the facility may take some work, but advocating, as much as is possible, for patrons' access is one of the activities that librarians and information professionals should be prepared to do. Adopting formal policies for materials review that mirror those used in the library may be a convenient fallback, but it is much more likely that issues of censorship or the contestation of library materials will arise with floor-level carceral staff who individually disagree with the inclusion of specific materials (Higgins, 2017). In these cases, it is useful to have a planned mode for responding to expected concerns. For instance, biographies of people who have been incarcerated may be challenged by a correctional officer who oversees library service for the day. Addressing this concern involves listening to the staff member in order to best identify the appropriate response and determining how strongly the officer feels about censoring the given material (Higgins, 2017). A preplanned response to this type of challenge might be to state that few nonfiction books are published that simply glorify violence and harm, that books that depict the realities of people's lives give them an anchor in the world and can be tools for reflection, and that the topic addressed is relevant to the experiences of many people in the area of a given facility. These responses reflect biases in publishing that align with some of the narratives of carceral facilities (but this does not have to be addressed with carceral facility staff). Advocating for patron information access requires that facility staff's concerns are addressed in some manner and that staff come to know that librarians are consistent, meticulous, and thoughtful in their collection development practices. As Higgins states, this must be done on a case-by-case basis, and the method for response will depend on the attitude of the staff, their commitment to the challenge, their overall perspective on whether or not incarceration is supposed to serve a rehabilitative or punitive function, and the likelihood that librarians will encounter the staff over time as they conduct library service.

In instances of ongoing challenges to a specific type of material or a specific title, it may be useful to go beyond the process of gathering reviews and supporting evidence for the work's inclusion in the collection. In some instances, it may make more sense to turn to other people who provide programming or services in the carceral facility. For instance, medical staff or groups who provide HIV-awareness training may be inclined to advocate for the inclusion of books on sexual health, including LGBTQIA+ sexual health and information related to medical gender transition. Psychology services staff may be willing to advocate for increased access for people who are in restrictive housing who have been diagnosed with or are perceived to have psychological difficulties that are compounded by incarceration, including people who are on psychological observation (suicide watch). Educators may advocate alongside librarians under the premise of increased literacy or engagement with texts that incarcerated people find to be personally meaningful. Using the library collection to support the facility's existing medical, psych, and educational and other programs, as far as possible, can strengthen ties between the librarian and the program staff and facilitate their coordination in response to attempts to censor materials or otherwise restrict patron access.

BUILDING PARTNERSHIPS AND INTRODUCING SERVICES

Library programming and services for people who are incarcerated, people who were previously incarcerated, and people most impacted by incarceration have to be scaled to fit the available resources and circumstances. Carceral institutions vary in their philosophical approach to programming and engagement, their willingness to invite oversight of conditions in the facility, their physical organization, their security levels and visitor restrictions, their hierarchical structures, how they interpret their legal obligations to provide information access, and a host of other criteria that shape whether or not facility administrators will look favorably upon the introduction of new programs. Approaching carceral facility staff is probably one of the surest routes into the carceral facility, but creating established partnerships between the library and other programs in a facility, or between the library and locally based resources and groups, may communicate to the carceral facility administration that library and information professionals understand the realities of incarceration, and will be able to abide by the facility's role as the ultimate arbiter of access to services or programming. Moreover, the facility administration must believe that the new library services are designed to provide a return on the time investment involved in introducing them (including the time spent by facility staff running background checks and granting clearance, enforcing security measures for bringing materials into the prison, and overseeing the library's day-to-day services).

Establishing in-library support for services or programs is one of the first steps to creating an institutional partnership that facilitates information access. Many individual librarians are probably already providing some level of direct or indirect library service to people who are incarcerated. They may volunteer with Books to Prisoners programs, set aside withdrawn library materials as donations to prison libraries, local shelters, and transitional housing, partner with community organizations and groups that are focused on addressing the local impact of incarceration, screen films related to mass incarceration and facilitate discussions with and between formerly incarcerated people, answer information requests from people who are incarcerated, or critically engage with information about policing and incarceration and alternative systems for addressing harm. These types of programs and services often grow out of the awareness that library patrons *are* directly impacted by ongoing cycles of violence perpetuated by these systems. The informed and innovative work of many individual librarians who have acknowledged the impact of policing and incarceration on the public goes largely unrecorded, but it should be recognized as an ongoing thread of responsive library services that seek to understand the widespread social impact of incarceration. These types of services and programs create a means to counter how the removal of people from society shapes the idea of the public.

A review of the long history of library services and information provision to people who are incarcerated reveals that, outside of a brief period in the 1970s, librarians' concerns and approaches to these services have not substantially changed over time. Aside from the ongoing circumstances of limited funding for services and limited field-wide concern for the information access and practices of people who are incarcerated, these services have been situated in most of the literature within the logics of carceral facilities. Librarians and information professionals have reiterated the philosophies of rehabilitation and punishment that have often limited access to information. While the connection to punitive approaches is clear, the reliance on rehabilitation as a driving force of librarianship inside of jails, juvenile detention centers, immigrant detention centers, and prisons limits collections—through a process of selection that is often rooted in whiteness.

More recent publications on library services in carceral facilities have justified the use of a public library model, but this model may not serve if the public of the library is not inclusive of people who are incarcerated.

The field of library and information science is at a turning point, largely due to the dedicated efforts of various groups of librarians, information professionals, and LIS educators. The work of librarians and information professionals who have championed information access in carceral facilities (often alongside people who are incarcerated) is supported in the field by ongoing campaigns and efforts that align with this goal. For instance, professional conversations and movements about the role and necessity of representative materials have generated ongoing attention to how libraries often do perpetuate systemic inequalities through their collection development practices. Discussions of the whiteness of the field and the middle-class culture of librarianship, largely led by Black, Indigenous, and Latinx librarians and library staff and students, and by librarians and library students of color, have provided room for addressing these failures and how they impact librarianship and information services. The calls for more socially just, racially diverse, and responsive library services have been taken up by some library administrations and city governments, which have reallocated funding to better align with these goals. These changes are supported by statements from the American Library Association that emphasize the need to acknowledge and address mass incarceration and its impact on information access, as well as the role of libraries in the process of reentry.

ADMINISTRATIVE SUPPORT FROM THE LIBRARY AND THE USE OF FORMAL AGREEMENTS

Librarians and information professionals who are not employed through a state's Department of Corrections, the federal prison system, or through an existing program in a carceral facility will need to work with their own library's administration in order to create enduring programs. Practical support will need to come from the administration, but this support is also symbolically important. A library administration's support for new library services and programming that address the realities of incarceration conveys to carceral institutions that new programming and services will continue over time.

Informed administration and management will be better equipped to approach carceral facility administrators or other government departments, such as juvenile or adult probation, about the possibilities of implementing new programs or services. They will also be able to anticipate that, in at least some instances, professional ethics and values may have to be balanced against the opportunity to create new programs and services in the facility, if this opportunity should arise.

A supportive library administration can facilitate formal agreements, such as a Memorandum of Understanding (MOU), between the carceral facility and the library system. MOUs are useful in maintaining services and programming as carceral facility administrators, wardens, and captains change over time and implement their own carceral policies. In instances where incoming administrators wish to implement a more restrictive and punitive approach to the facility, it is quite possible that library services will be reduced to the bare terms spelled out in the MOU. Any MOU should be written to allow as much information and library service as possible, with only limited information related to censorship or selection, and with an eye toward expanding the services should this possibility arise.

Discussions with the library administration can lead to established funding for formal programming. The budgeting concerns to take into account may involve consideration of the specific nature of the programming and services, the number of people incarcerated in the facility, the number of librarians and library staff who will provide programs and services, the facility's limitations on the number of materials that can be kept per person, and the costs of bringing in outside speakers and the materials for indirect programs. When possible, it is best for the library system to provide the materials budget for the collections, but there are instances of the funding being shared between a library system and a carceral facility, or solely by the facility. Given that some libraries in prisons have been funded through commissary spending (which is often exploitative of people who are incarcerated) (Conrad, 2017), librarians and library administrators may want to trace the route of carceral facility-provided funding in the course of their financial deliberations. If programs, services, or materials are co-funded, library administrators should advocate for a line item in the carceral facility's budget. This is rarely the funding reality for libraries in carceral institutions, and negotiators should enter into deliberations expecting some amount of pushback from the facility on committed funding, especially if the agreement does not specify the level of oversight that the carceral facility administration will have over what library materials are selected (Conrad, 2017).

Even in instances where library administrators or managers hold negative views or are simply uninterested in library services for people who are incarcerated, it is possible to make a convincing argument for the need for these services. Librarians might invite local groups or staff from transitional housing and similar services to speak at library staff meetings or to meet with administrators, or they can hold a short series of programs focused on incarceration and use the feedback from those programs to justify ongoing programming (Cottrell, 2017). They might draw upon the literature cited in this book to discuss the impact of incarceration on the local area and whether people impacted by incarceration are served by the library or not. If the library administration is particularly data-driven, librarians can turn to locally gathered or federally maintained statistics (such as those created by the Office of Justice Programs' Bureau of Justice Statistics or by the Prison Policy Initiative) that provide insight into the impact of incarceration, especially along lines of race and class, to bolster their arguments for greater access and library efforts.

COMMUNITY-BASED PARTNERSHIPS

Community-based partnerships with groups that provide services to people who are incarcerated can be a step toward starting a formal library service and can help to create a network between the library and other service providers. In addition to their established social services (such as caseworkers, medical staff, and psychological services staff), some carceral facilities have programming that is offered through outside groups or institutions. Creating supportive partnerships with these groups can facilitate the provision of library materials or services through the partner organization, and can also provide the partner organization with opportunities to hold public presentations or programming at the library.

Some possible areas of programming in carceral facilities include:

- Conflict resolution
- Creative arts and theater

- Education
- Employment and entrepreneurship
- Family support
- Health and wellness
- Language-specific service and language learning
- Legal resources
- LGBTQIA+ services
- Professional development
- Reentry services
- Substance use, harm reduction, and recovery

This list does not illustrate the full range of programming inside of carceral facilities.

Some carceral facilities will list the types of programming (and their providers) on their websites. Others may share this information in informal conversations with library staff. Community-based groups focused on services related to reentry are often familiar with the programs and services that take place in the local carceral facility. Probation and parole officers or administrators may also have information about the existing programming. Some facilities, such as juvenile detention centers, will be under mandate to provide educational and other services.

Library and information professionals who are seeking to identify services inside of a specific facility may want to reach out to established community groups. Some national-evel groups include:

- All of Us or None
- American Friends Service Committee
- Center for Constitutional Rights
- Critical Resistance
- Families Against Mandatory Minimums
- Human Rights Defense Center
- Immigration Advocates Network
- Justice Now
- Legal Services for Prisoners with Children
- National Resource Center on Children and Families of the Incarcerated
- Root & Rebound
- Transgender, Gender-Variant, and Intersex (TGI) Justice Project

Many of these groups have established communications with or have members who are currently detained or incarcerated.

Library and information professionals can identify state-level programs in resource guides that are created specifically for distribution to people who are incarcerated. For example, the Prison Activist Resource Center creates an annual guide of resources for incarcerated people. This guide, available on their website at www.prisonactivist.org, can be organized by location. The Education Justice Project (https://educationjustice.net/resources/) and the Alliance for Higher Education in Prison (www.higheredinprison.org/national-directory) have created similar resources for higher education programs available to people who are incarcerated. There are also many state- and local-level programs that have been created by formerly incarcerated people and involve direct support to those who are currently incarcerated. Connecting with these groups can lead to strong collaborations and exchanges. Librarians and information professionals can invite members of the groups as paid speakers at library programs, thus providing a platform for them to share insight and information about their programs. Librarians and information professionals can also ground their library services and collection development in the experience and knowledge of people who were formerly incarcerated or who are directly impacted by incarceration, should they choose to share that information.

Librarians and information professionals approaching community groups as partners need to do so with an awareness of how the scale of incarceration and the limited amount of funding available to these groups shapes their available resources. Libraries are uniquely positioned to assist existing programming by providing relevant materials, partnering to fund speaker series, and showcasing the work of these programs in the larger community. Librarians seeking to build partnerships with existing programs should approach these programs with the goal of creating a mutually beneficial exchange. Working with community-based groups and service providers can help the library to establish some level of library service in carceral facilities, can communicate to carceral facility administration that the library is able to provide informed services to incarcerated and formerly incarcerated people, and can open avenues for raising awareness and facilitating conversations about systems of incarceration among the general public. Existing program staff are also likely to know the best ways to create and establish services in a specific facility—they are aware of the culture and goals of the facility and its administration, can connect library and information professionals to the appropriate staff for establishing programs, and can give insight into which library services are best suited for a specific context.

SCALING SERVICES AND STARTING SMALL

Many prison librarians are employees of the facility, and their roles and services are often predefined. In contrast to this, initiating library and information services from outside of a carceral facility involves an array of considerations that will shape the services which are eventually offered. The scale of services offered can depend on institutional support from the library administration, the existing connections to community organizations, the administration of the carceral facility, whether or not library services are already offered there, and the amount of staff time and financial resources that are available for the project.

Librarians and information professionals who are designing services and programs for currently or formerly incarcerated people should create plans that can grow in scale over time, with an awareness that a greater opportunity to provide services or programs may arise with little warning. The current work of librarians and information professionals and of community groups that are providing information and materials to incarcerated people offers some models that can be used to create smaller-scale services and programs that might eventually lead to larger and more established ones.

A simple approach to scaling programs when opportunities or resources are limited is to assess how information about the life-shaping impact of incarceration can be incorporated into existing library and information services. This involves assessing whether or not a library's existing programs that might be useful in the process of reentry include information relevant for people who have been incarcerated, are on probation, parole or under supervised release, or have a felony conviction history. For example, including information in an employment workshop about how a felony conviction or time spent in prison or jail can impact the job-seeking process conveys to the participants in that workshop that librarians and information professionals are aware that some patrons may be formerly incarcerated. This removes the responsibility of formerly incarcerated people to self-identify, and simultaneously may raise the awareness among people who do not have that lived experience.

Outreach services can be reconfigured or extended to better recognize the aftereffects of incarceration. Outreach conducted with this intent provides a premise for approaching community groups, local, state, or federal supervisory agencies, and groups focused on reentry with a mutual goal of increasing access to information. Considering that incarceration occurs along the lines of systemic oppression, assessing outreach practices and identifying outreach opportunities can move beyond conducting outreach to specific sites related to reentry to offering materials and services to the communities most impacted, if the library does not already do this. New outreach projects can turn to local information sites and community centers to begin to identify ways that the library can support their efforts.

A library trying to increase its outreach efforts to formerly incarcerated people first needs to identify its own barriers to access. Some barriers to access, such as the library's punitive policies that involve fines and requirements for specific types of identification, can be addressed by changing library policy or by giving librarians and staff the agency to reduce barriers to access on a case-by-case level. Other barriers are maintained through the general culture of librarianship and of individual libraries. Staff training about the realities of incarceration and trainings that directly address the prevalence of whiteness in library culture and that dismantle the dehumanizing stereotypes of racialized criminality are an essential step in addressing the profession's neglect of services to people who are or have been incarcerated.

Coordinating with other groups to provide programming and materials in carceral facilities or in areas whose inhabitants are most negatively impacted by incarceration allows library and information professionals to support existing work outside of the library, learn effective strategies for service provision, and share the library's resources. Partnerships build awareness of how the library's resources might support patrons who have, in many instances, received formal or informal messages that they are not considered part of the public served by the library. Librarians and information professionals can create reentry-specific resources (fliers, resource guides, or similar materials) that are distributed at outreach events and locations and are also made available within the library. Outreach events present opportunities to amplify the voices of people who are already advocating for greater information and communications access for people who are incarcerated.

The direct, indirect, and reentry services described in previous chapters represent a variety of courses of action and levels of scale at which library and information services can be modified or created to address the impact of incarceration in publics served and as yet not served by libraries. Given that the impact of incarceration is so vast, the practice of incarceration so constant, and the ramifications of incarceration on Black, Indigenous, and people of color, LGBTQIA+ people, and people living in poverty so continuous, even a small-scale response can create a meaningful and needed change.

CONCLUSION

Library and information services to people who are incarcerated are not often prioritized by library systems or in the field of library and information science. Given this reality, establishing these services involves advocating for change within librarianship, in individual libraries, and in discussions with library administrations. Awareness of the impact of incarceration and the frequency with which Black, Indigenous, and people of color and their communities, LGBTQIA+ and gender non-conforming people, people living in poverty, and people who are disabled are targeted for incarceration—and that the mission and vision of many library systems and institutions align with providing services to people impacted by or experiencing incarceration—can work to shift library cultures toward better practices and models. Incorporating awareness of the impact of incarceration across library systems can help librarians to modify programs, identify new partners, and establish mutually beneficial connections to people in the areas that are most likely to experience policing, surveillance, and incarceration.

Building awareness and establishing programming can facilitate the creation of direct or indirect services for people who are incarcerated. Including information about the impact of incarceration creates room for patrons who have been incarcerated, who are previously incarcerated, or who are impacted by the incarceration of friends and family to engage with the library system about the realities of incarceration. It also raises general awareness of the realities of incarceration and its aftereffects. With so much information available about incarceration and the scope of policing, some of which is included in the first portion of this text, the responsibility to begin this work or to refine it to better fit the needs of library patrons should not fall on people who have already been most negatively impacted.

Administrative support for new or modified programming can lead to increased institution-wide implementation of trainings, and can build awareness and begin to shift libraries' culture. Administrative support also facilitates connections to carceral facilities and the departments that manage what types of information and programming are available inside of them. The library's administrative involvement and commitment to services conveys to carceral facility administrators and staff that the new services or programs will continue over time and will be operated under the limitations placed on them by the carceral facility. These formal, institutional networks and agreements can provide a foundation for established services that are not solely dependent on the work of a few dedicated librarians, library staff, or information professionals. Administration can also facilitate formal agreements between the library and carceral facility.

Even in the absence of administrative support or system-wide awareness training, individual librarians continue to advocate for increased services for people who are negatively impacted by incarceration. Their ongoing work reveals large and small ways that librarians can, and do, build critical awareness around policing and incarceration, network with community members and groups, create and distribute library resources, and directly support the information access of people who are incarcerated. The projects and possibilities highlighted throughout this half of the book reveal that there are many ways to apply a critical, informed, and reflective understanding of how incarceration shapes the social landscape while facilitating greater information access.

REFERENCES

American Library Association. 2019. "Prisoners' Right to Read: An Interpretation of the Library Bill of Rights." www.ala.org/advocacy/intfreedom/librarybill/interpretations/prisonersrightoread.

Arford, T. 2016. "Prisons as Sites of Power/Resistance." In *The SAGE Handbook of Resistance,* ed. D. Courpasson and S. Vallas, 224-43. London: Sage Publications.

Association of Specialized and Cooperative Library Agencies. 1992. "Library Standards for Adult Correctional Institutions." American Library Association.

Clark, S., and E. MacCreaigh. 2006. *Library Services to the Incarcerated: Applying the Public Library Model in Correctional Facilities*. Santa Barbara, CA: Libraries Unlimited.

Conrad, S. 2012. "Collection Development and Circulation Policies in Prison Libraries: An Exploratory Survey of Librarians in US Correctional Institutions. *The Library Quarterly: Information, Community, Policy* 82, no. 4: 407-27.

———. 2017. *Prison Librarianship: Policy and Practice*. Jefferson, NC: McFarland.

Cottrell, M. 2017. "Keeping Inmates on the Outside: Libraries Offer Services and Support to Ease Prisoner Reentry. *American Libraries* 48, no. 1-2: 48-55.

Fife, D., and K. Fong. 2015. "Comparing Notes: A Conversation about Library Service to County Jails." *Public Libraries* 54, no. 3: 31-34.

Glaberson, W. 2010. "Prison Books Bring Plot Twist to Cheshire Killings." *New York Times*, July 22. www.nytimes.com/2010/07/22/nyregion/22cheshire.html.

Higgins, N. 2013. "Family Literacy on the Inside." *Public Libraries* 52, no. 1: 30-35.

———. 2017. *Get Inside: Responsible Jail and Prison Library Service*. Chicago: Public Library Association.

PEN America. 2019. "Literature Locked Up: How Prison Book Restriction Policies Constitute the Nation's Largest Book Ban." https://pen.org/wp-content/uploads/2019/09/literature-locked-up-report-9.24.19.pdf.

CONCLUSION

The control, monitoring, and censorship of information is part and parcel of carceral systems. People who are incarcerated and people who are under state supervision bear the brunt of these practices in ways that affect their opportunities to access information, make choices, and pursue interests that affirm their humanity. The consequences of these practices go beyond immediate recognizable forms of incarceration. Communities that are heavily policed and experience high rates of detainment, both pre- and post-adjudication, are composed of people who have experienced state practices of information regulation and control. Carceral systems and practices also take hold in other institutions that have purportedly sustained information access. This is well documented in accounts of the school-to-prison pipeline, but it also manifests in more subtle forms. It can be found in what are often presented as regular library practices—such as enacting policies that permanently curtail an individual's access to the library as a form of punitive response to infractions or disturbances there, with limited warning that this would occur.

Librarians and information professionals need to reassess and change their approaches to the intersections and overlaps between incarceration, librarianship, and information access and to hold these in conversation in the field. The first half of this book contains tools for understanding the scope of carceral systems and how they entwine with information access and technology. By grounding a discussion of information and incarceration in a review of the arguments that have been most widely used to justify carceral practices in America, that section provides a critical lens for interrogating the normalization of carceral systems in librarians' discussions and the provision of their services.

Focusing on librarians' positioning of services along the lines of carceral logics of punishment and rehabilitation also stands in stark contrast to claims within the field about librarianship's neutrality and the possibility of professional neutrality in general. Reviewing the history of library services in carceral facilities reveals that they most often were undertaken through, and shaped by, adherence to belief systems that normalized and mirrored the logics that informed carceral practices in the United States. Tracing those logics back to their antecedent practices of colonial control and enslavement enables librarians and information professionals to begin to identify the flawed approaches that have shaped library services in carceral facilities over time, and to think about new ways to approach those services both in facilities and in the larger field.

It is, after all, these practices that have led to the multifold instantiations of carceral facilities and systems as they currently manifest. Looking to the overlaps and divergences between carceral practices of juvenile detention, incarceration and immigrant detention, and probation, supervised release, and parole not only makes clear the articulated nature of these institutions, it also troubles the popular narrative that people who have experienced incarceration and people who are in the public are groups walled off from one another. And this, in turn presents an opportunity to reconceptualize the public. Given that policing, incarceration, and surveillance have targeted Black, Indigenous, and people of color and their communities, LGBTQIA+ and gender non-conforming people, people living in poverty, and people who are disabled, and that they work along lines of extraction, confinement, and dispossession to physically remove people from the larger society, the profession needs to examine how library and information services are discussed and implemented. This would be the case even if incarceration and obligations to supervisory state systems did not directly shape the experiences of over six million people in America at any given moment (Phelps, 2018).

Comparing the more recent literature on library services to incarcerated people to a few published accounts of the importance they give to access to books and materials reveals a disconnect between people's lived experiences and the practices within the LIS field. The accounts in chapter 4 speak to the importance of information access and the complex relationships that people (incarcerated or not) form with and through texts and information. For people who are incarcerated, reading and information access have an even greater importance because these processes counter the impetus of carceral systems to control, dehumanize, and curate people's existence. Other forms of media and expression are grounds to be explored further in future research. For instance, librarians and information professionals might examine the artistic and aesthetic practices of people who are incarcerated, and the constraints placed on those practices (Fleetwood, 2020). Alternately, there may be ways to incorporate information and media created by people who are detained and incarcerated within the library collection. This could draw from the Reveal Digital online archive of prison newspapers (2021) to include prison newspapers, involve podcasts that feature people who are most impacted by incarceration, and bring media produced by youth (such as *The Beat Within*) into the library. Looking to other forms of information practice might provide ground to counter some of the same machinations of control and direction that have been discussed in the recent literature on library services to incarcerated people. These information and media practices also present opportunities for libraries and other information sites to display and promote the creative work of people who are incarcerated and those impacted by the long reach of incarceration.

Further practices and research can build on the review of technologies that is offered in this book. The lack of attention given within the field to the technologies in carceral settings and their capacity for greater surveillance and control is telling. With the patchwork availability of needed and desired books and recreational libraries within carceral facilities, tablets and similar technologies are often one of the few means by which people can access information and communicate with their families and social support networks. Yet, the tablets and other technologies within carceral contexts are marketed chiefly for their ability to surveil, catalog, and retain information and have been refined over the course of their implementation in carceral facilities across the United States. This is of obvious concern to the field of library and information science.

The second half of this book focuses on how libraries can implement library services in carceral facilities. It draws upon approaches to information access in carceral systems that do not necessarily situate information access as a tool for either rehabilitation or punishment. Drawing from the information practices of incarcerated people and the writings of formerly incarcerated people about the importance that access to books and information had during their incarceration, it looks to models both within and outside of the LIS field to create an overview of the types of services that outside libraries currently provide to people held in carceral facilities. Most of the models discussed in this part of the book consist of established and successful programs that represent the existing possibilities for service. They also highlight shortcomings in those services, potential areas for growth, and the need for increased funding and collaborations. Looking to established and successful models is only useful to the field when these are counterposed against the dearth of information access in many carceral facilities, as evidenced in the limited opportunities to choose what to read there—and in the continued calls for funding and other forms of support from vital library programs which have found ways to provide information access to their incarcerated patrons despite ongoing challenges and censorship practices.

Carceral systems have functioned through processes of erasure—both physical and psychological ones. The "mass" in mass incarceration has scaled up to such an extent that people's experiences of incarceration or the incarceration of their loved ones has led to widespread calls that range from substantive change, to encompassing reforms, or to abolition, and yet carceral systems continue unabated by legislation or even a global pandemic. It is indisputable that "prisons do not disappear problems, they disappear human beings" (Davis, 1998). The direct, indirect, and reentry-based services attended to in this text provide some footing for centering the humanity of people who are incarcerated through the implementation of library and information services. The range of library and information services described here shows that there are multiple opportunities for libraries and information professionals to increase information access. The models described in chapters 5 through 7 reveal that successful and effective library services can and do occur in carceral facilities, as well as in the places people live after they are released.

It is revealing that the services and programs described in this book have not been incorporated into most library and information science education, nor has there been any overall recognition that incarceration and other carceral forces have influenced and continue to shape the practice of librarianship. The difficulty of providing services that are not aligned with carceral aims, the lack of resources to support increased information access for people who are incarcerated, and the ways in which power flows are centered in carceral systems mean that speaking to the truth of providing these services and the realities of incarceration can often hamper or curtail the possibility of actually facilitating information access. These constraints will have to be negotiated and tested as new and more far-reaching services are established. The final chapter of this book addresses some of the manifestations of these broad concerns and focuses on patron privacy, collection development policies and challenges, first steps, and ways to raise general awareness of incarceration and its multifold negative impacts.

Even though information has been utilized by carceral systems for control, regulation, and state-enforced dehumanization, information access has been a life-sustaining force for people who are incarcerated, one they have used to affirm their relationships to family, community, and the larger world. Monica Cosby, a formerly incarcerated person, beautifully captures this in her opening essay in an issue of *Bound Struggles*, where she writes

> Reading lent me the courage and strength to refuse erasure. This erasure I speak of is of the self, which happens slowly but steadily in the prison. Society's refusal to see prisons and prisoners is no minor contribution. We are isolated in the prisons, cut off from our communities and our families. The cost of phone calls and visits contributes to this isolation. Even the cost of purchasing a book to send to someone in prison is too much—the $30 or so that it would cost to buy a book or two is too much for some families; oftentimes it is the choice to either get a book or be able to purchase personal hygiene items from the prison commissary, because the prisons do not provide those

things for free. Sending letters and books into prison is a way of communicating to us in the prisons that we are seen, that we are cared about. (Cosby, 2017, 3-4)

MOVING FORWARD

This text serves to disrupt the erasure of people who are incarcerated and to question the effects of incarceration from within the field of library and information science. It differs from many other works on the topic by taking a critical and situated approach to librarianship and incarceration in the United States. It supplements existing publications on these topics by stepping back from practical guides and reviews of services and instead approaching the topic from multiple and interlocking angles and by drawing upon a variety of academic disciplines. By doing this, it provides a broad overview of how carceral power operates through information control and how library and information professionals can work to address, interrupt, and push against these flows of power.

As an introductory work, this book is defined by its omissions and the impossibilities that shaped the moment of its creation. Future scholars and practitioners will likely benefit from a more comprehensive review of what library and information services are being provided in jails and prisons, what challenges and successes take place in these contexts, and how libraries can work across their institutional lines to support one another in providing information access to people who are incarcerated. Conrad's 2017 review of prison libraries and existing library standards lays the foundation for doing this, but library and information professionals would probably benefit from a comprehensive survey and review similar to LeDonne's extensive 1974 survey of library services in carceral institutions, a survey that also examined related legislation, analyzed nationwide and state protocols, and provided a bibliography. This type of comprehensive review might facilitate a more thorough analysis of how types of carceral systems interconnect, especially in relation to policing and surveillance.

The racialized, gendered, and ability-centric processes of incarceration are named in this text, but more focused reviews and research could further untangle the ways in which information access—as determined by information production, publishing, and purchasing—aligns with the broad-based policing, surveillance, and incarceration of people at the intersections of their identities in U.S. society (Crenshaw, 1991). This line of investigation could well lead to discussions of the overlaps between the practices of librarianship on the one hand and those of carceral systems on the other, as well as the possibilities for library systems to disinvest from prison labor and the carceral implications that often exist in libraries' claims to neutrality.

Divestment is not figurative. Some public libraries have taken advantage of incarcerated people's labor, and others have been approached by carceral staff as possible employment sites. Incarcerated workers are paid low wages, sometimes not compensated at all, and have little agency over the type of work they must do (McDowell and Mason, 2020). In many instances, the work done by incarcerated people does not often involve job training that will be applicable upon their release. Divestment campaigns led by people negatively impacted by incarceration have called for more funds to be moved from systems of policing and incarceration and to community resources (Freedom to Thrive, n.d.). Utilizing incarcerated people's labor, or purchasing products produced through their labor, runs counters to calls for true social change.

Thinking through the ways in which library and information professions are connected to carceral systems provides an opportunity for the field to reassess current approaches to library regulations and security practices. When reviewed at scale, it is obvious that carceral systems are expansive and attached at many points, including in individual interactions, the culture of various institutions, and how security practices within institutions may reiterate or draw from carceral practices overall. This is not to state the powerlessness of library and information professionals. Rather, critiquing the practices and effects of carceral systems can help ensure that LIS does not mimic these systems and their inherent limitations to information access. This may involve considerations of the technologies, including biometric technologies, that have been utilized in or are being promoted to libraries and other information institutions, including how these technologies were created, refined, and how they might further open flows of power that support and are reiterated by carceral systems (Sweeney and Davis, 2020). It will also probably involve a cost-benefit analysis that considers resource reallocation away from security and policing and investment into library and information services that are created to address the historical harms of exclusion, both within the culture (and demographic makeup) of the profession and through library and information practice that have often centered whiteness and the protection of whiteness. This can be grounded in a recognition that some of the costs of security practices and policies around initiating contact with the police include damage to existing relationships with communities who bear the brunt of policing and incarceration.

This text has held traditional library science and more contemporary technology and data driven information science approaches together in order to illustrate that each, in some way, finds its reflection and possible counter in the other when viewed through the lens of carceral practices. These two areas of the field are relevant throughout, but the carceral control of technologies and access to information through them leaves the second half of the book concentrated heavily on what have been considered traditional library practices. The examination of technologies in carceral facilities in this book sits at the interstices between information access and control. Technologies within carceral facilities largely fall in line with historical practices around information regulation and control found in the early overlaps between library practices and incarceration, including eugenicist approaches that have informed racial criminalization. Abundant research on technological surveillance, policing, cataloging, and detainment exists, but there is a lack of attention to this research within the LIS field and an overall lack of critical academic or professional attention paid to information and technology in carceral settings and practices. Library and information science needs to more heavily engage with the implications of these technologies and examine their role in the lives of people who are incarcerated, the people they communicate with outside, and in society as a whole.

Reiterating carceral logics within library and information practice forecloses the possibility of addressing some of the historical harms that have rooted the field. Focusing energy elsewhere—into collaborations with community members and groups most negatively impacted by (and most often targeted through) incarceration, and into prioritizing services that address the difficulties that people who are incarcerated or have experienced incarceration have expressed—are means by which the profession can come to work against carceral logics. Like carceral systems, library and information science has often functioned through the gatekeeping of information, both in carceral contexts and in the public. Library and information science can counter this precedent by centering the experiences of people who have been heavily impacted by cycles of incarceration and other forms of state violence; by turning to alternative forms of addressing disruptions, grievances, and harms (such as deescalation and restorative and transformation justice-based approaches); and by working from a recognition that while carceral systems are extensive and insidious, they are not totalizing. Librarians and information professionals, whether in the larger public or in carceral institutions, do not have to adhere to or replicate carceral logics, nor are they traversing unknown terrain if they attempt to push against the manifestations of these logics in library and information practice. This book has outlined one path—through the development, implementation, and support of library and information services that are designed with and for people who are incarcerated, and which are based on critical assessments of both carceral systems and library and information science—but there are probably many other, yet unplumbed, ways to shift the boundaries of how library and information science defines the public, and, through that recognition of the public, itself.

REFERENCES

The Beat Within. n.d. www.thebeatwithin.org/.

Conrad, S. 2017. *Prison Librarianship: Policy and Practice*. Jefferson, NC: McFarland.

Cosby, M. 2017. (Untitled introduction.) *Bound Struggles*, 7. Chicago: Chicago Books to Women in Prison.

Crenshaw, K. 1991. "Mapping the Margins: Intersectionality, Identity Politics, and Violence against Women of Color." *Stanford Law Review* 43: 1241-99.

Davis, A. 1998. "Masked Racism: Reflections on the Prison Industrial Complex." Colorlines. www.colorlines.com/articles/masked-racism-reflections-prison-industrial-complex.

Fleetwood, N. 2020. *Marking Time: Art in the Age of Mass Incarceration*. Cambridge, MA: Harvard University Press.

Freedom to Thrive. n.d. Our Work. https://freedomtothrive.org/our-work/#our-work.

LeDonne, M. 1974. *Survey of Library and Information Problems in Correctional Institutions*. U.S. Department of Health, Education, and Welfare.

McDowell, R. & Mason, M. 2020. "Cheap Labor Means Prisons Still Turn a Profit, Even During a Pandemic." *PBS Newshour*. www.pbs.org/newshour/economy/cheap-labor-means-prisons-still-turn-a-profit-even-during-a-pandemic.

Phelps, M. S. 2018. "Ending Mass Probation: Sentencing, Supervision, and Revocation." *Future of Children* 28, no. 1: 124-46.

Reveal Digital. 2021. American Prison Newspapers 1800-2020: Voices from the Inside. https://about.jstor.org/revealdigital/american-prison-newspapers/.

Sweeney, M. E., and E. Davis. 2020. "Alexa, Are You Listening? An Exploration of Smart Voice Assistant Use and Privacy in Libraries." *Information Technology and Libraries* 39, no. 4.

Library Literature on Adult Incarceration, 1992–2019

T his appendix includes citations for articles, chapters, books, and other materials on the topic of library services to incarcerated adults, published between 1992 and 2019. Materials are listed in chronological order. Asterisks indicate that materials are book chapters, books, or guides.

Suvak, D. 1993. "Evaluating LSCA: The Evidence from Prison Libraries." *Public Libraries* 32, no. 2: 86–90.

Mongelli, W. 1994. "De-Mystifying Legal Research for Prisoners." *Law Library Journal* 86: 277–98.

Westwood, K. 1994. "Prison Law Librarianship: A Lesson in Service for All Librarians." *American Libraries* 25, no. 2: 152–54.

*Rubin, R. J., and D. Suvak. 1995. *Libraries Inside: A Practical Guide for Prison Librarians*. Jefferson, NC: McFarland.

Stevens, T., and B. Usherwood. 1995. "The Development of the Prison Library and Its Role within the Models of Rehabilitation." *The Howard Journal of Criminal Justice* 34, no. 1: 45–63.

*Vogel, B. 1995. *Down for the Count: A Prison Library Handbook*. Metuchen, NJ: Scarecrow.

Vogel, B. 1995. "Meeting Court Mandates: The CD-ROM Solution." *Corrections Today* 57, no. 7: 158, 160.

Vogel, B. 1995. "Ready or Not, Computers Are Here." *Corrections Today* 57, no. 6: 160, 162.

Bratt, L. 1996. "Birthplace of My Redemption." *American Libraries*, 27, no. 6: 65–66.

Chepesuik, R. 1996. "Unlocking Doors through Literacy." *American Libraries* 27, no. 10: 46–48.

Schneider, J. 1996. "Prison Libraries Change Lives." *American Libraries* 27, no. 10: 46–48.

Vogel, B. 1996. "The Prison Law Library: From Print to CD-ROM." *Corrections Today* 58, no. 3: 100.

Sullivan, L. E. 1998. "Reading in American Prisons: Structures and Strictures." *Libraries & Culture* 33, no. 1: 113–19.

Westwood, K. 1998. "'Meaningful Access to the Courts' and Law Libraries: Where Are We Now?" *Law Library Journal* 90, no. 2: 193–95.

Wilhelmus, D. W. 1999. "A New Emphasis for Correctional Facilities' Libraries." *Journal of Academic Librarianship* 25, no. 2: 114–20.

Bouchard, J., and A. Winnicki. 2000. "'You Found What in a Book?' Contraband Control in the Prison Library." *Library & Archival Security* 16, no. 1: 47–61.

Franklin, P. 2000. "'Read to Succeed': An Inmate to Inmate Literacy Program in Washington State." *Journal of Correctional Education* 51, no. 3: 286–92.

Knudsen, M. 2000. "How My Library Affects My Life in Prison." *Education Libraries* 24, no. 1: 20. (Special issue.)

Lehmann, V. 2000. "Prison Librarians Needed: A Challenging Career for Those with the Right Professional and Human Skills." *IFLA Journal* 26, no. 2: 123–28.

London, D. 2000. "Conduit for Restoration: The Prison Library." *Education Libraries* 24, no. 1: 21. (Special issue.)

Median, L., R. Purifoy, M. Knudson, and D. London. 2000. "The Prison Library as Viewed by Four Inmates." *Education Libraries 24, no.* 1: 17–22. (Special issue.)

Purifoy, R. 2000. "You Are Here: A Guided Tour of the Oshkosh Correctional Institution Prison Library." *Education Libraries* 24, no. 1: 18. (Special issue.)

Singer, G. 2000. "Prison Libraries Inside Out." *Education Libraries 24, no.* 1: 11–16. (Special issue.)

Sullivan, L. 2000. "The Least of Our Brethren: Library Service to Prisoners." *American Libraries* 31, no. 5: 56–58.

Bowden, T. 2002. "A Snapshot of State Prison Libraries with a Focus on Technology." *Behavioral & Social Sciences Librarian* 21, no. 2: 1–12.

Lehmann, V. 2002. "The Prison Library: A Vital Link to Education, Rehabilitation, and Recreation." *Education Libraries* 24, no. 1: 5–10.

Bouchard, J., and L. Kunze. 2003. "Teaching Diverse Students in a Corrections Setting with Assistance from the Library." *Journal of Correctional Education* 54, no. 2: 66–69.

Geary, M. 2003. "Trends in Prison Library Service." *Bookmobiles and Outreach Services* 6: 79–91.

Gerken, J. L. 2003. "Does *Lewis v. Casey* Spell the End to Court-Ordered Improvement of Prison Law Libraries?" *Law Library Journal* 95, no. 4: 491–513.

Shirley, G. L. 2003. "Correctional Libraries, Library Standards, and Diversity." *Journal of Correctional Education* 54, no. 2: 70–74.

Lehmann, V. 2003. "Planning and Implementing Prison Libraries: Strategies and Resources." *IFLA Journal* 29, no. 4: 301–7.

*Sullivan, L. E., and B. Vogel. 2003. "Reachin' behind Bars: Library Outreach to Prisoners 1798–2000." In *Libraries to the People: Histories of Outreach, ed.* R. S. Freeman and D. M. Hovde, 113–27. Jefferson, NC: McFarland.

de la Peña McCook, K. 2004. "Public Libraries and People in Jails." *Reference & User Services Quarterly* 44, no. 1: 26–30. Stearns, R. 2004. "The Prison Library: An Issue for Corrections, or a Correct Solution for Its Issues?" *Behavioral & Social Sciences Librarian 23, no.* 1: 49–80.

Stearns, R. 2004. "The Prison Library: An Issue for Corrections, or a Correct Solution for Its Issues?" *Behavioral & Social Sciences Librarian* 23, no. 1: 49–80.

Asher, C. 2006. "Interlibrary Loan Outreach to a Prison: Access Inside." *Journal of Interlibrary Loan, Document Delivery, & Electronic Reserve* 16, no. 3: 27–33.

*Clark, S., and E. MacCreaigh. 2006. *Library Services to the Incarcerated: Applying the Public Library Model in Correctional Facilities.* Santa Barbara, CA: Libraries Unlimited.

Preddie, M. 2006. "The Lone Ranger, Part I: Charting New Grounds in Prison Hospital Librarianship." *Journal of Hospital Librarianship* 6, no. 1: 87–93.

Seamone, E. 2006. "Fahrenheit 451 on Cell Block D: A Bar Examination to Safeguard America's Jailhouse Lawyers from the Post-Lewis Blaze Consuming Their Law Libraries." *Yale Law & Policy Review* 24, no. 1: 91–147.

Shirley, G. 2006. "Library Services to Disadvantaged User Groups. Library Services to Adult Prisons in the United States." *LIBREAS. Library Ideas*, 6. https://libreas.eu/ausgabe6/003shir.htm.

Tubbs, C. 2006. "Electronic Research in State Prisons." *Legal Reference Services Quarterly* 25, no. 1: 13–38.

Greenway, S. A. 2007. "Library Services behind Bars." *Bookmobiles and Outreach Services* 10, no. 2: 43–64.

Payne, W., and M. J. Sabath. 2007. "Trends in the Use of Information Management Technology in Prison Libraries." *Behavioral & Social Sciences Librarian* 26, no. 2: 1–10.

Preddie, M. 2007. "The Lone Ranger, Part II: Meeting the Challenges of Prison Hospital Librarianship: Charging Forward with a Strategic Plan." *Journal of Hospital Librarianship* 6, no. 4: 75–83.

Sullivan, Larry E. 2008. "'Prison Is Dull Today': Prison Libraries and the Irony of Pious Reading." *PMLA* 123, no. 3: 703-6.

*Vogel, B. 2009. *The Prison Library Primer*. Lanham, MD: Scarecrow.

Shepard Smith, E. 2010. "May It Please the Court: Law Students and Legal Research Instruction in Prison Law Libraries." *Legal Reference Services Quarterly* 29, no. 4: 276-317.

Lehmann, V. 2011. "Challenges and Accomplishments in U.S. Prison Libraries." *Library Trends* 59, no. 3: 490-508. (Special issue, "Library and Information Services to Incarcerated Persons: Global Perspectives.")

Conrad, S. 2012. "Collection Development and Circulation Policies in Prison Libraries: An Exploratory Survey of Librarians in US Correctional Institutions." *The Library Quarterly: Information, Community, Policy* 82, no. 4: 407-27.

Abel, J. 2013. "Ineffective Assistance of Library: The Failings and the Future of Prison Law Libraries." *Georgetown Law Journal* 101, no. 5: 1171-1215.

Morris, J. 2013. "Free to Learn: Helping Ex-Offenders with Reentry." *Public Library Quarterly* 32, no. 2: 119-23.

Sorgert, R. 2014. "Forgotten and Elusive Partners: Academic Libraries and Higher Education in Prison." *Saint Louis University Public Law Review* 33: 429-519.

Drabinski, E., and D. Rabina. 2015. "Reference Services to Incarcerated People, Part I: Themes Emerging from Answering Reference Questions from Prisons and Jails." *Reference & User Services Quarterly* 55, no. 1: 42-48.

Rabina, D., and E. Drabinski. 2015. "Reference Services to Incarcerated People, Part II: Sources and Learning Outcomes." *Reference & User Services Quarterly* 55, no. 2: 123-31.

Couvillon, E., and A. Justice. 2016. "Letters from the Big House: Providing Consumer Health Reference for Texas Prisons." *Journal of Hospital Librarianship* 16, no. 4: 281-86.

Kelmor, K. 2016. "Inmate Legal Information Requests Analysis: Empirical Data to Inform Library Purchases in Correctional Institutions." *Legal Reference Services Quarterly* 35, no. 2: 135-46.

Rabina, D., E. Drabinski, and L. Paradise. 2016. "Information Needs in Prisons and Jails: A Discourse Analytic Approach." *Libri: International Journal of Libraries & Information Services* 66, no. 4: 291-302.

*Shirley, G. 2016. "In a Place of Monotony and Despair: A Library!" In *Celebrating the James Partridge Award: Essays toward the Development of a More Diverse, Inclusive, and Equitable Field of Library and Information Science*, ed. D. L. Barlow and P. T. Jaeger, 77-88. Advances in Librarianship, vol. 42. Emerald Group Publishing.

Wright, B. N. 2016. "The Prison Law Library: A Fourteenth Amendment Necessity." *Advances in Librarianship* 41: 209-28.

*Conrad, S. 2017. *Prison Librarianship: Policy and Practice*. Jefferson, NC: McFarland.

Dunaway, S. E. 2017. "¿Dónde está la biblioteca? It's a Damn Shame: Outdated, Inadequate, and Nonexistent Law Libraries in Immigrant Detention Facilities." *Legal Reference Services Quarterly* 36, no. 1: 1-33.

Gladstone, J. 2017. "Prison Law Libraries: From US's *Bounds* to Canada's *Biever*." *Canadian Law Library Review* 42, no. 3: 15-20.

*Higgins, N. 2017. *Get Inside: Responsible Jail and Prison Library Service*. Chicago: Public Library Association.

*Rayme, M. 2017. "Prison Libraries: On the Fringe of the Library World." In *Librarians with Spines: Information Agitators in the Age of Stagnation,* ed. Y. S. Cura and M. Macias, 99-110. Los Angeles: Hinchas.

*Styslinger, M. E., K. Gavigan, and K. Albright, eds. 2017. *Literacy behind Bars: Successful Reading and Writing Strategies for Use with Incarcerated Youth and Adults*. Lanham, MD: Rowman and Littlefield.

Finlay, J., and J. Bates. 2018. "What Is the Role of the Prison Library? The Development of a Theoretical Foundation." *Journal of Prison Education and Reentry* 5, no. 2: 120-39.

*Jacobson, E. 2018. "Reference by Mail to Incarcerated People." In *Reference Librarianship & Justice: History, Practice, & Praxis, ed.* K. Adler, I. Beilin, and E. Tewell, 151-59. Sacramento, CA: Library Juice.

Austin, J., and M. Villa-Nicholas. 2019. "Information Provision and the Carceral State: Race and Reference beyond the Idea of the 'Underserved.'" *The Reference Librarian* 60, no. 4: 233-61.

APPENDIX B

Library Literature on Youth Incarceration, 1992–2019

This appendix includes citations for articles, chapters, books, and other materials on the topic of library services to incarcerated youth published between 1992 and 2019. Materials are listed in chronological order. Asterisks indicate that materials are book chapters or books.

Carlson, P. 1994. "Books, Books, Books – Let Us Read: A Library Serving Sheltered and Incarcerated Youth." *VOYA* 17, no. 3: 137–39.

Herald, D. 1995. "Booktalking to a Captive Audience." *School Library Journal* 41, no. 5: 35–36.

Carlson, L. 1997. "A Day in Detention." *ALKI* 13, no. 3: 18.

Angier, N., and K. O'Dell. 2000. "The Book Group behind Bars." *VOYA* 23, no. 5: 331–33.

Davis, V. A. 2000. "Breaking out of the Box: Reinventing the Juvenile Center Library." *American Libraries* 31, no. 10: 58–61.

Ganter, J. 2000. "Capture the Power of Reading." *Illinois Libraries* 82, no. 3: 176–80.

Angier, N. 2001. "Juvenile Justice Outreach: Library Services at Detention Centers." *PNLA Quarterly* 66, no. 1: 16.

Madenski, M. 2001. "Books behind Bars." *School Library Journal* 47, no. 7: 40–42.

Puffer, M., and L. Burton. 2002. "Correctional Education Reform—School Libraries." *Journal of Correctional Education* 53, no. 2: 52–57.

Jones, P. 2004. "Reaching out to Young Adults in Jail. *Young Adult Library Services* 3, no. 1: 14–17.

———. 2005. "Partners in Anticrime." *Library Journal* 130: 32.

———. 2007. "600 Pod: Learning Resource Center and Library: Juvenile Detention Center Branch of the Pima County Public Library, Tucson, Arizona." *VOYA* 30, no. 5: 410–11.

McLellan, K., and T. Suellen. 2007. "Serving Teens Doing Time. (Johnson County Library Programs for Juveniles)." *VOYA* 30, no. 5: 403–7.

Wilhelm, E. 2007. "Here's My Heart, Handle with Care." *VOYA* 30, no. 5: 408–9.

Bodart, J. R. 2008. "It's All about the Kids: Presenting Options and Opening Doors." *Young Adult Library Services* 7, no. 1: 35–45.

Fenster-Sparber, J. 2008. "New York City's Most Troubled Youth: Getting Caught Reading at Passages Academy Library." *Knowledge Quest* 37, no. 1: 30–33.

Gilman, I. 2008. "Beyond Books: Restorative Librarianship in Juvenile Detention Centers." *Public Libraries* 47, no. 1: 59–66.

Parker, M. 2008. "Life as a Library Media Specialist within a Juvenile Detention School." *Library Media Connection* 26, no. 7: 50–51.

Czarnecki, K. 2009. "Dream It, Do It: At the Library! Technology Outreach at a Juvenile Detention Center." *Young Adult Library Services* 7, no. 2: 22–24, 31.

McLellan, K. 2009. "From Classroom to Courtroom: Our Role in the Community." *Public Libraries* 48, no. 1: 62–65.

Joseph, B. 2010. "Global Kids uCreate Project: Extending Collaborative Learning to Incarcerated Youth in Two Cities." *Youth Media Reporter* 4: 82–85.

Fenster-Sparber, J., A. Kennedy, C. Leon, and R. Schwartz. 2011. "E-Reading across the Digital Divide: How We Got to Be the First School Library Serving Incarcerated and Detained Youth to Get iPads into the Hands of Our Students." *Young Adult Library Services* 10, no. 4: 38–41.

*Sweeney, J. 2011. "Interagency Cooperation in Juvenile Detention Center Library Services: An Introduction to the Issues." In *Advances in Library Administration and Organization,* 30, ed. D. Williams and J. Golden, 187–206. Bingley, UK: Emerald Group.

Zettervall, S. 2011. "When There Is No Frigate but a Book." *American Libraries* 42, no. 1-2: 48–51.

Austin, J. 2012. "Critical Issues in Juvenile Detention Center Libraries." *Journal of Research on Libraries and Young Adults,* July. www.yalsa.ala.org/jrlya/2012/07/critical-issues-in-juvenile-detention-center -libraries/.

Roos, B. 2012. "Beyond the Bars: Serving Teens in Lockdown." *Young Adult Library Services* 10, no. 2: 12–14.

*Sweeney, J. 2012. *Literacy: A Way Out for at-Risk Youth.* Santa Barbara, CA: Libraries Unlimited.

Zeluff, K. 2012. "Collection Development Policies in Juvenile Detention Center Libraries." *Library Media Connection* 30, no. 5: 36–38.

Zeman, M. E. 2013. "Juvenile Ex-Offenders Need Libraries, Too." *Public Libraries Online.* http:// publiclibrariesonline.org/2013/11/juvenile-ex-offenders-need-libraries-too/.

*Coyle, J., J. Austin, and R. A. Montague. 2014. "Library Services to Incarcerated Youth: A Case Study." In *Youth Community Informatics: New Media for Community and Personal Growth*, ed. B. C. Bruce, A. P. Bishop, and N. R. Budhathoki, 119–33. New York: Peter Lang.

*Zeman, M. E. 2014. *Tales of a Jailhouse Librarian: Challenging the Juvenile Justice System One Book at a Time.* Brooklyn, NY: Vinegar Hill.

Montague, R. A. 2015. "Mix IT Up! A Blending of Community Informatics and Young Adult Librarianship to Further Social Justice in Library and Information Science Education." *Library Trends* 64, no. 2: 444–57.

Ownes, D., and C. Tadgh. 2015. "Tech Pilots in Juvenile Facilities Support Skills." *Library Journal* 140, no. 4: 25.

Austin, J. 2017. "Reform and Revolution: Juvenile Detention Center Libraries in the 1970s." *Libraries: Culture, History, and Society* 1, no. 2: 240–66.

*Styslinger, M. E., K. Gavigan, and K. Albright, eds. 2017. *Literacy behind Bars: Successful Reading and Writing Strategies for Use with Incarcerated Youth and Adults.* Lanham, MD: Rowman and Littlefield.

YALSA. 2018. "Interview with NPL Staff on Serving Incarcerated Youth." *Young Adult Library Services* 17, no. 1: 5–7.

Austin, J. 2019. "Literacy Practices of Youth Experiencing Incarceration: Reading and Writing as Points of Regulation and Escape." *Libri: International Journal of Libraries and Information Studies* 69, no. 1: 77–87.

INDEX

Page numbers followed by the letter "f" indicate figures.

CPSIA information can be obtained
at www.ICGtesting.com
Printed in the USA
LVHW011227210423
744932LV00009B/305